The Impact of Global En͓ Cultural Identities in the 1 Arab Emirates

This book provides a nuanced portrait of the complexities found within the cultural and linguistic landscape of the United Arab Emirates, unpacking the ever-shifting dynamics between English and Arabic in today's era of superdiversity. Employing a qualitative phenomenological approach which draws on a rich set of data from questionnaires to focus groups with Emirati students, Emirati schoolteachers, and expatriate university teachers, Hopkyns problematizes the common binary East-West paradigm focused on the tension between the use of English and Arabic in the UAE. Key issues emerging from the resulting analysis include the differing attitudes towards English and in particular, English Medium Instruction, the impact of this tension on identities, and the ways in which the two languages are employed in distinct ways on an everyday scale. The volume will particularly appeal to students and scholars interested in issues around language and identity, language policy and planning, multilingualism, translanguaging, and language in education.

Sarah Hopkyns is Assistant Professor in the College of Education, Zayed University, United Arab Emirates. She is also a Fellow of the Higher Education Academy. She has presented and published widely in the field of Sociolinguistics, with a focus on global English, English Medium Instruction (EMI), and cultural identities.

Routledge Studies in Language and Intercultural Communication

Edited by Zhu Hua, Birkbeck College, University of London
Claire Kramsch, University of California, Berkeley

Interculturality, Interaction and Language Learning
Insights from Tandem Partnerships
Jane Woodin

Beyond Native Speakerism
Current Explorations and Future Visions
Stephanie Ann Houghton, Damian J. Rivers and Kayoko Hashimoto

Screens and Scenes
Multimodal Communication in Online Intercultural Encounters
Edited Richard Kern and Christine Develotte

Glocal Languages and Critical Intercultural Awareness
The South Answers Back
Edited Manuela Guilherme and Lynn Mario T. Menezes de Souza

Redefining Tandem Language and Culture Learning in Higher Education
Edited by Claire Tardieu and Céline Horgues

Tertiary Language Teacher-Researchers Between Ethics and Politics
Silent Voices, Unseized Spaces
Chantal Crozet and Adriana R. Díaz

The Impact of Global English on Cultural Identities in the United Arab Emirates
Wanted not Welcome
Sarah Hopkyns

www.routledge.com/Routledge-Studies-in-Language-and-Intercultural-Communication/book-series/LICC

The Impact of Global English on Cultural Identities in the United Arab Emirates

Wanted not Welcome

Sarah Hopkyns

Routledge
Taylor & Francis Group

LONDON AND NEW YORK

First published 2020 by Routledge

2 Park Square, Milton Park, Abingdon, Oxon OX14 4RN
605 Third Avenue, New York, NY 10017

Routledge is an imprint of the Taylor & Francis Group, an informa business

First issued in paperback 2022

Library of Congress Cataloging-in-Publication Data
A catalog record for this book has been requested

ISBN: 978-0-367-23003-6 (hbk)
ISBN: 978-1-03-233674-9 (pbk)
DOI: 10.4324/9780429277870

Typeset in Sabon
by Apex CoVantage, LLC

Contents

Figures and Tables

Figures

Tables

Preface

Much has been written about the role that English as a global language has played in supplementing and even displacing local national languages in international workplaces, publishing industries, and educational institutions. The current interest in bi- and multilingualism in applied linguistics is a response to the pressure around the world to learn English, the world's inescapable lingua franca, in addition to one's own native language. But learning English is not just learning another linguistic system; it is also, especially when used as a medium of instruction in schools and at universities, learning another system of knowledge, another system of thought. Educators and politicians in Japan, China, South Korea, Singapore justly worry that, by learning English, youngsters in those countries learn a whole new way of thinking and being that might clash with the social and cultural identity transmitted to them by the society they grew up in.

This book offers fascinating insights into the effects of global English on the local cultural identities of English learners in another particular country – the United Arab Emirates. Sarah Hopkyns, Assistant Professor of Education at Zayed University in Abu Dhabi, has lived for many years in the UAE and is able to give us a vivid sense of the status of English there through her survey of Emirati university students, Emirati primary school teachers, and expatriate university teachers like herself. Through survey questionnaires and participant observation of student focus groups, as well as through her own reflexive research journal, she is able to draw the reader into the complex world of a country with a short but spectacular history. Founded in 1971 after its separation from Britain, the UAE has sought to transform itself into high modernity through its rich oil resources, but at the price of an extraordinarily stratified society in which only 10% are Emirati citizens and all others are foreigners. In the UAE, as in other 'rentier' states in the Arab world, whose economy depends largely on the income obtained from 'renting', i.e., selling, natural resources to the outside world, there is a clear distinction between the Emirati capital owners and the multilingual foreign labour force. English is therefore the indispensable language of communication both for domestic purposes and for the UAE's relations to the outside world of business, finance, and politics.

The teaching of English in the UAE is a prime example of the effects of globalization and its concomitant linguistic 'imperialism', but at the same time it complexifies the notion of imperialism as at once historically determined and pragmatically self-imposed. The book illustrates dramatically the tension between linguistic imperialism and pragmatism in the Arabian Peninsula and the power, generational, and ideological struggles that the use of English as medium of instruction brings about. Seeking to define one's English-speaking identity necessarily entails having to redefine one's Arabic speaking identity; both are woven into the very fabric of the nation, requiring a fundamental rethinking of what constitutes both 'Western' and 'Arabic' culture. The book documents admirably the conflict of desires between projecting power and competing on the global English-speaking stage on the one hand and maintaining social and political stability and promoting Muslim and Arabic values on the other.

Beneath the glitter of modernity lie the complexities, multiplicities, and hybridities of history, which Hopkyns encourages both teachers and learners of English in the Gulf to embrace. For researchers holding post-structuralist views of language (translanguaging, superdiversity, hybridity), this book advances our knowledge of how global Englishes affect the local political cultures in various areas of the world. It can help applied linguists and intercultural communication scholars better understand what the challenges are and what the prospects are of finding solutions.

Claire Kramsch, UC Berkeley

Acknowledgements

The research in this book was conducted over a period of seven years beginning with the start of my doctorate in 2012, which was the same year I arrived in the United Arab Emirates. There are many people I would like to thank for making this book possible. Firstly, I am extremely grateful to the participants in this study who, especially due to the qualitative nature of the research, committed a significant amount of their time and energy when their days were already long and busy. During the transcribing phase of the study and from reading responses repeatedly during the data analysis phase, I often had feelings of excitement and gratitude over the richness of the data collected. I owe this to the participants for giving such detailed, candid, and insightful responses and demonstrating full engagement with the research topics. I would also like to thank the university teachers who allowed me to visit their classes, introduce the project, and collect data. Especially, Dr. Raymond Sheehan went out of his way to help me gain access to the Emirati primary school teacher participants, despite interrupting their intense exam-preparation course.

I would also like to acknowledge my colleague Dr. Habibul Khondker for the inspiration behind the expression 'wanted not welcome', which not only appears in the title of the book, but is a theme running throughout the volume. This expression was originally used in his 2010 article in *Encounters Journal* with reference to foreign workers in the UAE. Upon my wish to expand the term to refer to English as a global language, Dr. Khondker was both supportive and encouraging. I am also grateful to colleagues Dr. Wafa Zoghbor and Ayeda AlObathani who provided me with valuable insights into the Arabic language, Khaleeji dialects, and Arabic-English linguistic hybridity as well as nuances in cultural practices (such as naming conventions), all of which would not have been easy to find reference to in academic texts.

I also want to express gratitude to my editor at Routledge, Elysse Preposi, and to Helena Parkinson, Routledge's Editorial Assistant, for encouraging me to move forward with this project and believing in it. This book would not have been possible without their support, as well as the valuable input of three anonymous reviewers. I thank the reviewers greatly for the effort and expertise that they contributed to reviewing both the book proposal and final draft which ultimately strengthened the final product. I would also like to thank my doctoral supervisor, Dr. Julie Norton, who provided me with valuable advice and encouragement as well as constructive feedback throughout the research process.

It is also important to recognize the support of the Zayed University Office of Research. Shortly after the completion of my pilot study, I was awarded a 'Research Incentive Fund' (RIF), which is a generous grant that allowed me to hire two Arabic-English translators, Dina Osman and Raieda Ishak, for the main study. I am grateful to Dina and Raieda for giving numerous hours to translation work as well as checking each other's work along the way for increased accuracy.

The Office of Research also funded numerous professional development trips to local and international conferences. Presenting my findings at major conferences, such as the American Association for Applied Linguistics (AAAL), TESOL International, the International Association of Teaching English as a Foreign Language (IATEFL), and the Gulf Research Meeting (GRM) at Cambridge University, provided me with valuable experiences. These events allowed me to receive feedback from diverse audiences and provided me with the opportunity to be at the forefront of research activity in my field. I have gathered inspiration from many cutting-edge plenary talks and through illuminating conversations at social events. I was extremely fortunate to meet Claire Kramsch, whose work I have long admired, at TESOL Arabia conference in Dubai in 2016. Since then, she has been a firm supporter of my work and an encouraging mentor and role model. Her suggestion of the writing of this book as part of the Routledge Studies in Language and Intercultural Communication series was instrumental in me achieving this goal.

I would also like to thank my colleagues at Zayed University, other Gulf-based universities, and beyond for their support of my work as well as many fascinating discussions about English, Arabic, culture, and identity. I would especially like to recognize the encouragement and enthusiasm of friends and colleagues Melanie van den Hoven, Telma Steinhagen, Wafa Zoghbor, Peter Hassall, Timothy Nicoll, Sara Hillman, Kevin Carroll, Kay Gallagher, David Palfreyman, Louisa Buckingham, Joanne Seymour, Glenda El Gamal, Ahmad Al-Issa, Sue Garton, and many more.

Finally, an enormous thank you goes to my wonderfully supportive family. I am especially grateful to my father Dr. Nigel Jepson for his valuable comments and feedback on various draft chapters of the book. I also want to thank my much-appreciated husband, Daniel Hopkyns, and son, Thomas Hopkyns. They have been tirelessly supportive of my studies, even when it has meant long weekends in my office at the university. I am most grateful to Dan and Thomas for forcing me to relax and have fun between bouts of writing.

1 Introduction

A precarious edge between one era and another – between the society's idea of a person and a person's sense of self.

– Utayba (2015)

1.1 East-West Paradigm in Media Reports

When opening any number of Arabian Gulf newspapers (Table 1.1), three major themes hit the reader: the seductive nature of English, declining levels of Arabic, and the need for bolstering local cultural identities.

Table 1.1 Arabian Gulf Newspaper Headlines

Gulf Newspaper Headlines	*Newspapers and Year*
English proficiency comes at a cost	Gulf News, 2011
Teach us English but without its cultural values	Saudi Gazette, 2013
Poor literacy in Arabic is 'the new disability' in the UAE	The National, 2013
Embrace English . . . without losing Arab Identity	The Arab News, 2013
Cultural identity in danger in the GCC (Gulf Cooperation Council countries)	Gulf News, 2013
English language 'seducing' UAE pupils	The National, 2014
World Arabic Language Day: the fight to keep Arabic relevant	The National, 2017
Learning Arabic should be a joy, not a chore	The National, 2019

When reading the articles attached to the headlines, it becomes clear that these issues mainly relate to English and Arabic in education. Numerous accounts testify to the dominance of English in schools, often to the detriment of Arabic. For example, director of Dubai-based Jumeira Baccalaureate School, Imad Nasr, states:

It was a shock when I first came to this school and noticed that the majority of the native-Arabic-speaking children talk to each other and even their parents in English. It's not just the students here but I would say in general in Dubai, Arabs do not converse in their native language.

("World Arabic Language Day", 2017)

Not only in Dubai but also across the United Arab Emirates (UAE), poor literacy in Arabic has been identified as the nation's 'new disability'. These were the words of Dr. Sheikha Al Ari, who is a member of the Federal National Council (local governing body), after overseeing students in local schools and witnessing shockingly low proficiency levels in Arabic ("Poor literacy in Arabic", 2013).

While the headlines in Table 1.1 and the articles that follow them, in true journalistic style, are both eye-catching and disturbing, they tend to reflect a binary East-West paradigm which portrays English as the aggressor and Arabic as the victim in need of saving. Emotive and positional words such as 'fight', 'danger', and 'seduce' attached to English, and words such as 'lose', 'chore', and 'disability' connected to Arabic, paint a picture of disharmony between two competing languages. While sensationalism sells, it is important to explore the intricacies that lie beneath black and white media coverage. Delving beyond surface-level reporting of these issues, the aim of this book is to investigate the inevitable complexities behind such headlines, from the multiple perspectives of Emirati university students, Emirati primary school teachers, and expatriate university faculty members.

Before doing so, however, it is important to discuss the central concepts that run through the book, which include: English as a global language, postmodern cultural identities, and interculturality in the age of superdiversity. Following this, a brief description of the study will be given before providing synopses for the following chapters.

1.2 English as a Global Language – the Debate

English has been given, at various points in time, the labels *world English* (since the 1920s), *international English* (since the 1930s), and most recently *global English* (since the mid-1990s). These labels have subtle differences in meaning with 'the third being linked (often negatively) to socio-economic globalization' (McArthur, 2004, p. 3). The terms are used somewhat interchangeably in public discourse, though, and all relate to the fact that English, as a language, stands in a category of its own with regard to its far-reaching and immense influence. Whereas in the past, English was but one language amongst others, it is now, without dispute, in a category of its own. The success of the British colonial empire and the subsequent rise of American industrial and technological power have combined to create a situation in which English, uniquely, has come to be accepted as the symbol of a modern technologically advanced society. It is true to say that 'whereas once Britannia ruled the waves, now English rules them' (Phillipson, 1992, p. 1). De Swaan (2001) defines English as the world's only 'hypercentral' language as it is estimated that a staggering 'one in three of the world's population are now capable of communicating to a useful level in English' (Crystal, 2012, p. 155), which is a number that is on the rise. As Al-Dabbagh (2005) states, English has become 'the Latin of the contemporary world' or, as Morrow and Castleton (2011) say, 'the Walmart of the language universe', meaning, just like the American megastore, which has replaced numerous smaller stores across the USA, it serves all needs and is omnipresent. It is the only language spoken on all five continents and is the official language of 52 countries (CIA World Fact Book, as cited in Deument, 2000, p. 393). Consequently, its influence reaches almost every corner of the globe and affects language use on an unprecedented scale. As English now occupies an important position in many education systems around the world, which is certainly the case in the Gulf Cooperation Council (GCC) states (Bahrain, Kuwait, Oman, Qatar, Saudi Arabia, and the UAE), it has become the 'global academic lingua franca' (Jenkins, 2014, p. 10) and a high stakes gatekeeper to success in education. Globalization, with English and technology as its 'two inseparable mediational tools' (Tsui & Tollefson, 2007, p. 1), now has a profound impact on world communication, politics, science, technology, entertainment, social and cultural relations, international business, and socioeconomics worldwide. One would suppose that such a powerful language could not fail to affect its speakers on multiple levels.

Although there is a consensus amongst scholars that global English does indeed affect language, culture, and identity around the globe, there is significant disagreement as to the nature and extent of such effects. Is the spread of global English a process of top-down linguistic and cultural homogenization or one promoting creative hybridization whereby speakers autonomously shape language to suit local needs? Or is it somewhere in between? Scholars are divided over where on the spectrum global English lies. Bakhtin's (1981) discussion of centripetal (moving towards the centre) and centrifugal (moving away from the centre) forces is useful here where it is recognized that these competing forces often result in tensions. Such competing forces are most evident in the polarized views regarding the effects of English as a global language expressed in the 'Englishization versus Hybridization debate' (Hopkyns, 2016).

Englishization

Proponents of the former lens of 'Englishization' see English as a 'killer language' (Fishman, 1999), an aggressive 'Tyrannosaurus Rex' type tongue (Swales, 1997), or 'pushy auntie English' (Troudi & Al Hafidh, 2014). English from this perspective is seen as 'linguistic imperialism' (Phillipson, 1992), 'linguistic dystopia' (Dovchin, 2018), or a new form of Western cultural colonialism, where its spread represents a push to emulate not only language but also Western lifestyles and ways of think-ing, resulting in 'a system of mono-cultural or even mono-lingual domi-nance' (Harrison et al., 2007, p. 20). Such dominance has been described as a new form of 'western cultural colonialism' (Ahmed, 2011, p. 120) or 'mental colonialism: the subtle push to emulate everything Western including the English language' (Suzuki, 1999, p. 145). As Qiang and Wolff (2005) powerfully describe, English in the eyes of many is 'a mod-ern day Trojan horse filled with EFL teachers/soldiers or missionaries, armed with English words rather than bullets, intent upon re-colonizing the world to remake it in the image of Western democracy' (p. 60). In this sense, globalization, with English as its accomplice, has been linked to 'McDonaldization' or 'makdana' in Arabic (Hammond, 2007, p. 33), whereby the principles of the fast-food restaurant are coming to dom-inate more and more societies around the world. Similarly, and more specifically, the spread of English has been called 'McCommunication' (Block, 2002, p. 117) due to its perceived homogenizing nature.

Hybridization

While some fear global English is an extension of British and American imperialism, others argue that 'hybridization' or 'glocalization', in which local versions of imported language and cultural artifacts are created, overpowers 'Englishization' in many societies. Here an interdependent relationship between the global and the local exists rather than the domi-nance of the former over the latter. Globalization, from this angle, pres-ents opportunities to engage with post-traditional order and create new identities, with an emphasis on moving forward not backward. This could be seen, in a neutral sense, as a natural process of transformation or 'a happenstance rather than planning' (Brumfit, 2004, p. 165) where Eng-lish is used voluntarily and creatively adapted by local communities. For example, Blommaert (2016) gives examples of how hybridized language often emerges in unexpected places, such as the unique versions of English or French seen throughout Japan on shop signs. In this sense, there is an attitude of 'we're going to make our own English, but only in this context'. Therefore, the target language is being used without care or knowledge of a native-speaker model. Here localization and appropriation of Eng-lish in local communities occurs and creative expression takes place often through linguistic hybridization (e.g. Dovchin, 2018; Kachru, 1992). Such a perspective argues that rather than English being viewed as an imperial-istic language, it is often altered by speakers to fit local contexts.

Colonial-Celebration and Functionalism

In addition to the two sharply contrasting lenses of Englishization and Hybridization, two further perspectives regarding the global spread of

English include: Colonial-celebration and Functionalism. The former takes an arrogant view of the spread of English around the globe. As Kuppens (2013) explains, colonial-celebration is 'built on the colonial Eurocentric image of the West as inherently superior to the rest of the world' (p. 332). Here, the Anglophone West is associated with modernization, wealth, and development, and therefore spreading English is seen as a 'good deed' or a moral obligation.

Moving away from such a view, the lens 'Functionalism' positions English as a communication tool rather than celebration of colonialism or a threat to culture and identity. It is argued that English has a minimal effect on cultural identity due to the belief that global English is 'native-culture-free' (Polzl, 2003), a 'linguistic masala' (Meierkord, 2002), or 'a mere tool, bereft of collective cultural capital' (House, 2003). The most well-known proponent of this view is Crystal (1997), who emphasizes that the dominance of English is not problematic as bilingualism or multilingualism allows speakers of English as a second language to use their first language(s) for expressing their identity and English for international communication.

Post-Colonial Performativity

A fifth perspective can be found in Pennycook's (2010) 'Post-Colonial Performativity', which is influenced by postmodern notions of identity. Here a more flexible way of seeing the connection between language and identity is stressed, with an emphasis on agency. The focus is placed on how different varieties of English are used to perform alternative identities. As Pennycook (2007) states, 'when we talk of global English use, we are talking of the performance of new identities' (p. 112). Pennycook's (2001, 2003a, 2003b, 2007, 2010) work extends the ideas of appropriation or centrifugal forces (Bakhtin, 1981) to look at how English is used amongst speakers to perform transcultural and tranlinguistic identities. Pennycook's lens of 'Post-Colonial Performativity' more thoroughly accounts for the hybrid, transcultural, and translingual phenomena that exist in most societies where global English is present. Here, through transcultural flows, identities performed through English are neither fully global nor fully local but rather part of a transcultural interplay through which languages are fluid and interconnected. The focus is on the creation of new plural identities. As Higgins (2009) states, 'a transcultural approach is rewarding because it examines how people create new spaces, new cultures, and new languages with their local and global resources' (p. 12). In this sense, there is an emphasis on using both English and local languages to create something unique and new, but in ways which vary according to time, space, or interaction patterns. However, complexities involved in such hybridity often result in a 'tension between the global flow of an ideology and the local fixity of what authenticity means and how it should be realized' (Pennycook, 2007, p. 112), as the opening quote of this chapter implies.

The five lenses of global English, explained previously, are summarized in Table 1.2. Although all are worthy of contemplation, it is the fifth lens of 'post-colonial performativity' which is most useful for exploring the relationship between global English and cultural identities in superdiverse contexts, such as the UAE, due to its emphasis on multiplicity and flexibility within identity construction.

Table 1.2 Five Lenses on Global English

	Lenses on Global English	*Viewpoint*
1	Englishization/Linguistic Imperialism	Linguistic and cultural globalization causes homogenization.
2	Hybridization/World Englishes	New varieties of English and use of hybridization can be used as a form of anti-colonial resistance.
3	Colonial-Celebration	English brings wealth, development, and 'modernization' to the rest of the world.
4	Functionalism	English is a neutral language. It is used merely as a communication tool for bilingual speakers.
5	Post-Colonial Performativity	English can be used in different ways in different contexts to represent multiple identities.

We will now turn to look at the second key concept of the book, which is the construction of cultural identities in modern times. The understanding of both the terms culture and identity have changed significantly since the 1990s, as we will see in the following section.

1.3   Modern Cultural Identities

The concepts *culture* and *identity* share a similar pattern of understanding by scholars in the field. In the view of many scholars (Block, 2007; Kramsch, 1998; Norton, 2000; Risager & Dervin, 2015; Zhu, 2014, 2017), the concepts have evolved significantly partly due to globalization, hypermobility, and superdiversity and partly due to the increased recognition of the importance of the interpretivist paradigm in intercultural studies, with its central ontological tenant being constructivism. Constructivism recognizes the presence and importance of subjective meanings in relation to social interaction. This approach leads to an understanding of culture and identity as being primarily socially-constructed as well as fluid, changeable, negotiated, and far from straightforward. The concepts of culture and identity epitomize what Dervin and Liddicoat (2013) describe as a 'conceptual jungle', in that defining these terms often involves analyzing 'what they are not', as if brushing aside heavy branches or climbing over thick undergrowth to arrive at one's destination, which is a tentative definition of these highly complex concepts.

Culture

Culture, in its anthropological sense, was traditionally seen as 'the whole way of life of a people' (Young, 1996, p. 37). However, much controversy now surrounds such a definition due to the fact that as the world is becoming more and more globalized and cosmopolitan in nature, it is becoming increasingly rare to find groups of people sharing an identical way of life. Instead, members of cultural groups tend to show 'family resemblances' (Spencer-Oatley, 2000) meaning that it is almost impossible to fully distinguish one cultural group from another. Rather than culture being associated with a physical place, such as a country, it is viewed as a 'social force which is evident wherever it emerges as being significant' (Holliday, 2005, p. 23). In this sense, cultural identity is constantly evolving and leaking at the boundaries. It is not static or neatly packaged, and it is connected to several smaller overlapping groups rather than one large 'catch-all' group, such as nationality (Hopkyns, 2014, p. 4).

In today's globalized and highly mobile world, individuals tend to create cultures through multiple smaller social groupings such as families, colleagues, friendship circles, special interest groups, contemporaries, etc., which are known as 'small cultures' (Holliday, 1999). Here, notions of monolithic cultures are put aside, with an emphasis on differences that exist within cultures. Small cultures, however, differ from subcultures in that they do not necessarily have a 'Russian doll or onion-skin relationship with parent large cultures' (Holliday, 1999, p. 239). For example, a small culture such as 'English as a Medium of Instruction (EMI) learners' can extend beyond the borders of large cultures such as a nation. Here, we see certain educational environments around the world are very similar in terms of teacher-student behaviour despite national cultural differences. Whereas notions of large culture divide the social world into 'hard', essentially different ethnic, national, or international cultures, the small culture notion 'leaves the picture open, finding "softer cultures" in all types of social grouping, which may or may not have significant ethnic, national or international qualities' (Holliday, 1999, p. 240). In this sense, the small culture approach focuses on social processes as they emerge. As part of this softer and less rigid approach to cultures comes a marked awareness of the dynamic and changeable nature of culture. As Ingold (1994, as cited in Atkinson, 1999, p. 632) sums up well, nowadays 'people live culturally' rather than living *in* cultures. This more minimal and operational notion of culture allows it to be discovered rather than presumed. Cultures are often unrooted, ever-developing, and highly changeable. Individuals frequently find ways to adjust, dismiss, or reject cultural norms, making them active players in the formation of their cultural identities rather than merely 'cultural dopes' (Crane, 1994, p. 11). Considering the previous points, culture can, generally, be defined as a way of life or outlook adopted by a community, making it a form of 'collective subjectivity' (Alasuutari, 1995). This definition reflects the complexity and socially-constructed nature of 'cultures'.

Identity

The concept of identity has been named one of the most pivotal concepts of our times (Risager & Dervin, 2015, p. 7). Like the concept of culture, however, due to its complexity identity is considered a 'fuzzy concept' (Strauss & Quinn, 1997, p. 7) or a 'slippery' term (Riley, 2006, p. 296). As with cultural studies, recent years have seen a paradigm shift moving away from 'inter-group approaches' to identity, which tended to over-simplify and essentialize differences between large groups such as nationality or language, while paying less attention to the multiplicities within groups. Although there has not been a full-scale replacement of essentialist views (Lytra, 2016), identities in recent times are generally recognized by most scholars as plural, rich, complex, and sometimes contradictory (Mercer, 2011; Norton, 2000; Suleiman, 2003; Zhu, 2017). Considering these factors, identity can be defined as 'how a person understands his or her relationship to the world, how that relationship is constructed across time and space, and how the person understands possibilities for the future' (Norton, 2000, p. 5).

Plurality and Positioning in Identity Construction

Scholars such as Norton (2000), Pavlenko and Blackledge (2004), and Tracy (2002) have highlighted the plural nature of identity in numerous ways. For Tracy (2002), there are four categories of identity which are Master (gender, ethnicity, age, nationality), Interactional (specific roles people enact such as mother, teacher, customer), Relational (interpersonal relationships such as power difference or social distance which are context-dependent), and Personal (personality, attitudes, character), making one's identity multifaceted and complex. Pavlenko and Blackledge (2004, p. 21) also recognize the plurality of identities by categorizing them as follows: *imposed identities* (which are not negotiable in a particular time and space), *assumed identities* (which are accepted and not negotiated), and *negotiable identities* (which are contested by groups and individuals). Imposed (or non-negotiable) identities are those assigned to individuals that they cannot resist such as compulsory name changes for immigrants in the early 1900s in the United States. Assumed (or non-negotiated) identities are those that individuals are usually happy with and do not wish to negotiate or contest. These are usually legitimized by traditionally dominant discourses, such as being heterosexual, white, monolingual, etc. Negotiable identities, which are arguably the most interesting types to investigate, refer to all identity options that can be contested and resisted by individuals and groups. Examples include race, ethnicity, nationality, sexuality, religious affiliation, and 'linguistic competence and ability to claim a "voice" in a second language' (Pavlenko & Blackledge, 2004, p. 22). It is the latter form of negotiable identity that is particularly relevant to the study context. Due to the dominance of English in multiple domains, there is a sense of vulnerability surrounding Arabic and local cultural identities, as indicated in the newspaper headlines at the start of this chapter, which affects identity options.

Positioning theory, which is rooted in Davies and Harre's (1990) seminal work and was expanded upon by Pavlenko and Blackledge (2004), looks at how individuals see themselves (*reflective positioning*) or are seen by others (*interactive positioning*). Such positioning affects identities in a variety of settings and in multiple ways. Based on the combination of *reflexive* and *interactive positioning*, identity becomes a process of analyzing and reanalyzing, reflecting and re-reflecting, negotiating and renegotiating; it is not something one *has*, rather it is 'something which people *use* to justify, explain, and make sense of themselves in relation to other people and to the contexts in which they operate' (MacLure, 1993, p. 312). Reflective positioning is often contested by others causing ongoing tension between self-chosen identities and others' attempts to position them. As individuals participate in discourses related to a range of roles such as *university student, daughter, shopper, traveller, schoolteacher, mother, etc.*, various identities are co-constructed, and at times contested. The complex interplay between reflective and interactive positioning, in this sense, is shaped to serve specific purposes, affiliations, contexts, and spaces.

Power and Negotiation of Identities

Identity becomes particularly interesting, important, and relevant when it is in crisis or when something assumed to be fixed and stable becomes questionable or uncertain. The series of newspaper headlines discussed at the start of this chapter point towards identities in the Gulf countries being 'contexts of crisis' due in part to the binary ways in which English and Arabic are positioned by the media and in public discourses, as well as the overt power English yields over Arabic in multiple public domains, particularly in education. French sociologist Bourdieu's (1977, 1991) concept of linguistic stratification is useful here, in that language often acts as a form of symbolic, economic, and social capital which tends to be unevenly distributed according to the social setting, making individuals favourably or unfavourably positioned according to the context or space. For example, in the context of the UAE, the power surrounding English and its gatekeeper status in education can unfavourably position those struggling to meet EMI university standards.

Language ideologies, which can be defined as a set of beliefs of a group or an individual, are far from neutral, particularly in multilingual societies where Orwellian perceptions of languages and identity result in some being seen as 'more equal than others' (Selvi, 2016, p. 62). Negotiation is a logical outcome of such inequality. When some identity options are more valued than others, people often not only have to negotiate and defend their cultural identities but also construct each other's perceptions. In postmodern societies, languages may serve as sites of solidarity, empowerment, resistance, disempowerment, or discrimination. How one positions oneself depends upon the level of inclusion and acceptance one feels amongst certain communities. In contexts such as the UAE, young citizens may feel the English-speaking aspect of their identities receives a greater level of acceptance in their English Medium Instruction (EMI) university setting, whereas their Arabic-speaking (Emirati dialect) self receives greater inclusion at home, especially with older family members for which speaking English is often not an option nor desirable.

1.4 Interculturality and Superdiverse Contexts

Considering the definitions and discussions of culture and identity thus far, the theoretical perspective of 'Interculturality' (IC), which originates in Nishizaka's seminal work (1995) and was extended by Mori (2003) and Zhu (2010, 2014), is particularly useful and relevant as a way of explaining complexities within modern cultural identities.

The Principles of Interculturality (IC)

Drawing upon social constructivism, the theoretical perspective of interculturality (IC) problematizes cultural differences and emphasizes the 'inter' nature of interactions. IC proposes that although an individual belongs to several different membership categories such as Emirati, female, student, art-lover, etc., not all identities are salient or relevant in the same way at a given point in time. The theory of IC has traditionally been used in two different ways: *IC as being* and *IC as doing*. The first way of viewing IC is as a state *of being* 'intercultural'. In this sense, people have cultural values and cultural differences, which are part of their state of being. By taking this view, previous studies have tended to concentrate on the search for cultural values that underlie cultural differences and theories and models that bridge differences in communication. Although popular between the 1970s and 1990s with Hofstede's often-cited work (1980) exemplifying this approach, recently criticisms have been launched against IC *as being* due to it being seen as essentialist, reductionist, and lacking problematization. In contrast, IC *as doing*, which has become increasingly popular in recent years due to the paradigm shift with regard to identity studies, views cultural identities as multidimensional and socially-constructed. Instead of seeing cultural identity as static or given, the theoretical lens of *IC as doing* 'problematizes the notion of cultural identities and emphasizes the emergent, discursive and inter-nature of interactions' (Zhu, 2014, p. 209).

The Age of Superdiversity

Although IC has been present throughout the different stages of world history (Pieterse, 2004), it has become particularly salient in today's globalized world. The term globalization, which was coined by Theodore Levitt in the May/June 1983 edition of the Harvard Business Review, was made particularly popular by Robertson (1992). Globalization can be defined as 'a system of interrelationships between regions and territories, places and settings, actors and actions, marked by massively increased velocity, intensity, reach, and impact' (Held et al., 1999, cited in Jayyusi, 2010, p. 154). Despite the label 'globalization' having been in circulation only relatively recently, the concept has been around for hundreds of years dating back to the fifteenth century with explorers mapping the planet. Just as the concept of globalization is not new, the resulting effects such as increased diversity of populations are also not new. What *is* new, however, is the pace at which globalization has spread due to the diffusion of capitalism, the fall of communism, and significant technological advances leading to faster and more efficient communication (Harris et al., 2002, p. 3). Thus, the speed with which people can move around the earth (hypermobility) and connect online at the click of a button is distinct to the last three decades. With more people moving to and from a greater number of places than in any other time in history, unprecedented forms of social, cultural, and linguistic diversity, especially in large urban centres of the world, has become commonplace. Vertovec (2007) explains that this increase in pace and scale of movement since the early 1990s has transformed 'diversity' into 'superdiversity'. The term 'superdiversity' thus refers to 'the diversification of diversity' (Vertovec, 2007) or 'diversity on the move' (Meissner & Vertovec, 2015). The increased spread, speed, and scale (the three S's) of diversification affects power, politics, and policy (the three P's) with respect to migration patterns, legal states, gender and age, and variance in human capital (Meissner & Vertovec, 2015). This concept has been adopted across a wide variety of social science disciplines including sociology and migration studies (Knowles, 2012), social work, demography, and linguistics (Blommaert & Rampton, 2012) where connections have been made between the three S's and the three P's to inform the fields. The UAE undoubtedly fits the description of a superdiverse context due to its heterogeneous population where it is estimated that over 100 languages are spoken by approximately 200 nationalities (Solloway, 2018, p. 459). In the UAE's most populous city, Dubai, 91.8% of the population are non-Emirati (Dubai Statistics Centre,

2017), making multilingualism and multiculturalism part of daily life, as will be expanded upon in Chapter 2 of this book.

As the concept of 'superdiversity' will be used throughout this book with reference to the study setting and comparable global contexts, it is important to recognize various critiques of the term before justifying its use. Firstly, the term 'superdiversity' has been criticized for its 'simple, catchy, youthful, and relentlessly optimistic and bright' connotation, which conjures images of a rosy world of peaceful diversity skirting around complexities and power dynamics. Makoni (2012) argues that the only beneficiaries of this celebration of diversity are Western scholars, whereas those from other parts of the world feel 'the idea of diversity is a careful concealment of power differences' (p. 192). It has also been argued that the vagueness of the term allows it to be used superficially with reference to global demographics, time, people, language, and media, thus appealing to the 'widest range of consumers' (Strutton & Roswinatho, 2014). Such criticisms of the term superdiversity have mainly targeted European contexts where scholars based in Western Europe have used the term superdiversity to describe a high concentration of migrants in a 'shrinking pool of prime destination countries' (Czajka & de Haas, 2014, p. 315) such as the UK, Germany, and France. This is said to reflect a 'Eurocentric worldview' (Czajka & de Haas, 2014, p. 314) of the notion of immigration becoming more diverse globally. However, as Pavlenko (2018) argues, the centres of linguistic diversity are not primarily in Western Europe but rather located in Africa, Asia, and the Pacific. Yet, little attention is given to such areas due to lack of research funds and grants available as well as a notable lack of interest in periphery contexts.

Taking the previous criticisms into consideration, the use of the term of superdiversity in this book aims to go further than equating it to demographic diversity in European migration hubs. Rather diversity in terms of cultures, identities, and languages are explored in relation the Asian context of the UAE with regard to not only migration patterns but also the everyday interactions of transnationals and locals in a range of domains including physical spaces and online contexts. Here, it is recognized that in addition to the complexity of greater physical movement between and within countries worldwide, 'global contact zones' (Clifford, 1997) or 'network societies' (Castells, 1996) have arisen not only in face-to-face contexts but also online due to the global spread of the Internet. It is also recognized that within these global contact zones people, 'meet, clash, and grapple with each other, often in highly asymmetrical relations of domination and subordination' (Pratt, 1992, p. 4). In this sense, superdiversity in the UAE does not equate to all nationalities and languages holding equal power and strength. Rather, uneven social and linguistic power exists through prominent social stratification, as will be explored in detail in Chapter 2 of this book.

Interculturality (IC) and Cultural Identities (CI)

The lens of Interculturality (IC) has been successfully used to analyze complex cultural identities often found in superdiverse contexts such as multilingual cities as well as diasporic communities. For example, Zhu's (2010) study investigated the process of language socialization in Chinese diasporic families in the United Kingdom using the theory of IC. Here tensions within communities, especially between different generations, were frequently found. For example, often adolescent children of immigrant parents were exposed to conflicting sets of cultural values and practices which led to challenges and complexities when constructing their own sociocultural identities. A further issue common in superdiverse and diasporic contexts is the potential tensions arising from conflicting language ideologies. For instance, older generations tend to view the target language (usually English) as the 'they-code' (Gumperz, 1982) and therefore prefer to use their mother tongue for family interaction. On the other hand, the younger generation often consider English as a 'we-code' and prefer it to ethnic languages. Such discrepancies in language ideologies challenge language maintenance and can result in 'conflict and tension regarding what language to use, when and to what extent' (Zhu, 2010, p. 191). Findings from the present study, which will be shared in subsequent chapters of the book, as well as findings from previous empirical research in the Gulf region mirror such descriptions of 'they-code vs. we-code' tensions, (Findlow, 2005, 2006; Hopkyns, 2014, 2016; O'Neill, 2016; Solloway, 2016). The question of to how to use English without marginalizing Arabic is one of the central challenges facing the Gulf region.

Translingual and Transcultural Identities

In superdiverse settings such as the UAE, as well as diasporic communities, younger generations tend to 'not only internalize the social and cultural norms of a community, but also actively participate in the construction of their own social and cultural identities' (Zhu, 2010, p. 191). In the context of the UAE, where English is used as the lingua franca as well as in education, cultural identity tends to display itself in what Baker (2009, p. 567) describes as 'a hybrid, mixed and liminal manner, drawing on and moving between global, national, local, and individual orientations'. Originally a term associated with biology, hybridity is now often used in cultural studies to describe the mix and plurality of identity that results from the phenomenon of 'togetherness-in-difference' (Ang, 2001) or 'double belonging' (Lam & Warriner, 2012). As Pavlenko and Black-ledge (2004, p. 17) explain, 'At times, fragmentation and splintering give birth to new, hybrid, identities and linguistic repertoires'. Such hybridity in positioning, or a creation of a 'third space' (Bhabha, 1994) is common

in such contexts. Exploring the way in which individuals reconfigure and/
or establish 'new centres' is, therefore, of direct relevance to the UAE
context as well as other superdiverse regions.

Translingual Identities

In settings where daily life is richly multilingual, 'collaborative work'
(Blommaert, 2010, p. 9) is common, where linguistic hybridity or 'translingual practice' (Canagarajah, 2013) is used as a way of easing communication or expressing oneself in a more natural and precise manner.
Universal forms of linguistic hybridity include code-switching and translanguaging. The former involves bilingual or multilingual speakers swap-
ping between or combining languages at the grammar, word, or phrase
level or at style levels. This happens not only between distinct languages
such as Arabic and English, but it can also happen within diglossic languages such as Arabic which includes Modern Standard Arabic (MSA),
Classical Arabic, and Khaleeji dialects. Going beyond code-switching,
translanguaging refers to the practices of bilinguals whose aim is to maximize communication potential, so it includes, but it is not limited to,
code-switching (Garcia, 2009). Translanguaging in both speaking and
writing is typical in superdiverse contexts. There are also other forms of
linguistic hybridity that are region-specific. In the case of the UAE, for
example, 'Arabizi', which is a combination of the word *Arabi* (Arabic)
and *Engliszi* (English), involves the mixing of English and Arabic words
using a modified Latin script (Bianchi, 2012; Palfreyman & Al Khalil,
2003) and English numbers to replace Arabic sounds that have no spelling equivalent in English (Al Fardan & Al Kaabi, 2015). For example, the
Arabic letter 'ع' (Ain) is represented as the English number '3'. Arabizi
has become popular on social media, as using Latin script for writing
Arabic words online is generally deemed easier than using the Arabic
script due to the dominance of English on the Internet. Texting using Arabizi is also popular as not all cell phones are Arabic-friendly and many do
not support the Arabic language in their built-in systems (Hopkyns et al.,
2018). As Arabizi has no definite rules, it is a friendly and accessible way
of communicating. For example, in the name 'Mohammed' the number
7 is used for the epiglottal fricative /ħ/ (a heavy /h/ sound not found in
English) but there is freedom over the spelling, meaning both 'Mu7am-
mad' or 'm7md' may be used. This allows young Emiratis to exercise linguistic creativity and provides agency and freedom to 'make up the rules'.
As a result, translingual practice becomes very much users' own and an
active part of identity construction in superdiverse contexts. Translingual identities can also emerge through creative ways of avoiding dominant languages such as English. In the UAE, for instance, a phenomenon,
which is rarely discussed in English publications, is *White Dialects*. This
term refers to hybridity within the Arabic language rather than between

languages, and it is used by speakers intentionally or unintentionally to maximize communication potential, as with translanguaging (Hopkyns et al., 2018). The concept of white dialects was coined only recently by Ahmed Esmael at the 2016 Arabic Conference in Dubai and arose from linguists' desire to protect the Arabic language and maintain its position as the language of the Arabic identity and everyday life (Hopkyns et al., 2018). White dialects act as a middle ground between all dialects of Arabic. However, unlike MSA, which is naturally assumed to be the default version of Arabic used between Arabic speakers, white dialects are more fluid and changeable in nature as they are the linguistic product that speakers produce while communicating. Translingual practice, in this sense, may be used as a form of resistance to the dominance of English, as will be explored further in Chapter 3 of this book.

Although linguistic hybridity in multilingual contexts has been recognized by scholars as both natural and commonplace (Blommaert, 2015; Canagarajah, 2013; Dovchin, 2017; Dovchin & Lee, 2019), attitudes towards such practice vary greatly, with some multilingual speakers supporting linguistic hybridity and others lamenting the loss of language purity. In formal domains such as education, translingual practice is often not readily accepted (Carroll & van den Hoven, 2017). Instead, common ideologies centre around monolingualism or 'double monolingualism' (Al-Bataineh & Gallagher, 2018), where it is felt languages should be pure and separate or remain as 'two solitudes' (Cummins, 2007). Such monolingual ideologies often jar with natural language use in multilingual contexts, causing a clash between ideas of what 'should be' and what 'is'.

Transcultural Identities

Together with monolingual ideologies is a tendency to try and simplify the concept of culture by mistakenly using the words 'culture' and 'country' as synonyms. Billig (1995) describes this notion as 'banal nationalism' where the concept of a national language and a national culture is treated as unproblematic. Even though nationality still plays a significant role in defining one's identity in intercultural relationships, it should be recognized that this strand is only one element of intercultural relations. Defining culture by nationality alone hides a multiplicity of differences between individuals such as 'unequal power relations, including poverty, violence, structural inequalities such as racism and the possibilities of multiple identities' (Hoskins & Sallah, 2011, p. 114). When we talk of 'Western culture' or 'Emirati culture', therefore, we must do so with the understanding that there are variations and fluidity within these categories, and recognize the multifaceted, co-constructed nature of participants' cultural identities. In the case of millennials growing up in superdiverse contexts, arguably more prominent than *national cultural identities* are emerging *transcultural identities*. Here we find individuals in superdiverse contexts not relating to any specific national culture. In today's postmodern society, many scholars and writers emphasize a self which is unrestricted by any specific cultures. In this sense, people are fluid and many-sided, endlessly changing and recreating identities, which Lifton (1999) refers to as 'the protean self' after Proteus, the Greek sea god of many forms. Building on this perspective, Mathews (2000, p. 4) compares modern cultural identity to shopping in a 'cultural supermarket', arguing that 'we have come to live in a world of culture as fashion, in which each of us can pick and choose cultural identities like we pick and choose clothes'. Mathews' study (1996), investigating cultural identity in the shadow of Hong Kong's return to China in 1997, found that university graduates, teachers, and alumni enjoyed choosing or 'shopping for' Western names for themselves to be used in public (e.g., Vivian, Alice, Henry), feeling that 'Chinese names were "old-fashioned", and restricted for use at home'. Similarly, Emirati teenagers also frequently adopt Western names in order to present a certain image, especially online (Hopkyns, 2014).

Although to a certain extent, the presence of a cultural supermarket exists in superdiverse contexts where individuals can 'choose the best of the West' and reject other parts of what English symbolizes, it should be recognized that identity is not entirely a 'free-floating concept' (Zhu, 2017, p. 131) or a 'choose your own adventure novel', where each choice takes one in seemingly undefined directions (Mulcock, 2001, p. 171). Rather, restrictions do exist, especially in the Middle Eastern context. As Mathews (1996, p. 401) recognizes:

> One's choices from the cultural supermarket are deeply influenced by one's given cultural shaping, and also by the array of social and institutional rules one must conform to and the roles one must fit. They are also shaped by the array of competing voices aimed at molding one's mind, from the propaganda of nations, to the blandishments of advertisements and the allure of popular culture, to the pressures of one's immediate social world.

Here we are reminded of the opening quote in this chapter, which describes the existing tensions between personal choices or notions of identity and society's expectations.

The Bound Nature of Language, Culture, and Identity

Not only are social groupings, societal norms, behaviour, and artifacts connected to cultural identity formation, but there are undisputable connections between language, culture, and identity to the point where language is viewed a fundamental element of any discussion on cultural identity. As Kramsch (1998) states, 'Language is the principal means whereby we conduct our social lives. When it is used in contexts of communication, it is bound up with culture in multiple and complex ways' (p. 3). Scholars researching in the Gulf region draw parallels between the far-reaching power English has as a language and Islam has as a religion. Both are far more than their labels suggest. As Harris (1991, p. 90) states, 'English is not just a language, any more than Islam is just a religion', in that neither can be easily restricted or contained. Morrow and Castleton (2011, p. 329) point out the pervasive nature of both Islam and English in the context of the Gulf by stating, 'Even those who are briefly in an Arabic speaking country will find themselves, without conscious thought, utilizing the more common Allah phrases. Who, then, can learn English without learning all that comes along with it?'. In this sense, language, culture, and identity are intrinsically intertwined, making them prone to the 'domino effect' (Hopkyns, 2014, p. 5), in that if one is affected, the others are not far behind. As Said (2011) powerfully states, 'losing a language is losing a culture and losing culture is losing one's identity' (p. 191). This strong statement which focuses on 'losing' rather than 'gaining' does, however, imply that without one's own language, one is left with nothing, which is certainly not the case. While language is an important part of identity, it should be recognized that it is one of many aspects contributing to identity construction. These multifaceted aspects of a person's identity are fluid, changeable, and constantly evolving. It therefore is not possible, or desirable, to remain in a state in which one's culture, language, and identity remain unchanged. Indeed, changes to identity through the use of English may be welcomed changes, which add rather than subtract from a person's sense of identity. Block (2008) challenges the term 'loss' in relation to multilingualism and multiculturalism, stating that for many individuals the focus is not on what they might be losing but rather on what they seek to develop. As Cheng (2010, cited in Dervin, 2014, p. 193) correctly states, 'Every culture changes; otherwise it is not culture, but a museum piece'. In alliance with the theory of IC, it should be emphasized that 'culture permeates and means different things to different people' (Zhu, 2015, p. 23). In this sense, cultural identities, especially in superdiverse contexts, are complex and should be recognized as such.

Together with the theory of interculturality, it is the intertwined nature of the three key concepts, culture, identity, and language (Figure 1.1), which form the core theoretical and conceptual framework of the study.

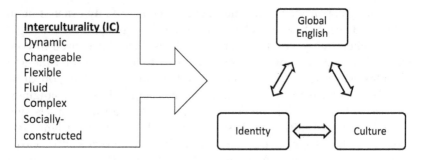

Figure 1.1 The Theoretical and Conceptual Framework of the Study

1.5 Research Notes and Overview of the Book

Complexity within identity construction is present in multiple contexts across the globe. However, due to the unique combination of linguistic, social, demographic, historical, and cultural factors in the UAE, this complexity intensifies, making the effects of global English on local cultural identities especially vital and timely to investigate. Rather than accept the binary position of English vs. Arabic or West vs. East pushed forward by the headlines seen at the start of this chapter, where English is seen as a bully and Arabic as a sitting target, the effects of global English on cultural identity in the UAE instead need to be recognized as complicated and multidimensional.

This book explores such complexities through extensive research in the capital city of the UAE, Abu Dhabi. The approach taken (which will be discussed further in Chapter 4 of this book) is a phenomenological case study. This innovative hybrid approach was used to investigate multiple participants' perspectives. The phenomenon investigated in the study was 'global English, and its effect on local cultural identities' and the cases or units of analysis were three groups of participants (Emirati university students, Emirati primary school teachers, and expatriate university teachers). Each group had a vested interest in the topic due to all living in the UAE and all being affected to varying degrees by the issues discussed.

A key feature of phenomenology is its emphasis on the existence of multiple realities. As Denscombe (2010) states,

> Phenomenology rejects the notion that there is one universal reality and accepts, instead, that things can be seen in different ways by different people at different times in different circumstances, and that each alternative version needs to be recognized as being valid in its own right.

Phenomenological research essentially aims to 'to make the invisible visible' (Kvale, 1996, p. 53) and focuses on the life world of participants with an openness to their experiences. The study provides illuminating insights into the many nuances and complexities involved in identity construction in the modern superdiverse landscape of the UAE. Specific real-life examples paint a vivid picture of both the challenges and growth connected to linguistic and cultural change. With 164 participants in total completing open-response questionnaires and partaking in lively and fruitful focus group discussions, the data shared in this book are both rich and poignant. The data were analyzed using thematic data analysis (TA), and methodological triangulation was employed for added validity.

Chapter Synopses

This chapter has explored the key concepts of the book: global English, modern cultural identities, and interculturality in superdiverse contexts. It has also briefly introduced the study. We will now turn to look at what is to come in subsequent chapters. Following the introductory chapter, the second chapter examines the context of the UAE by providing the background to issues reflected in the newspaper headlines at the start of the book. Contextual factors contributing to such tensions between English, Arabic, and cultural identity are analyzed. These include the UAE's climate of fast-paced change, its demographic imbalance, its complex history with English-speaking nations, the increased amount of English in education, the prevalence of global English in multiple domains, and Arabic diglossia (use of different versions of Arabic in different contexts). While such a combination of factors is unique to the UAE context, taken individually many of the factors, such as multinational demographics and English in education (EMI), apply to multiple contexts worldwide.

The third chapter presents examples of many forms of resistance to the dominance of English in the region. This includes the country's 'Emiratization initiative', a surge of conferences and symposia on the theme of cultural identity, as well as a marked Arabic language drive. Top-down nation-wide projects to boost Arabic and local cultural identity are explored as well as bottom-up grassroots efforts seen amongst Emirati students. Comparisons are made with neighbouring Gulf states and other countries worldwide. It is argued that despite the various forms of resistance highlighted in this chapter, the pragmatic importance of English continues to grow and this seems to outweigh resistance efforts. The chapter explores a distinct 'conflict of desires' in terms of English being both needed and resented.

The fourth chapter provides the background to the study by explaining who the participants were and how their views are particularly valuable to explore. The chapter also explains the nature of the study in terms of approach, data collection, and data analysis. The fifth, sixth, and seventh chapters draw on data from the study. Chapter 5 discusses language and symbolism. The image of English and Arabic from both Emirati and expatriate points of view are explored. The chapter contains a series of striking word clouds which show in an instant the image of both languages. The word clouds consist of words the participants associated with the languages. Very little overlap could be seen between the two languages, with English representing the outside world and Arabic symbolizing inner worlds. Comparisons are made with other global settings, where binary ways of viewing English and mother tongue languages are also apparent. Chapter 6 explores the effects of global English on various layers of Emirati cultural identity. Major themes include power and agency, English as additive and subtractive, complexities in modern cultural identities, and feelings of English being wanted but not welcome. Chapter 7 looks at the sociolinguistic implications of EMI. In the UAE, where EMI dominates all levels of education, there is almost no choice but to study in the medium of English in higher education. Key questions explored include: How much EMI? Which English should be taught in EMI courses? And who should teach EMI courses? Comparisons are made with other global contexts with regard to attitudes to EMI and sociolinguistic implications.

The eighth chapter, which is the concluding chapter, looks back at the findings and provides concrete suggestions for addressing key issues raised in the study's findings. Practical pedagogical implications are discussed and recommendations are provided as to how to achieve a discourse of balance and inclusion, promote hybridity over purity, and focus on an element of choice regarding medium of instruction in higher education.

References

Ahmed, K. (2011). Casting Arabic culture as the 'other': Cultural issues in the English curriculum. In C. Gitsaki (Ed.), *Teaching and Learning in the Arab World* (pp. 119–137). Bern: Peter Lang.

Alasuutari, P. (1995). *Researching Culture: Qualitative Method and Cultural Studies*. London, Thousand Oaks, New Delhi: Sage Publications.

Al-Bataineh, A., & Gallagher, K. (2018). Attitudes towards translanguaging: How future teachers perceive the meshing of Arabic and English in children's story books. *International Journal of Bilingual Education and Bilingualism*. https://doi.org.10.1080/13670050.2018.1471039.

Al Dabbagh, A. (2005). Globalism and the universal language. *English Today*, 21 (2), 3–12.

Al Fardan, H., & Al Kaabi, A. (2015). *Spoken Emirati Phrasebook*. Abu Dhabi: Cultural Programs and Heritage Festivals Committee, Abu Dhabi.

Ang, I. (2001). *On Not Speaking Chinese. Living Between Asia and the West*. London: Routledge.

Atkinson, D. (1999). TESOL and culture. *TESOL Quarterly*, 33 (4), 625–654.

Baker, W. (2009). The cultures of English as a lingua franca. *TESOL Quarterly*, 43 (4), 567–592.

Bakhtin, M. (1981). *The Dialogic Imagination* (M. Holquist, Ed., C. Emerson, & M. Holquist, Trans.). Austin: University of Texas Press.

Bhabha, H. K. (1994). *The Location of Culture*. London: Routledge.

Bianchi, R. M. (2012). Glocal Arabic online: The case of 3arabizi. *Studies in Second Language Learning and Teaching*, 2 (4), 483–503.

Billig, M. (1995). *Banal Nationalism*. London: Sage Publications.

Block, D. (2002). McCommunication. In D. Block, & D. Cameron (Eds.), *Globalization and Language Teaching* (pp. 117–133). London: Routledge.

Block, D. (2007). *Second Language Identities*. New York: Continuum.

Block, D. (2008). On the appropriateness of the metaphor LOSS. In P. Tan, & R. Rubdy (Eds.), *Language as Commodity: Global Structures, Local Marketplaces* (pp. 187–203). London: Routledge.

Blommaert, J. (2010). *The Sociolinguistic of Globalization*. Cambridge: Cambridge University Press.

Blommaert, J. (2015). *Ethnography, Superdiversity and Linguistic Landscapes: Chronicles of Complexity*. Bristol, UK: Multilingual Matters.

Blommaert, J. (2016, November). *Connecting the Dots Nonlinearly: Language, Globalization and Complexity*. Paper presented at the Third International Conference on Language, Linguistics, Literature and Translation – Connecting the dots in a Glocalized World, Sultan Qaboos University, Muscat, Oman.

Blommaert, J., & Rampton, B. (2012). *Language and Superdiversity*. MMG Working Paper 12–09, Max Plank Institute for the Study of Religious and Ethnic Diversity. Göttengen.

Bourdieu, P. (1977). The economics of linguistic exchanges. *Social Science Information*, 16, 645–668.

Bourdieu, P. (1991). *Language and Symbolic Power*. Cambridge: Polity Press.

Brumfit, C. J. (2004). Language and higher education: Two current challenges. *Arts and Humanities in Higher Education*, 3 (2), 163–173.

Canagarajah, S. (2013). *Translingual Practice: Global Englishes and Cosmopolitan Relations*. New York: Routledge.

Carroll, K. S., & van den Hoven, M. (2017). Translanguaging within higher education in the United Arab Emirates. In C. M. Mazak, & K. S. Carroll (Eds.), *Translanguaging in Higher Education: Beyond Monolingual Ideologies* (pp. 141–156). Bristol: Multilingual Matters.

Castells, M. (1996). *The Rise of the Network Society: The Information Age*. Oxford: Blackwell.

Clifford, J. (1997). *Routes, Travel and Translation in the Late Twentieth Century*. Cambridge, MA: Harvard University Press.

Crane, D. (1994). Introduction: The challenge of the sociology of culture to sociology as discipline. In D. Crane (Ed.), *The Sociology of Culture* (pp. 1–19). Oxford: Blackwell.

Crystal, D. (1997). Vanishing languages. *Civilization*, 40–45.

Crystal, D. (2012). A global language. In P. Seargeant, & J. Swann (Eds.), *English in the World: History, Diversity, Change* (pp. 151–177). New York: Routledge.

Cultural identity in danger in the GCC (2013, December 17). *Gulf News*. Retrieved from: https://gulfnews.com/going-out/society/cultural-identity-in-danger-in-the-gcc-1.1268187.

Cummins, J. (2007). Rethinking monolingual instructional strategies in multilingual classrooms. *Canadian Journal of Applied Linguistics*, 10, 221–240.

Czajka, M., & de Haas, H. (2014). The globalization of migration: Has the world become more migratory? *International Migration Review*, 48 (2), 283–323.

Davies, B., & Harre, R. (1990). Positioning: The discursive production of selves. *Journal for the Theory of Social Behaviour*, 20 (1), 43–63.

Denscombe, M. (2010). *The Good Research Guide* (4th ed.). New York: Open University Press.

Dervin, F. (2014). Exploring 'new' interculturality online. *Language and Intercultural Communication*, 14 (2), 191–206. http://dx.doi.org/10.1080/147084 77.2014.896923.

Dervin, F., & Liddicoat, A. J. (2013). Introduction: Linguistics for intercultural education. In F. Dervin, & A. J. Liddicoat (Eds.), *Linguistics for Intercultural Education* (pp. 1–28). Amsterdam: John Benjamins Publishing.

Deument, A. (2000). Language planning and policy. In R. Mesthrie, J. Swann, A. Deumert, & W. L. Leap (Eds.), *Introducing Sociolinguistics* (pp. 371–405). Edinburgh: Edinburgh University Press.

Dovchin, S. (2017). The ordinariness of youth linguascapes in Mongolia. *International Journal of Multilingualism*, 14, 144–159.

Dovchin, S. (2018). *Language, Media and Globalization in the Periphery: The Linguascapes of Popular Music in Mongolia*. New York: Routledge.

Dovchin, S., & Lee, J. W. (2019). Introduction to special issue: 'The ordinariness of translinguistics'. *International Journal of Multilingualism*. doi:10.1080/149 0718.2019.1575831

Dubai Statistics Centre (2017). Retrieved from: www.dsc.gov.ae/en-us.

Embrace English . . . Without Losing Arab Identity (2013, December 24). *The Arab News*. Retrieved from: www.arabnews.com/news/497601.

English Language "Seducing" UAE Pupils (2014, December 8). *The National*. Retrieved from: www.thenational.ae/uae/english-language-seducing-uae-pupils-speaker-at-panel-says-1.269234.

English Proficiency Comes at a Cost (2011, February 27). *Gulf News*. Retrieved from: https://gulfnews.com/uae/education/english-proficiency-comes-at-a-cost-1.768125.

Findlow, S. (2005). International networking in the United Arab Emirates higher education: Global-local tension. *Compare*, 35 (3), 285–302.

Findlow, S. (2006). Higher education and linguistic dualism in the Arab Gulf. *British Journal of Sociology of Education*, 27 (1), 19–36.

Fishman, J. A. (1999). The new linguistic order. *Foreign Policy*, 113, 26–34.

Garcia, O. (2009). *Bilingual Education in the 21st Century: A Global Perspective*. Oxford: Wiley-Blackwell.

Gumperz, J. (1982). *Discourse Strategies*. Cambridge: Cambridge University Press.

Hammond, A. (2007). *What the Arabs Think of America*. Cairo, Egypt: Greenwood World Publishing.

Harris, R. (1991). English versus Islam: The Asian voice of Salman Rushdie. In M. Chan, & R. Harris (Eds.), *Asian Voices in English* (pp. 87–96). Hong Kong: Hong Kong University Press.

Harris, R., Leung, C., & Rampton, B. (2002). Globalization, diaspora, and language education in England. In D. Block, & D. Cameron (Eds.), *Globalization and Language Teaching* (pp. 29–46). London: Routledge.

Harrison, D., Kamphuis, D., & Barnes, M. (2007). Linguistic imperialism in 21st century Arabia. In A. Jendli, S. Troudi, & C. Coombe (Eds.), *The Power of Language: Perspectives from Arabia* (pp. 20–34). Dubai: TESOL Arabia.

Higgins, C. (2009). *English as a Local Language*. Bristol, UK: Multilingual Matters.

Hofstede, G. (1980). *Culture's Consequences: International Differences in Work-related Values*. London: Sage Publications.

Holliday, A. (1999). Small cultures. *Applied Linguistics*, 20 (2), 237–264.

Holliday, A. (2005). *The Struggle to Teach English as an International Language*. Oxford: Oxford University Press.

Hopkyns, S. (2014). The effects of global English on culture and identity in the UAE: A double-edged sword. *Learning and Teaching in Higher Education: Gulf Perspectives*, 11 (2).

Hopkyns, S. (2016). Emirati cultural identity in the age of 'Englishization': Voices from an Abu Dhabi university. In L. Buckingham (Ed.), *Language, Identity and Education on the Arabian Peninsula* (pp. 87–115). Bristol: Multilingual Matters.

Hopkyns, S., Zoghbor, W., & Hassall, P. (2018). Creative hybridity over linguistic purity: The status of English in the United Arab Emirates. *Asian Englishes*, 20 (2), 158–169.

Hoskins, B., & Sallah, M. (2011). Developing intercultural competence in Europe: The challenges. *Languages and Intercultural Communication*, 11 (2), 113–125. doi:10.1080/14708477.2011.556739.

House, J. (2003). Developing pragmatic competence in English as a lingua franca. In K. Knapp, & C. Meierkord (Eds.), *Lingua Franca Communication* (pp. 245–268). Frankfurt: Peter Lang.

Ingold, T. (1994). Introduction to culture. In T. Ingold (Ed.), *Companion Encyclopedia of Anthropology: Humanity, Culture, and Social Life* (pp. 329–349). London: Routledge.

Jayyusi, L. (2010). The Arab world, the global moment, and the struggle over representation. *Encounters* (2), 153–182. Dubai: Zayed University Press.

Jenkins, J. (2014). *English as a Lingua Franca in the International University: The Politics of Academic English Language Policy*. London: Routledge.

Kachru, B. B. (Ed.). (1992). *The Other Tongue. English Across Cultures* (2nd ed.). Chicago: Illinois University Press.

Knowles, C. (2012). Nigerian London: Re-mapping space and ethnicity in super-diverse cities. *Ethnic and Racial Studies*, 36 (4), 651–669.

Kramsch, C. (1998). *Language and culture*. Oxford: Oxford University Press.

Kuppens, A. H. (2013). Cultural globalization and the global spread of English: From 'separate fields, similar paradigms' to a transdisciplinary approach. *Globalizations*, 10 (2), 327–342.

Kvale, S. (1996). *InterViews*. London: Sage Publications.

Lam, W. S. E., & Warriner, D. S. (2012). Transnationalism and literacy: Investigating the mobility of people, languages, texts, and practices in contexts of migration. *Reading Research Quarterly*, 47 (2), 191–215.

Learning Arabic Should Be a Joy, Not a Chore (2019, August 1). *The National*. Retrieved from: www.thenational.ae/opinion/editorial/learning-arabic-should-be-a-joy-not-a-chore-1.893605.

Lifton, R. J. (1999). *The Protean Self: Human Resilience in an Age of Fragmentation*. Chicago: University of Chicago Press.

Lytra, V. (2016). Language and ethnic identity. In S. Preece (Ed.), *Handbook of Language and Identity* (pp. 131–145). New York: Routledge.

MacLure, M. (1993). Arguing for your self: Identity as an organizing principle in teachers' jobs and lives. *British Educational Research Journal*, 19 (4), 311–323.

Makoni, S. (2012). A critique of language, languaging, and supervernacular. *Muitas Vozes*, 1 (2), 189–199.

Mathews, G. (1996). Names and identities in the Hong Kong cultural supermarket. *Dialectical Anthropology*, 21, 399–419.

Mathews, G. (2000). *Global Culture/Individual Identity: Searching for Home in the Cultural Supermarket*. London: Routledge.

McArthur, T. (2004). Is it world English or international English or global English, and does it matter? *English Today*, 20 (3), 3–5.

Meierkord, C. (2002). 'Language stripped bare' or 'linguistic masala'? Culture in lingua franca communication. In K. Knapp, & C. Meierkord (Eds.), *Lingua Franca Communication* (pp. 245–268). Frankfurt: Peter Lang.

Meissner, F., & Vertovec, S. (2015). Comparing Super-diversity. *Ethnic and Racial Studies*, 38 (4), 541–555.

Mercer, S. (2011). Language learner self-concept: Complexity, continuity and change. *System*, 39 (3), 335–346.

Mori, J. (2003). The construction of interculturality: A study of initial encounters between Japanese and American students. *Research on Language and Social Interaction*, 36 (2), 143–184.

Morrow, J. A., & Castleton, B. (2011). The impact of global English on the Arabic language: The loss of the Allah lexicon. In A. Al-Issa, & L. S. Dahan (Eds.), *Global English and Arabic* (pp. 307–334). Bern, Switzerland: Peter Lang.

Mulcock, J. (2001). Creativity and politics in the cultural supermarket: Synthesizing indigenous identities for the r/evolution of spirit. *Continuum: Journal of Media and Cultural Studies*, 15 (2), 169–185.

Nishizaka, A. (1995). The interactive constitution of interculturality: How to be Japanese with words. *Human Studies*, 18, 301–326.

Norton, B. (2000). *Identity and Language Learning*. Harlow, England: Longman.

O'Neill, G. T. (2016). Heritage, heteroglossia and home: Multilingualism in Emirati families. In L. Buckingham (Ed.), *Language, Identity and Education on the Arabian Peninsula* (pp. 13–38). Bristol: Multilingual Matters.

Palfreyman, D., & Al Khalil, M. (2003). A funky language for teenzz to use: Representing Gulf Arabic in instant messaging. *Journal of Computer-Mediated Communication*, 9, 23–44.

Pavlenko, A. (2018). Superdiversity and why it isn't: Reflections on terminological innovation and academic branding. In B. Schmenk, S. Breidbach, & L. Küster (Eds.), *Sloganization in Language Education Discourse: Conceptual Thinking in the Age of Academic Marketization* (pp. 142–168). Bristol: Multilingual Matters.

Pavlenko, A., & Blackledge, A. (2004). Introduction: New theoretical approaches to the study of negotiation of identities in multilingual contexts. In A. Pavlenko, & A. Blackledge (Eds.), *Negotiation of Identities in Multilingual Contexts* (pp. 1–33). Clevedon: Multilingual Matters.

Pennycook, A. (2001). *Critical Applied Linguistics: A Critical Introduction.* Mahwah, NJ: Erlbaum.

Pennycook, A. (2003a). Global Englishes, Rip Slyme, and performativity. *Journal of Sociolinguistics*, 7 (4), 513–533.

Pennycook, A. (2003b). Beyond homogeny and heterogeny: English as a global and worldly language. In C. Mair (Ed.), *The Politics of English as a World Language* (pp. 3–17). Amsterdam: Rodopi.

Pennycook, A. (2007). *Global Englishes and Transcultural Flows.* London: Routledge.

Pennycook, A. (2010). The future of Englishes: One, many or more. In A. Kirkpatrick (Ed.), *The Routledge Handbook of World Englishes* (pp. 673–687). London: Routledge.

Phillipson, R. (1992). *Linguistic Imperialism.* Oxford: Oxford University Press.

Pieterse, J. N. (2004). *Globalization and Culture: Global Mélange.* Lanham: Rowman & Littlefield.

Polzl, U. (2003). Signaling cultural identity: The use of L1/Ln in ELF. *Vienna English Working Papers*, 12 (2). 3–23. Retrieved from: www.univie.ac.at/Anglistik/views/03_2/POEL_SGL.PDF.

Poor literacy in Arabic is 'the new disability' in the UAE, FNC (Federal National Council) told (2013, June 12). *The National.* Retrieved from: www.thenational.ae/uae/education/poor-literacy-in-arabic-is-the-new-disability-in-the-uae-fnc-told-1.647654.

Pratt, M. L. (1992). Art of the contact zone. *Professions*, 91, 33–40.

Qiang, N., & Wolff, M. (2005). Is EFL a modern day Trojan horse? *English Today*, 21 (4), 55–60.

Riley, P. (2006). Self-expression and negotiation of identity in a foreign language. *International Journal of Applied Linguistics*, 16 (3), 295–318.

Risager, K., & Dervin, F. (2015). Introduction. In K. Risager, & F. Dervin (Eds.), *Researching Identity and Interculturality* (pp. 1–24). New York: Routledge.

Robertson, R. (1992). *Globalization: Social Theory and Global Culture.* London: Sage Publications.

Said, F. F. S. (2011). Ahyaan I text in English 'ashaan it's ashal': Language in crisis or linguistic development? The case of how Gulf Arabs perceive the future of their language, culture and identity. In A. Al-Issa, & L. S. Dahan (Eds.), *Global English and Arabic* (pp. 179–212). Bern, Switzerland: Peter Lang.

Selvi, A. F. (2016). Native or non-native English-speaking professionals in ELT: 'That is the question!' or 'Is that the question?' In F. Coupland, S. Garton, & S. Mann (Eds.), *LETS and NESTS: Voices, Views and Vignettes* (pp. 53–69). London: British Council.

Solloway, A. (2016). English in the United Arab Emirates: Innocuous lingua franca or insidious cultural Trojan horse? In L. Buckingham (Ed.), *Language, Identity and Education on the Arabian Peninsula* (pp. 176–196). Bristol: Multilingual Matters.

Solloway, A. (2018). 'Make them take an 'IELTS test' in Arabic'! Resentment of and resistance to English and English-medium instruction in the UAE. *Arab World English Journal*, 9 (3), 458–478.

Spencer-Oatley, H. (2000). *Culturally Speaking.* London: Continuum.

Strauss, C., & Quinn, N. (1997). *A Cognitive Theory of Cultural Meaning.* Cambridge: Cambridge University Press.

Strutton, D., & Roswinatho, W. (2014). Can vague brand slogans promote desirable consumer responses? *Journal of Product and Brand Management*, 23 (4–5), 282–294.

Suleiman, Y. (2003). *The Arabic Language and National Identity*. Edinburgh: Edinburgh University Press.

Suzuki, T. (1999). *Why the Japanese People are no Good at English*. Tokyo: Iwanami Shoten.

Swaan, A. de. (2001). *Words of the World: The Global Language System*. Cambridge: Polity Press.

Swales, J. (1997). English as Tyrannosaurus Rex. *World Englishes*, 16 (3), 373–382.

Teach us English but Without Its Cultural Values (2013, January 29). *The Saudi Gazette*. Retrieved from: http://live.saudigazette.com.sa/article/30286.

Tracy, K. (2002). *Everyday Talk: Building and Reflecting Identities*. New York: The Guilford Press.

Troudi, S., & Al-Hafidh (2014, June). *The Dilemma of English and Its Roles in the United Arab Emirates and the Gulf*. The Gulf Research Meeting. Paper presented at Cambridge University, Cambridge, UK.

Tsui, A. B. M., & Tollefson, J. W. (2007). *Language Policy, Culture, and Identity in Asian Contexts*. London: Lawrence Erlbaum Associates.

Utayba, M. (2015). Sayyidat al-qamar: The allure of storytelling, the pain of remembering. In M. Utayba (Ed.), *On Narration and Critical Practice: Readings in Arabic and World Literature*. Cairo: Al-Haya Al-amma li-qusur al-thaqafa.

Vertovec, S. (2007). Super-diversity and its implications. *Ethnic and Racial Studies*, 30 (6), 1024–1054.

World Arabic Language Day: The Fight to Keep Arabic Relevant (2017, December 18). *The National*. Retrieved from: www.thenational.ae/arts-culture/world-arabic-language-day-the-fight-to-keep-arabic-relevant-1.685324.

Young, R. (1996). *Intercultural Communication*. Clevedon: Multilingual Matters Ltd.

Zhu, H. (2010). Language socialization and interculturality: Address terms in intergenerational talk in Chinese diasporic families. *Language and Intercultural Communication*, 10 (3), 189–205.

Zhu, H. (2014). *Exploring Intercultural Communication: Language in Action*. Abingdon: Routledge.

Zhu, H. (2015). Negotiation as the way of engagement in intercultural and lingua franca communication: Frames of reference and interculturality. *Journal of English as Lingua Franca*, 4 (1), 63–90.

Zhu, H. (2017). New Orientations to identities in mobility. In S. Canagarajah (Ed.), *Routledge Handbook of Migration and Language* (pp. 117–132). London: Routledge.

2 Linguistic Angst and Cultural Tensions in the United Arab Emirates

Adults who were Bedouins, tending goats and farming dates, have children driving Land Cruisers and studying in America.

– Winslow et al. (2002, p. 572)

The past is a foreign country, they do things differently there.

– Hartley (1953)

Every context has a different sociolinguistic reality. For the UAE, this reality is complex, dynamic and full of multiplicities. Today's Arabian Gulf could be described as a parallel universe when comparing it to how it was less than five decades ago. The changes that have taken place within this period in many of the Gulf countries, including the UAE, are unfathomable, even to those who have seen them with their own eyes. Labelled the 'land of superlatives', the UAE's physical transformation can most obviously be seen in the creation of country-wide urban megaprojects which include architecturally unique skyscrapers, state-of-the-art hospitals, dazzling megamalls with 4D cinema complexes, futuristic-designed schools and universities, five-star-plus hotel resorts, and even whole 'entertainment islands'.

Dramatic changes in wealth, demographics, infrastructure, and lifestyle are a result of industrialization, urbanization, modernization, and, perhaps most strikingly, globalization in terms of the English language and all that accompanies it. Figure 2.1 shows the difference in terms of infrastructure and lifestyles affected by the surrounding environments, by contrasting the UAE's natural desert landscape, which once covered the country, with today's highly-developed Dubai skyline, landscaped gardens, and high-speed motorways.

To look back in time, the UAE started as seven Trucial Sheikdom States of the Persian Gulf coast with the UK having taken control of their defense and foreign affairs in a series of treaties made in the

2.1.1: Timeless Liwa Desert   *2.1.2:* The highly-developed Dubai skyline

Figure 2.1 From Desert to City

Photographs by the author

1800s. The Trucial States were never given the status of colony under the British Empire due to the region being extremely poor at the time (Gobert, 2019, p. 113), but the power relations involved resembled 'informal colonialism' (Onley, 2005). After over 150 years of British rule of what was a mainly impoverished population of Bedouin tribes, traders, and pearl divers thinly spread across vast and desolate desert lands, the British announced their planned departure in 1968, and three years later the United Arab Emirates as a country was formed. The British presence in the region was regarded as in some ways beneficial but also exploitative, especially once oil was discovered in the late 1950s (Al-Fahim, 1995, p. 42). After the discovery of oil, the UAE established itself as a 'rentier state' (Minnis, 2006), whereby it acquired a significant portion of its national revenues from the sale of indigenous resources (oil, in the case of the UAE) to external customers, with the government being the primary recipient of this external rent. As a consequence, the government was able to use the newly acquired petrodollars to boost the economy and infrastructure of the country in dramatic and dynamic ways.

Although the UAE is often held up as a 'shiny success story' or 'zero to hero tale', as with any rollercoaster ride of insatiable momentum, complications or reservations often only become apparent with time. A kaleidoscope of contextual factors contributes to current linguistic angst and cultural tension in the region. These factors include the UAE's climate of fast-paced change, hypermobility, and superdiversity, the dramatic and sudden increase of English in education and society in general, its complex history with English-speaking nations, and the presence of *diglossia* in Arabic (different types of Arabic spoken at home and in educational contexts) (Figure 2.2).

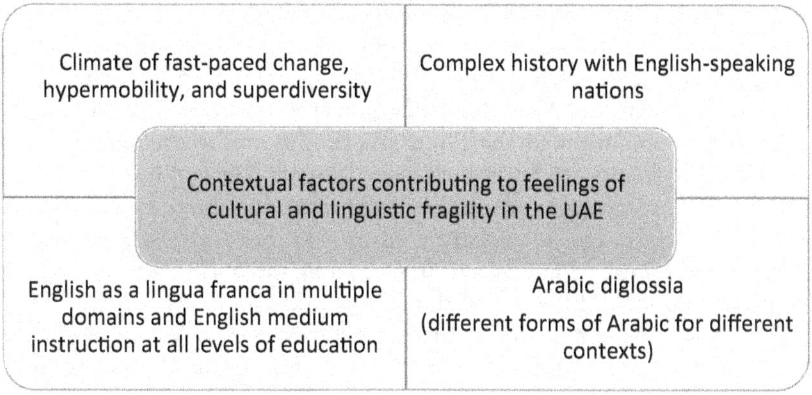

Climate of fast-paced change, hypermobility, and superdiversity	Complex history with English-speaking nations
English as a lingua franca in multiple domains and English medium instruction at all levels of education	Arabic diglossia (different forms of Arabic for different contexts)

Contextual factors contributing to feelings of cultural and linguistic fragility in the UAE

Figure 2.2 Contextual Factors Contributing to Feelings of Cultural and Linguistic Fragility in the UAE

2.1 Climate of Fast-Paced Change, Hypermobility, and Superdiversity

The dramatic transformation described at the start of the chapter has happened at a startling pace and, as the Emirate of Abu Dhabi alone is now home to one of the largest sovereign wealth funds in the world in terms of total assets, estimated at $627 billion in 2012 (Burton, 2012, p. 22), there are no signs of this financial development slowing down. This climate of extreme fast-paced change could be said to contribute towards feelings of cultural fragility, where the current generation struggle with uncertainty over what was, what is, and what is to come. Such feelings were observed during the pilot phase of the study (Hopkyns, 2016, p. 103) when expatriate English university teacher, Matthew (pseudonym), summarized:

> For such a young, fast changing country, I think the students see their culture changing around them. They have grandparents who seemingly could come from a completely different culture, and I think they see themselves as a new generation. I can only imagine it is difficult to identify with something so nebulous.

Hand in hand with accelerated change in terms of infrastructure and development has been a steady influx of expatriate workers, since the discovery of oil in the UAE in the late 1950s. This has led to dramatic transformations of the population, job market, power, and status within the lifespan of the young nation. With a population of just over 2.5 million and an annual growth of over 8%, which is one of the highest in the world (UAE Yearbook, 2013, p. 54), Abu Dhabi is a rapidly expanding capital city. However, most of the UAE's resident population of 9.5 million is not Emirati but rather expatriate. Expatriates from India, Philippines, Pakistan, Sri Lanka, Nepal, Ethiopia, Egypt, Russia, UK, USA, Canada, South Africa, Australia, and New Zealand and other countries now outnumber the native population to the point where only approximately 11% of the UAE's residents are Emiratis (United Nations Development Program, 2018), a figure projected to decline further to only 10% in 2020 (Harris, 2013, p. 87). This is in sharp contrast to other Arab nations such as Yemen and Egypt where expatriates account for only 1.4% and 0.2%, respectively (Shah, 2004, as cited in Ahmad, 2016, p. 31).

It is the UAE's alluring tax-free packages that have attracted the 1.5 million foreign construction workers, almost 900,000 retail employees, and over 55,000 teachers and educational administrative staff to the UAE (UAE Yearbook, 2013, p. 159). Globally, although superdiverse societies are not rare, the fact that expatriates outnumber locals to such a degree is unusual. The country's 'intensive and increasing dependency on expatriates in all labor sectors' (Al-Shaiba, 2014, p. 76) partly arose due to the relatively small local population not being able to meet the human resources requirements of developmental plans. The immense wealth brought to the UAE by its natural resources also gave Emiratis a special status by which they could choose not to take certain jobs, especially those deemed physically demanding, low-status, or those requiring rigorous training. For this reason, as Al Ali (2008, p. 367) states, although 'the pace of growth continues . . . UAE nationals are not employed in their own country'. Expatriates have an overwhelmingly high profile (91%) in the Emirati labour market, meaning only 9% of jobs are taken by Emiratis. From this 9%, 8% are in the public sector and just 1% is in the private sector (TANMIA, 2006). Public sector jobs, or government jobs, are far more popular amongst Emiratis due to more flexible working hours, culturally sensitive environments (e.g., no work on Fridays), higher pay and generous holidays. However, due to this preference, many public-sector organizations are now considered overstaffed. This imbalance in the workforce and population at large is increasingly being recognized as an urgent social issue in the UAE.

Social Stratification and Wasta

The importation of skilled and unskilled workers working in public and private sectors has led to a society where divisions between groups are numerous. As Calafato and Tang (2019, p. 135) state, such a diverse expatriate population has led to 'complex socio-cultural, political, linguistic, and economic interactions between the different groups residing in the country'. Although on the surface the UAE appears to be the apex of multiculturalism, there is a reluctance to readily embrace 'outsiders' as equals, whether they be strangers, colleagues, friends, or family members, which indicates uneven social and linguistic power given to various ethnicities, nationalities, and languages. Such inequities between nationalities in the UAE has been referred to as 'ethnocracy' (Piller, 2018) or social stratification (Davidson, 2005). Ethnocracy can be seen at a micro-level (within Emirati society) and at a macro-level (within society in the UAE as a whole). It relates to both social and linguistic inequities.

On a micro-level, diversity amongst citizens is not fully accepted. Mixed marriages account for around 20% of marriages involving Emirati nationals (Shaaban, 2012), and such marriages usually occur with other Gulf nationals. Marriages involving Emirati husbands and non-Emirati wives are far more common, however the reverse also occurs. Locals with an Emirati mother and a foreign father are colloquially known as 'mumeratis' and tend to experience discrimination. 'Mumerati' students at the university in which the study takes place, for example, have the letter 'M' before their student identification number, to indicate their background. Generally, they are regarded as 'different' by students with 'pure' Emirati heritage. As Aydarova (2012, p. 292) states, 'prejudice against certain tribes and racism against certain racial groups are a commonplace occurrence in students' daily lives and in the classroom'. In addition to the two groups mentioned previously, Kanna (2010, p. 105) identifies a third group who are known locally as 'Ayam' and are of Iranian descent. Within Emirati society, therefore, 'pure' Emiratis who can trace their ancestors back to the Arabian Peninsula, such as those from the Al Bu Falasah section of the Bini Yas tribe (Davidson, 2008, p. 153–158), occupy the highest status in society, Ayam are in the middle, and Emiratis from mixed marriages are at the bottom and 'regarded as second class' within Emirati society (Kanna, 2010, p. 105), as seen in Figure 2.3.1.

On a macro-level, social stratification based on nationality, ethnicity, and employment status is deeply embedded in UAE society. Generally, society in the UAE can be divided into three main classes: 'labor, brains, and bank' (Burton, 2012, p. 71). In Davidson's (2005) social pyramid (Figure 2.3.2), Emiratis are the *bank* at the top, the Westerners/Western-educated are the *brains*, and the bottom two layers are the *labour*. These divisions are infamous both inside and outside the country, leading to

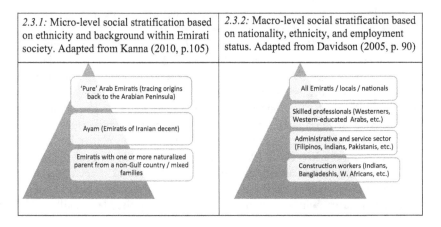

2.3.1: Micro-level social stratification based on ethnicity and background within Emirati society. Adapted from Kanna (2010, p.105)

'Pure' Arab Emiratis (tracing origins back to the Arabian Peninsula)

Ayam (Emiratis of Iranian decent)

Emiratis with one or more naturalized parent from a non-Gulf country / mixed families

2.3.2: Macro-level social stratification based on nationality, ethnicity, and employment status. Adapted from Davidson (2005, p. 90)

All Emiratis / locals / nationals

Skilled professionals (Westerners, Western-educated Arabs, etc.)

Administrative and service sector (Filipinos, Indians, Pakistanis, etc.)

Construction workers (Indians, Bangladeshis, W. Africans, etc.)

Figure 2.3 Social Stratification in the UAE on a Micro- and Macro-Level

common expressions such as '*Emirates* stands for *English-Managed, Indian-Run, Arabs Taking Enormous Salaries*' (Pieterse, 2010, p. 17). The division in social status between Emiratis and 'others' leads to 'cultural detachment' (James & Shammas, 2013, pp. 148–151) or even a 'cultural apartheid'. There are instantly noticeable distinctions between Emiratis and other nationalities in terms of dress, with Emirati women wearing the traditional black *abaya* (a full-length black cloak) and *shayla* (black headscarf) and Emirati men wearing the *kandoura* (long white robe) and *gutra* (white head wear). Not only clothing but also a range of other attributes and lifestyle factors such as local dialect, wealth, status, and connections distinguish Emiratis from foreigners.

As seen in Figure 2.3, the UAE is 'a culturally complex environment, with a myriad of unwritten rules and codes of conduct which serve to accentuate the "otherness" of those culturally dissimilar' (James & Shammas, 2013, p. 161). The layers of society within the macro-level social pyramid do not often waiver, with each having their own social networks. While many nationalities with different linguistic backgrounds share the same public spaces, such as restaurants, shopping malls and cafes, as Coles and Walsh (2010, p. 1322) state, 'as in other global(ising) cities, parallel social lives involving public tolerance, yet little meaningful interaction, are the norm'. Emiratis' interaction with transnationals tends to be transactional and service-based (Hopkyns, 2017, p. 39). Even in EMI government universities, where expatriate teachers typically interact with far more Emiratis than most professionals, such interaction is usually limited to the confines of the university (Burkett, 2016, p. 6). Occasional wedding invitations from students are eagerly accepted, but being invited to an Emirati's home would be unusual.

Being at the pinnacle of the macro-level social pyramid allows Emiratis to feel elite and privileged within their own society. Although they are the minority in number, they undisputedly hold the most power due to nationality alone. In addition to the power Emiratis' nationality affords them, a form of social capital or system of 'favouritism' known as *Wasta* is prevalent in almost all aspects of Emirati society, including education, job applications, government services, court decisions, and marriage arrangements. Known as *blat* in Russian and *Vitamin B* in German, *Wasta*, which is colloquially known as *Vitamin W* (Gallacher, 2009, p. 29), can be defined as a type of official favouritism where Emiratis can 'employ connections or perhaps an intermediary to reach certain goals or to speed up certain processes' (Kropf & Newbury-Smith, 2016, p. 12). It is an important part of society in Arab countries and success in life may depend largely on the scale and scope of *Wasta*. As Davidson (2014, p. 272) explains, in the Gulf monarchies, including the UAE, 'almost any bona fide citizen, regardless of background or education, can automatically assume a relatively high social standing'. In practice, this means citizens are often able to 'queue-jump expatriates, win arguments with the traffic police (especially if the adversary is an expatriate) and in general enjoy preferential treatment in public' (Davidson, 2014, p. 272). A further example of social and economic exclusivity experienced by Emiratis is the *Kafala* system, where expatriates wanting to start a business must seek an Emirati partner (usually silent partner) who is to own 51% of the business. This directly benefits nationals by providing them with an effortless and convenient source of income. It could be said that the existence of *Wasta* and *Kafala*, as well as other forms of state-sponsored social inequity, serve to deepen the social divide between Emiratis and expatriates.

Despite the privileged position and increased opportunities Emiratis have access to through the macro-social pyramid, *Wasta* and *Kafala*, the sheer number of transnationals in the UAE, using English as a lingua franca in all spheres of life, leads to a paradoxical shift in power relations in terms of language use. The fact that Emiratis have become a minority in their homeland leads to a general sense of unease and is seen by many to threaten the stability of society and language (Al-Kitbi, 2008, p. 3). This is especially felt due to expatriate workers being on short-term contracts, as the frequent coming and going of this population results in Emiratis living amongst ongoing demographic change. This demographic cycle of change and imbalance is regularly discussed in the media and amongst the local population with relation to the negative impacts of foreign labour on Emirati national identity. In fact, the phrase 'wanted but not welcomed' as seen in the title of this book was originally used to refer to conflicting feelings towards foreign workers by some in the Gulf today (Khondker, 2010).

2.2   English as a Lingua Franca in Multiple Domains

Due to the UAE's history, unique demographics, and the impact of globalization, as discussed previously, English now dominates everyday public life and, to a lesser extent, private life too. As Altbach (2014, p. 99) explains, 'because of its location, population base and economy – the UAE, and other Gulf countries as well, are more affected by globalization trends than most other parts of the world'. It is estimated that around 100 languages, including Urdu, Malayalam, Hindi, Singhalese, Bengali, Farsi, and Tagalog, are spoken in the UAE by almost 200 nationalities (Constantine & Al Lawati, 2007). However, as most of the UAE's expatriate workers come from partly Anglophone countries such as India, Sri Lanka, and the Philippines and majority English-speaking countries such as the UK and USA, English, above other languages, has become a very practical tool as a lingua franca at every level of society.

English in Public Domains

The official language in the UAE, Arabic, is not the one spoken by the majority of residents, which is an extremely unusual phenomenon. As

Hundley (2010, p. 1) states, 'Arabic shares equal billing with English on street signs and in shopping malls, but one has to strain to actually hear it spoken in daily discourse'. Randall and Samimi (2010, p. 44) add that, 'there can be few societies in the world where a second language is necessary to carry out basic shopping tasks, from buying food in super-markets to clothes in shopping malls', meaning almost all aspects of daily life can be accomplished without ever using Arabic. Here it is apparent that on a social and practical level, English is essential for all types of daily economic transactions such as requesting information from a hotel receptionist or making a doctor's appointment as well as enjoying time at malls and cinemas. Although shop and restaurant signs are by law sup-posed to be in both languages, there are still plenty that appear only in English, or use an uneven mix of the two, skewed in favour of English. Similarly, many temporary or visiting events occur only in English with a token smattering of Arabic. In Figure 2.4, we can see a typical scene of a weekend festival in the glass-roofed courtyard at Abu Dhabi's largest mall. At first glance, one is pushed to find Arabic. At second glance, the mall's name 'Yas Mall' is in both English and Arabic as well as the small writing at the bottom right of the picture.

The same feeling of being surrounded by English occurs when walking into popular Abu Dhabi bookstores, where English publications clearly

Figure 2.4 The Dominance of English in UAE Public Spaces

Photograph by the author

outnumber the Arabic, and where Peppa Pig dominates the children's sections. Comparable feelings arise when picking up a copy of the Abu Dhabi free weekly magazine, 'Abu Dhabi World', which until recently was called 'Abu Dhabi Week' and only published in English. Although there is now a separate Arabic version, it is not as readily available. Similarly, when looking through the popular 'Time Out' magazine which is still in English only, the list of establishments and events catering to expatriate lifestyles including pubs, nightclubs, and bars is overwhelming. There are ladies' nights every day of the week and infamous Friday brunches which feature all-you-can-consume 'grape' or 'bubbly'. Parties and events centred around Western religious and cultural holidays also feature heavily, with Christmas and Easter, as well as Halloween and St. Patrick's Day being celebrated at multiple venues throughout the country, albeit with a local twist (Figure 2.5).

This could be pandering to the notion of 'the English abroad are more English than the English' in that expatriates tend to crave the traditions from home more than anything else. It certainly helps to make English-speaking expatriates feel comfortable living in the UAE, which is perhaps part of the reason so many stay for so long. Being able to use one's mother language, English, in every public sphere from hospitals to airports, from

Figure 2.5 Santa Claus Riding a Camel at a Christmas Event in the Liwa Desert, UAE
Photograph by the author

taxis to shops, and at schools and universities, makes life very comfort-able and convenient indeed. One cannot help but question how comfort-able this English-dominated public life is for Emiratis, however.

English in Private Domains

Not only does English dominate the public domain, it also affects private spheres. As well as children being immersed in English at nurseries to give them a 'head start' (Badry, 2011, p. 91), hiring foreign maids, who also act as nannies, baby sitters, foster mothers, companions, cooks, and teachers has become, as Taha-Thomure (2008, p. 190) states, 'a semi-new trend' in Arab societies. English-speaking housemaids and nannies, who are hired by 94% of Emirati families (Dubai Statistics Centre, as cited in Ahmed, 2014, p. 1), use English to communicate with the children in their care. When visiting any outdoor playground or indoor soft-play zone, it is often groups of nannies or maids watching the children rather than parents. The maids hired in the Gulf States typically come from impoverished backgrounds with little education and, in many instances, poor language skills. As Taha-Thomure (2008) states:

> They (foreign nannies/maids) are not trained to raise children and as such it becomes an extremely dangerous and superfluous enterprise socially, linguistically, ethically and educationally to put the task of raising Arabic children in the hands of largely uneducated maids. Children are growing up missing that interpersonal bond between them and their very busy parents and along the way they may lose their mother tongue (Arabic) and not acquire proficiency in any other language.
>
> (p. 190)

Bringing English, or a basic version of English, into homes in such an all-encompassing way cannot fail to affect language and cultural identity. Not only is English being used with nannies inside the home, it is also used between family members, which can lead to family rifts. For example, it is not uncommon for children in a family to communicate with each other through English with the parents and grandparents not being able to fully understand. In this sense, English becomes a 'secret language' which is used between siblings or friends for private discussions, intentionally or unintentionally, excluding certain family members. This was found in an earlier study by Johannsen (1996, pp. 76–86) which used Arabic ques-tionnaires to assess how often Emirati university students used English and with whom. Perhaps surprisingly, the most common area in which students used English every day after 'with servants' was 'with siblings'. The students commented that they interacted in English with their sisters and brothers so that their parents would not understand, resulting in the use of 'English as a secret language'. O'Neill's study (2016) produced similar findings, with participants commenting on finding it easier to use English at home with siblings than to use Arabic. O'Neill's participants did, however, comment on how older family members disapproved of this, feeling that the use of English and even Arabizi (using English letters and numbers to represent Arabic sounds) was invasive in the home context. English is also used at home for expressing private thoughts and feelings that are perhaps difficult to express in Arabic due to cultural restraints. Using English online while at home is a further example of the private domain being affected. It was found in the 2014 pilot phase of this study that the adoption of Anglicized names such as 'Joey' instead of 'Mohamed', for example, and using only English or Arabizi on social networking websites such as Twitter, is not uncommon amongst Emirati youth (Hopkyns, 2015, p. 24). Considering the various ways in which English penetrates home life, Burden-Leahy (2009, p. 536) concludes that, 'there is a pattern emerging of Arabic being replaced by English as the main language in some Emirati homes'.

English in Education

In addition to English being used as a lingua franca in public and private domains, there has been a sudden and seismic shift in terms of the amount of English at all levels of education in the UAE. Mirroring the pace of general change, this increase in the amount of English in education has been far from gradual. In Abu Dhabi, as Gallagher (2016, p. 139) explains,

> the recent radical reformation of the state school system has included a shift in the medium of instruction from the traditional use of 'Arabic-only' to teach all school subjects, to include the use of 'English-also' as a medium of instruction from kindergarten onwards.

With such changes, the UAE education system has veered from one extreme to the other by 'shifting paradigm from "late-late" immersion all the way down to "early-early" immersion' (Gallagher, 2013, p. 6). Due to this abrupt switch to EMI from the very start, in the eyes of many, Emirati education has been 'de-Arabicised' (Solloway, 2016, p. 178) and English has essentially replaced Arabic as 'the language of education' in the UAE.

The same extreme presence of English can be seen in higher education. The UAE's first university 'United Arab Emirates University' (UAEU), established in 1976, was originally Arabic-medium. However, due to expertise provided from mainly English-speaking countries, the primary instructional language at all the UAE's federal universities (UAEU, Zayed University, and Higher Colleges of Technology) is now English, apart from degrees in Emirati/Islamic studies, Arabic, and Shari'a Law. These universities employ mainly expatriate teachers to teach in foundation programs and content areas in EMI. In addition to federal EMI universities, numerous private EMI universities have also opened branches in the UAE in the last 20 years. Such universities include the American University of Sharjah, the American University of Dubai, Middlesex University Dubai (UK), the University of Wollongong (Australia), New York University Abu Dhabi (USA), and Paris Sorbonne Abu Dhabi (France). Ironically, and as a further testament to the power of English in the region, Paris Sorbonne Abu Dhabi offers almost all its master's programs entirely in English (Gobert, 2019, p. 7).

Educational Background of the United Arab Emirates

To understand how English has come to be such a dominant force in Emirati education, it may be helpful at this point to examine in more detail the context in which the UAE has developed over a period of time. Formal education in the UAE, like the country itself, has a very short history. Although schools in the Gulf region date back to the 1820s, these schools tended to focus only on religion and they were only for boys who were taught by the local Imam, the speaker of the mosque (Ridge, 2011, p. 59). As wealth came to increase due to a booming pearling industry, families wanted to invest in more structured schools. To meet this desire, the first Western-style schools, run by Emiratis educated abroad and Arab expatriates, were set up in the early twentieth century. It was not until 1953, when the first Kuwaiti educational mission opened a school in Sharjah, that formal education began. With the birth of the country in 1971, the Federal Government made education free and compulsory for all children with the aim of eradicating illiteracy and by 1985 a national curriculum, created by the Ministry of Education, was in full use (Ridge, 2011, p. 60). Within the private sector, the first foreign school in the UAE opened in the 1960s (Lootah, 2011, p. 31). With a growing expatriate population, more and more private schools opened and today there are 567, almost equal to public schools which is 659, (Reports and Statistics, 2018), primarily in Dubai and Abu Dhabi, which offer more than 17 different school curricula (Al-Qutami, 2011, p. 11). Whether studying in a private school with an imported curriculum (British or otherwise), or a government-sponsored state school, English Medium Instruction (EMI) plays a large role, particularly for the core subjects of science and mathematics.

Educational Reforms With an Emphasis on English

Since the formation of the nation, a series of reforms have shaped local education especially in terms of the adoption of Western educational models, the hiring of foreign consultants, teachers, and faculty, and increased emphasis on EMI. Starting in the early 1990s, significant educational reforms took place due to international and regional political developments. As Lootah (2011, p. 33) explains, the downfall of the Soviet Union resulting in Western capitalist domination, the Iraqi invasion of Kuwait, and increased American presence in the Middle East, globalization of economics, politics, and culture, and the erosion of the concept of national sovereignty, all affected educational policy. Subsequently, the aftermath of 9/11/2001 further influenced decision-makers and educational policy. Strong links between terrorism and Islamic fundamentalism were made in American political and media discourse, and education was pinpointed as the root cause of this. To eliminate what were viewed as fanatical trends in Islamic culture and Arab thinking it was felt that intervention in the educational process was necessary in terms of 'reforming school curricula, teaching methods, and the school environment in a manner that reinforces the culture of peace, tolerance and openness to other cultures and rejects extremism and violence' (Lootah, 2011, p. 37). This involved hiring foreign experts, consultants, schoolteachers and university faculty, implementing educational programs designed to reform education and revising school curricula. American models of education were favoured cross-nationally by Emirati universities, including the one in which the study takes place. This could be accredited to the USA's image as a superpower and its strong presence in the UAE in terms of the oil, military, and construction industries. Other higher education institutes looked to Singapore as a model due to the country's high performance on international tests, its ability to compete in the global economy, and, primarily, its citizens' ability to speak English.

In addition to the external pressures for local educational reform, the global trend of 'internationalizing' education to compete on the global stage appealed greatly to national leaders. Internally, in sync with the global 'discourse of opportunity' (Tollefson & Tsui, 2004), and under the directives of Sheikh Zayed bin Sultan Al Nahayn, English was promoted as the language of academic learning in federal and Emirate-funded institutions. As English was already the medium of instruction in higher education, the greatest focus was on producing high school graduates who would be ready to confidently and directly enter their EMI degree courses without the need for costly, time-consuming, and unpopular foundation programs. With these goals in mind, an initial reformative step was taken in 1994 with the creation of 'Model Schools', which were better funded, had a higher entrance requirement and used EMI for mathematics and science. In 2007, a further reform took place with the introduction of the 'Madares Al Ghad' or 'Schools of the Future' project in 50 schools distributed geographically and qualitatively all over the UAE. This involved reshaping school environments through the presence of foreign supervisors alongside school principles. Foreign teachers were hired to oversee class teachers and foreign training teams were introduced in schools as well as intervention in school curricula and teaching methods. Following this, a more significant and widespread initiative came into play with the introduction of the New School Model (NSM) in 2010. From the onset, one of the NSM's key learning outcomes was developing students' Arabic and English skills through the use of Arabic and English teachers jointly planning for, and teaching, classes. This involved the inclusion of English-medium education starting in all Kindergarten (KG) and Grades 1–3 classes in government schools in 2010, all Grade 4 classes in 2011, and all Grade 5 classes in 2012, which was introduced with the aim of students becoming bi-literate in Arabic and English by the time they reach university (ADEC, 2014). The NSM was later renamed the 'Abu Dhabi School Model' (ADSM) in 2015 (Pennington, 2015) and is now called the Emirati School Model (ESM) due to its expansion to all Ministry of Education (MoE) schools throughout the UAE (Gobert, 2019, p. 120). This model not only increased the amount of English in the curriculum but it also placed a high priority on the STEM subjects (Science, Technology, Engineering, and Mathematics) and twenty-first century skills, all taught through the medium of English. A policy which happened alongside the NSM was the introduction of the 'Public Private Partnership' (PPP) (Gobert, 2019, p. 121). In the PPP, for-profit and non-profit school providers and educational consultants such as *Nord Anglia* and *Mosaica* were hired to run over 176 MoE schools in Abu Dhabi (Thorne, 2011) and over 940 native-English-speaking licensed teachers from Britain, Australia, and North America (BANA) were hired (Hamilton, 2010).

Further to the strong presence of English in state schools through the 'Emirates School Model' (ESM), Emiratis have become increasingly attracted to private EMI international schools. Although generally associated with providing an education for children outside their own national context, private international schools have been attracting more and more nationals due to being classified as 'excellent', parents seeing certificates such as the International General Certificate of Secondary Education (IGCSE) and the International Baccalaureate (IB) as a golden ticket or 'magic ingredient' (Gobert, 2019, p. 122) which opens doors to international higher education (Mackenzie et al., 2003), or general dissatisfaction with national educational systems. Anecdotally, in my own son's Grade 1 class at a British-curriculum international school in Abu Dhabi, 6 of the 16 students are Emirati (37.5%), which according to the head teacher of the school is an average statistic these days but higher than was typical in the past. Certainly, when visiting the classroom, it is very much an 'English-dominated zone' with British teachers and all the six-year-old children, including Emiratis, communicating in fluent English. The British curriculum is followed rigidly to the point where in lessons on counting and money, the children do not use the local currency 'UAE dirham and fils' but rather 'British pounds and pence'.

Even before the age of five, UAE nursery education (from birth until three years old) is currently taught through the medium of English, with little attention paid to Arabic (Bennet, 2009). In Dubai, 89% of nursery staff are foreign with poor Arabic language skills (Bennet, 2009). British curricula, which start when children are as young as three years old, are popular due to their high academic and general performance in national inspections (Knowledge and Human Development Authority). However, British curricula's primarily focus is on the English language with little room left for other languages. The sociolinguistic consequences of EMI schooling at all levels of education may mean optimal English proficiency, but is this at the expense of Arabic language skills and a secure sense of cultural identity? This is the burning question, of course.

English Medium Instruction in Higher Education

Turning to look at EMI in higher education specifically, there is a 'rainbow of motives' (Coleman, 2006, p. 4) behind the global trend of internationalizing higher education. These include the rise of CLIL (Content and Language Integrated Learning), teaching and research materials, staff mobility, and graduate employability. English is clearly an omnipresent language in higher education worldwide. It is not only the language of instruction in English-speaking giants such as the USA, UK, Canada, and Australia but also the primary language of instruction in Singapore, India, Pakistan, Sri Lanka, and much of Anglophone Africa. English is, therefore, key for communicating knowledge worldwide. English is also the medium of the majority of internationally circulated scientific journals, and scientific and scholarly Internet websites. Furthermore, the largest number of international students also go to English-speaking universities (Altbach, 2014, p. 107). In this sense, academic power truly lies with English-speaking universities.

Although EMI is spreading globally (Dearden, 2015; Macaro, 2018), unlike other places in the world, which have taken a more partial or gradual approach towards internationalizing education, the UAE's search for the 'silver bullet' (Aydarova, 2012, p. 285), accelerated by the growing impact of globalization in multiple domains, has led to a particularly dramatic approach. In addition to importing Western models of education, which is common worldwide, 'Westernization in GCC higher education has gone further by relying on Western faculty and administrators to implement and lead their reforms' (Badry & Willoughby, 2016, p. 208). Some feel, however, such a dramatic approach is too much, too soon. As Aydarova (2012, p. 291) states,

> Importing these models into local contexts creates conflicts and tensions because Emiratis who are already outnumbered by foreigners in their own country feel threatened – their culture and language are being eroded by the introduction of foreign models and the English language.

2.3 Complex History With English-Speaking Nations

The UAE's complex history with English-speaking nations further contributes to how English is viewed in the region. Before the formation of the nation, when the UAE was known as the Trucial States, it was controlled and protected by truces with Britain, as mentioned at the start of this chapter. This was a relationship, which, although once viewed as mutually beneficial, had turned into 'unwanted dominance' (Al-Fahim, 1995, p. 27). Arab nationalism peaked after the United Nations' creation of the state of Israel in 1948, resulting in loss of land rights for 700,000 Palestinian Arabs (Darraj & Puller, 2009, p. 32), which was viewed as very much supported by the English-speaking superpower, the USA. Feelings of resentment over this decision continue, as can be seen by the placement of the Palestinian flag over Israel on world maps at the university in which the study takes place as well as on maps for sale in local stores and atlases in local school libraries which have Israel 'blacked out' before purchase or loan (Figure 2.6).

Decades later, the tragic events of 9/11/2001 and the post 9/11 media 'war of words' served to sharpen the debate on Huntington's (1993) theory of the 'Clash of Civilizations' (COC), which hypothesized that people's cultural and religious identities would be the main source of conflict in an increasingly globalized world. Bringing such a debate to the forefront, the events of 9/11 served to reinvigorate old and divisive stereotypes. It is true to say that the negative feelings surrounding the highly publicized and distressing events of 9/11/2001 and its aftermath have caused a deep rift between the Muslim and non-Muslim worlds which, although diffused significantly, is still felt over ten years later. This reality

2.6.1: Palestinian flag covering Israel on a world map in an Abu Dhabi university

2.6.2: Israeli flag blacked out in school library book (Abu Dhabi-based International school)

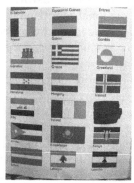

Figure 2.6 Attitudes Towards Israel as Demonstrated on Maps and Books

Photographs by the author

has created what Findlow (2005, p. 285) describes as 'a schizophrenic cultural climate'. At the same time as English is gaining more and more ground in the Gulf, so is 'sensitivity and mixed feelings about the pace and direction of modernization and globalization and resentment at the sheer numbers of foreigners on Emirati soil' (Findlow, 2005, p. 296).

This 'schizophrenic cultural climate' has fluctuated in strength over the last decade. In the approach to the 2016 USA presidential election, tensions intensified, perhaps peaking on 11 November 2016 with the triumph of Donald Trump. Known regionally and globally as 'the Islamophobia President' (Beydoun, 2016, p. 1), the day of the election was a distressing event for most in the Arabian Gulf. The atmosphere at the university in which the study took place, for example, was highly charged. In morning classes, the students found it difficult to focus on their work as they watched on their mobile devices newsflashes showing the red vote column rising. During my own morning class that day, a student asked for a short video of Michelle Obama's powerful speech on the importance of tolerance, peace, harmony, and unity amongst races and faiths to be shown, which resulted in a class discussion on the importance of this message. It was during the two-hour lunch break between classes that the final election result was revealed. This left teachers and students alike in a state of shock and disbelief. It was, however, moving to see students' support for their teachers, especially American teachers, during this difficult time which was shown through increased sensitivity, kind words, flowers, and gifts (Figure 2.7). Tellingly, not a single voice in support of the result could be heard.

2.7.1: 'Don't be sad'   *2.7.2:* 'Don't worry, we are all with you'

Figure 2.7 Students Show Support for Teachers on the Day Donald Trump Was Elected With Flowers and Notes

Photographs by the author

Although the election results did not negatively affect the students' attitudes towards their American teachers, who were for the most part extremely upset, there was a widespread feeling of contempt for Americans in general, who were seen to be directly responsible for electing such a figure, as well as fear for the future. Ultimately, it could be said that Trump's new role as president has served to deepen the notion of 'us and them' in the eyes of 'them'.

2.4   Arabic Diglossia

A final contextual factor influencing linguistic fragility in the UAE is the diglossic nature of Arabic. Diglossia, which means 'two or more varieties of the same language are used by some speakers under different conditions' (Ferguson, 1959, p. 325), is not unique to Arabic; rather it exists in multiple countries such as Switzerland, Greece, and Haiti, to name just a few. In the case of the UAE, it is common for Abu Dhabi locals to speak their local Emirati Arabic (EA) dialect 'Khaleeji' at home and amongst family and friends of the same dialect but use the standard language 'Modern Standard Arabic (MSA)' or 'Fusha' to communicate with speakers of other dialects or on public occasions, as well as Classical Arabic for religion. In this sense, Arabic could be described as a 'triglossic language' due to having three varieties or registers, rather than two, all in regular use. MSA, which descends from Classical Arabic, provides 'a pristine example of standard language ideology' (Hachimi, 2013, p. 272) as it is used in education, religion, and officially, and not commonly spoken in everyday life. This gives it distance and prestige. The local dialect, on the other hand, is generally considered less prestigious than MSA and has no standard written form. All formal written communication, including official documents, speeches, newspapers and magazines appear in MSA, and the Holy Quran is written in Classical Arabic. Although recently, with the increased use of social media, informal creative written forms, such as Arabizi (use of English letters and numbers to represent Arabic dialect sounds), can be seen on social networking sites such as Facebook, WhatsApp, and Instagram, etc. and there are even 'Khaleeji' phrase books for sale in local book stores. There is a sense, however, that these are seen more as a novel gift, in the same way a 'Glaswegian phrase book' might be seen in the UK, rather than a serious study aid. Ferguson (1959, p. 330) gives an example of the difference in the ways local dialects and MSA are seen by Arabic speakers.

> Speakers of Arabic may say (in their local dialect) that so-and-so doesn't speak Arabic. This normally means he does not know MSA, although he may be a fluent, effective speaker in the local dialect. If a non-speaker of Arabic asks an educated Arab for help learning to speak Arabic, the Arab will normally try to teach him the standard

forms, insisting that these are the only ones to use. Very often, educated Arabs will maintain that they never use the local dialect at all, in spite of the fact that direct observation shows that they use it constantly in all ordinary conversation.

Despite Ferguson's comment being made decades ago, the situation remains much the same in today's Emirati society. This is partly due to the ways of learning MSA and EA/Khaleeji being very different. The local dialect, Khaleeji, is learnt by children as a 'mother tongue', whereas MSA is heard by children from time to time but learnt primarily at school as part of a formal education. There are significant differences between Khaleeji and MSA, mainly in terms of grammatical structure. MSA has grammatical categories and an inflectional system of nouns and verbs, which is greatly reduced in Khaleeji. There are pronunciation differences too, such as the MSA sound /j/ being pronounced as /y/ in EA (Al Fardan & Al Kaabi, 2015, p. 12). It can be seen, therefore, that the diglossic nature of Arabic means that although MSA is the official language of over 20 countries, it does not belong to a socially, politically, geographically, or economically dominant group. In this sense, 'it is nobody's mother tongue' (Badry & Willoughby, 2016, p. 179).

It should be noted that despite what may have been implied so far, Arabic is still in a strong position globally. It is spoken by over 300 million people as a first language (Nydell, 2012, p. 93) and was even selected as one of the six official languages of the United Nations in 1997 due to the vast amount of people speaking it as a native or second language worldwide (Al Fardan & Al Kaabi, 2015, p. 11). In addition to this, Arabic remains strong worldwide through its intrinsic historical connection to Islam, and, being the language of the Quran, making it the religious language of over a billion Muslims around the world. Furthermore, Arabic is growing as a second language in Western countries. According to a survey conducted by the Modern Language Association in the USA, Arabic is now the eighth most studied language in US universities (Furman et al., 2010, cited in Gebril & Taha-Thomure, 2014, p. 1). However, such statistics do not reveal the complexities and challenges involved in being an Arabic native-speaker in the Gulf context. In the Gulf, in addition to the dominance of English in multiple domains, diglossia, or triglossia places an additional language-learning burden on Emiratis and makes Arabic less appealing as a language in comparison to the comparatively simple (non-diglossic) and readily available language of English (Hopkyns et al., 2018).

2.5 Parallels With Other Global Contexts

Although the complex web of factors contributing to linguistic vulnerability and cultural fragility described in this chapter may be unique to the context of the UAE, taken individually many of the factors also have relevance for other contexts globally. As Piller (2018) concurs, 'unique does not mean exceptional' (p. 91). There are many parallels which can be drawn between aspects of the UAE's sociolinguistic landscape and other areas of the world. Firstly, although the UAE's largest hub, Dubai, is currently the fastest growing city today (Smakman & Heinrich, 2018, p. 25), many other 'megacities' or urbanized countries are also expanding rapidly. For example, Hong Kong and Singapore have experienced a similar breathtaking pace of development in the last 100 years. Cityscape 'before and after pictures' of such regions produce the same levels of shock in terms of dramatic infrastructural and sociocultural change within a short period of time. In addition, neighbouring oil-rich countries such as Saudi Arabia, Kuwait, Oman, and Qatar have followed very similar patterns of growth in terms of extreme societal transitions. Thus, the contextual backdrop of fast-paced and dizzying change in the UAE is also of relevance to multiple other urban centres and societies.

Secondly, superdiversity found in the UAE in terms of its large expatriate or non-indigenous population and daily multilingualism can also be found in many other contexts, although perhaps not to the same extent. Europe's largest city London, for example, has one of the highest proportions of foreign-born residents across cities globally, with '3 million (34%) of its estimated population of 8.6 million being foreign born' (Fox & Sharma, 2018, p. 115). Los Angeles, California has become 'majority-minority' (Macias et al., 2018, p. 183) in terms of ethnicity and language due to its diverse population. Furthermore, Canada as a country has the highest number of foreign-born residents (20.6%) amongst the G8 countries (Statistics Canada, 2018). In both the global south and the global north, linguistic and cultural complexities inherent to superdiverse contexts can be found. In particular, the tensions surrounding English in the UAE context are shared with diasporic communities living in large Western migration hubs (e.g., London, New York, Toronto, etc.). Diasporic communities, which have moved from their original homeland to another country, are often forced to navigate multilingual environments in both public and private domains. A similar climate of fast-paced change is often felt in these communities given that what is left behind is rarely replicated exactly in the new environment. Such change exacerbates generational gaps and 'push and pull' relationships with the target language (Giampapa, 2004; Mills, 2004; Zhu, 2010). A conflict of desires is often felt, where global English is necessary or wanted but at the same time resented or not welcome due to its gatekeeper power in many realms of society.

A further bridging factor between the context of the UAE and other global settings is hypermobility. Many nations have highly transient populations with different international norms of English coming in and going out, making language use dynamic. While other contexts such as Singapore and Hong Kong, for example, may have longer histories of societal multilingualism and multiculturalism than the UAE, many of the factors discussed in this chapter are relevant to these 'semi-parallel' contexts.

Thirdly, many post-colonial or 'unofficial post-colonial' (Onley, 2005) countries other than the UAE share complicated histories with English-speaking countries. We can see again similarities between the UAE, Singapore, and Hong Kong, all having previously been governed by Britain. Post-colonial tensions surrounding the use of English and local languages are also well-documented in countries such as such as Kenya (Higgins, 2009), Singapore (Alsagoff, 2010), South Africa (Makalela, 2017), and Pakistan (Mahboob, 2009). In addition to post-colonial tensions, the UAE shares its complicated relationship with the United States due to the war on terror, with many other Muslim nations such as Saudi Arabia and Kuwait where policies such as Trump's 'Muslim ban' amplified tensions (Yang, 2018, p. 6).

Finally, even communities which cannot be defined as superdiverse or diasporic share some contextual factors mentioned in this chapter. One such example is the case of EMI. Increasingly, universities in many countries are adopting complete or partial EMI. For example, Korea's 2006 'Globalization Project' outlined a plan to increase EMI lectures by 10% annually and by 2010 all doctorate programs were to be taught in English (Cho, 2012, p. 18). In Europe too, EMI in higher education is spreading. For example, Finland has the largest share of EMI in higher education outside English-speaking countries, earning it the name 'Little England' (Lehikoinen, 2004, p. 46). Countries such as Cyprus, Germany, Denmark, and even France have also identified the need for more English-medium university courses and are accepting English as a lingua franca (Coleman, 2006, p. 8). With the acceleration of globalization comes the pressure to join the league of world-class English-medium universities. As Coleman (2006, p. 3) states, 'universities are no longer institutions but brands'. This is a phenomenon felt worldwide, and attitudes towards such a movement are mixed, as will be explored further in the following chapter. As we move on to look at top-down and bottom-up resistance to feelings of linguistic vulnerability and cultural fragility in the UAE in the next chapter, the picture becomes more intriguing still as the notion of English as 'wanted not welcome' moves to the forefront.

References

ADEC (2014). *The New School Model*. Abu Dhabi Education Council. Retrieved from: www.adec.ac.ae/en/Students/PS/Pages/New-School-Model.aspx.

Ahmad, R. (2016). Expatriate languages in Kuwait: Tension between public and private domains. *Journal of Arabian Studies*, 6 (1), 29–52.

Ahmed, K. (2014). *Language and Identity in Education*. The fifth Annual Gulf Comparative Education Society Symposium Conference Proceedings: Locating the National in the international: Comparative Perspectives on Language, Identity, Policy, and Practice, 104–111.

Al-Ali, J. (2008). Emiratisation: Drawing UAE nationals into their surging economy. *International Journal of Sociology and Social Policy*, 28 (9/10), 365–379.

Al-Fahim, M. A. J. (1995). *From Rags to Riches*. London: London Centre of Arab Studies Ltd.

Al Fardan, H., & Al Kaabi, A. (2015). *Spoken Emirati Phrasebook*. Abu Dhabi: Cultural Programs and Heritage Festivals Committee, Abu Dhabi.

Al-Kitbi, E. (2008, May 29). Prevent being side-lined. *The Gulf News*. Retrieved from: http://gulfnews.com/news/uae/culture/prevent-being-side-lined-1.107357.

Al-Qutami, H. E. H. M. O. (2011). Expected developments in the UAE economy over the next ten years. In the Emirates Center for Strategic Studies and Research (ECSSR). *Education in the UAE Current Status and Future Developments*, 9–13.

Alsagoff, L. (2010). English in Singapore: Culture, capital and identity in linguistic variation. *World Englishes*, 29 (3), 336–348.

Al-Shaiba, A. (2014). Key perspectives on preparing UAE nationals for employment. In the Emirates Center for Strategic Studies and Research (ECSSR). *The Future of Education in the UAE Innovation and Knowledge Production*, 67–95.

Altbach, P. G. (2014). Globalization and the university: The realities of the 21st Century. In the Emirates Center for Strategic Studies and Research (ECSSR). *The Future of Education in the UAE Innovation and Knowledge Production*, 97–121.

Aydarova, O. (2012). If not "the best of the West," then "look East": Imported teacher education curricula in the Arabian Gulf. *Journal of Studies in International Education*, 17 (3), 284–302.

Badry, F. (2011). Appropriating English: Language in identity construction in the United Arab Emirates. In A. Al-Issa, & L. S. Dahan (Eds.), *Global English and Arabic* (pp. 81–122). Bern, Switzerland: Peter Lang.

Badry, F., & Willoughby, J. (2016). *Higher Education Revolutions in the Gulf: Globalization and Institutional Viability*. New York: Routledge.

Bennet, J. (2009). *Early Childhood Education and Care in Dubai*. Retrieved from: www.khda.gov.ae/CMS/WebParts/TextEditor/Documents/Early%20Childhood%20Education%20&%20Care%20-%20Executive%20Report%20-%20Eng.pdf.

Beydoun, K. A. (2016). *Donald Trump: The Islamophobia President*. Retrieved from: www.aljazeera.com/indepth/opinion/2016/11/donald-trump-islamophobia-president-161109065355945.html.

Burden-Leahy, S. M. (2009). Globalization and education in the postcolonial word: The conundrum of the higher education system of the United Arab Emirates. *Comparative Education*, 45, 535–544.

Burkett, T. (2016). Emiratis Students' cultural norms and university teachers' awareness: A socio-cultural gap? *Perspectives*, 24 (1), 5–11.

Burton, S. (2012). *Staying Afloat: Three Years in Abu Dhabi*. Bloomington: I universe, Inc.

Calafato, R., & Tang, F. (2019). Multilingualism and gender in the UAE: A look at the motivational selves of Emirati teenagers. *System*, 84, 133–144.

Cho, J. (2012). Campus in English or campus in shock? *English Today*, 28 (2), 18–24.

Coleman, J. A. (2006). English-medium teaching in European higher education. *Language Teaching*, 39, 1–14.

Coles, A., & Walsh, K. (2010). From 'Trucial State' to 'postcolonial' city? The imaginative geographies of British expatriates in Dubai. *Journal of Ethnic and Migration Studies*, 36 (8), 1317–1333.

Constantine, Z., & Al Lawati, A. (2007, February 20). Mother tongue loses in the race of languages. *The Gulf News*. Retrieved from: https://gulfnews.com/uae/mother-tongue-loses-in-the-race-of-languages-1.162168.

Darraj, S. M., & Puller, M. (2009). *Creation of the Modern Middle East: United Arab Emirates*. New York: Infobase Publishing.

Davidson, C. M. (2005). *The United Arab Emirates: A Study in Survival*. Boulder, CO: Lynne Reinner Publishers.

Davidson, C. M. (2008). *Dubai: The Vulnerability of Success*. London: Hurst Publishers Ltd.

Davidson, C. M. (2014). Expatriates and the Gulf monarchies: Politics, security and the Arab spring. *Asian Affairs*, XLV (II), 270–288.

Dearden, J. (2015). English as a medium of instruction – a growing global phenomenon. *Report: British Council*. Retrieved from: www.britishcouncil.org/education/ihe/knowledge-centre/english-language-higher-education/report-english-medium-instruction.

Ferguson, C. A. (1959). Diglossia. *Word*, 15 (2), 325–340.

Findlow, S. (2005). International networking in the United Arab Emirates higher education: Global-local tension. *Compare*, 35 (3), 285–302.

Fox, S., & Sharma, D. (2018). The language of London and Londoners. In D. Smakman, & P. Heinrich (Eds.), *Urban Sociolinguistics* (pp. 115–129). London: Routledge.

Furman, N., Goldberg, D., & Lusin, N. (2010). Enrollments in languages other than English in United States Institutions of Higher Education, Fall 2009. *Modern Language Association of America*, 1–41.

Gallacher, D. (2009). *The Emirati Workforce: Tables, Figures, and Thoughts*. Dubai, UAE: Zayed University Press.

Gallagher, K. (2013, July). *From 'Late-late' to 'Early-early' Immersion: Discontinuities and Dilemmas in Medium of Instruction Policies and Practices in the UAE: Workshop 8 Paper*. The Gulf Research Meeting. Paper presented at Cambridge University, Cambridge, UK.

Gallagher, K. (2016). From 'late-late' to 'early-early' immersion: Discontinuities and dilemmas in medium of instruction of instruction policies and practices. In L. Buckingham (Ed.), *Language, Identity and Education on the Arabian Peninsula* (pp. 139–160). Bristol: Multilingual Matters.

Gebril, A., & Taha-Thomure, H. (2014). Assessing Arabic. In A. J. Kunnan (Ed.), *The Companion to Language Assessment* (1st ed., pp. 1781–1789). Oxford: John Wiley & Sons.

Giampapa, F. (2004). The politics of identity, representation, and the discourses of self-identification: Negotiating the periphery and the centre. In A. Pavlenko, & A. Blackledge (Eds.), *Negotiation of Identities in Multilingual Contexts* (pp. 192–218). Clevedon: Multilingual Matters.

Gobert, M. (2019). Transformation in English language education in the UAE. In K. Gallagher (Ed.), *Education in the United Arab Emirates: Innovation and Transformation*. Singapore: Springer.

Hachimi, A. (2013). The Maghreb-Mashreq language ideology and politics of identity in a globalized Arab world. *Journal of Sociolinguistics,* 17 (3), 269–296.

Hamilton, C. (2010, September 22). Teachers complain of visa chaos as 1,000 arrive to start work at once. *The National.* Retrieved from: www.thenational. ae/uae/education/teachers-complain-of-visa-chaos-as-1-000-arrive-to-start-work-at-once-1.501111.

Harris, J. (2013). Desert dreams in the Gulf: Transnational crossroads for the global elite. *Race and Class,* 54 (4), 86–99.

Hartley, L. P. (1953). *The Go-Between.* London: Penguin.

Higgins, C. (2009). *English as a Local Language.* Bristol: Multilingual Matters.

Hopkyns, S. (2015). A conflict of desires: English as a global language and its effects on cultural identity in the United Arab Emirates. In R. Al-Mahrooqi, & C. Denman (Eds.), *Issues in English Education in the Arab World* (pp. 6–36). Newcastle upon Tyne: Cambridge Scholars Publishing.

Hopkyns, S. (2016). Emirati cultural identity in the age of 'Englishization': Voices from an Abu Dhabi university. In L. Buckingham (Ed.), *Language, Identity and Education on the Arabian Peninsula* (pp. 87–115). Bristol: Multilingual Matters.

Hopkyns, S. (2017). *A Conflict of Desires: Global English and Its Effects on Cultural Identity in the United Arab Emirates.* Doctoral thesis, University of Leicester, UK. Retrieved from: http://hdl.handle.net/2381/40444.

Hopkyns, S., Zoghbor, W., & Hassall, P. (2018). Creative hybridity over linguistic purity: The status of English in the United Arab Emirates. *Asian Englishes,* 20 (2), 158–169.

Hundley, T. (2010, February 22). Is Arabic a dying language? *PRI Global Post.* Retrieved from: file:///Users/z9510/Desktop/Is%20Arabic%20a%20dying%20 language%3F%20%7C%20Public%20Radio%20International.webarchive.

Huntington, S. P. (1993). The Clash of Civilizations? *Foreign Affairs,* 72 (3), 22–49.

James, A., & Shammas, N. M. (2013). Developing intercultural intelligence: Dubai style. *Journal of International Education in Business,* 6 (2), 148–164.

Johannsen, K. L. (1996). Errors and identity: A world English perspective. In A. Holbrook, C. Coome, & S. Troudi (Eds.), *TESOL Arabia: Conference Proceedings Selected Papers 1995 & 1996* (pp. 76–86). Dubai: TESOL Arabia.

Kanna, A. (2010). Flexible citizenship in Dubai: Neoliberalism subjectivity in the emerging "city-corporation". *Cultural Anthropology,* 25 (1), 100–129.

Khondker, H. H. (2010). Wanted but not welcome: Social determinants of labor migration in the UAE. *Encounters,* 2, 205–233.

Knowledge and Human Development Authority (KHDA). Dubai Private Schools: A Decade of Growth. Retrieved from: https://khda.gov.ae/Areas/ Administration/content/FileUploads/Publication/Documents/English/ 20180507174427_KeyFindings_2008-2018_en.pdf.

Kropf, A., & Newbury-Smith, T. C. (2016). Wasta as a form of social capital? An institutional perspective. In M. A. Ramady (Ed.), *The Political Economy of Wasta: Use and Abuse of Social Capital Networking* (pp. 3–21). Switzerland. Springer International Publishing.

Lehikoinen, A. (2004). Foreign-language-medium education as a national strategy. In R. Wilkinson (Ed.), *Integrating Content and Language: Meeting the Challenge of a Multilingual Higher Education* (pp. 41–48). Maastricht: Universitaire Pers.

Lootah, M. S. (2011). Assessing educational policies in the UAE. In the Emirates Center for Strategic Studies and Research (ECSSR). *Education in the UAE Current Status and Future Developments*, 27–52.

Macaro, E. (2018). *English Medium Instruction*. Oxford: Oxford University Press.

Macias, R. F., Diaz, A., & Drane, A. (2018). Notes on the languages of the City of Angels. In D. Smakman & P. Heinrich (Eds.), *Urban Sociolinguistics* (pp. 181–203). London: Routledge.

Mackenzie, P., Hayden, M., & Thompson, J., (2003). Parental priorities in the selection of international schools. *Oxford Review of Education*, 29 (3), 299–314.

Mahboob, A. (2009). English as an Islamic language: A case study of Pakistani English. *World Englishes*, 28 (2), 175–189.

Makalela, L. (2017). Translanguaging practices in a South African institution of higher learning: A case of Ubuntu multilingual return. In C. M. Mazak, & K. S. Carroll (Eds.), *Translinguaging in Higher Education* (pp. 11–28). Bristol: Multilingual Matters.

Mills, J. (2004). Mothers and mother tongue: Perspectives on self-construction by mothers of Pakistani heritage. In A. Pavlenko, & A. Blackledge (Eds.), *Negotiation of Identities in Multilingual Contexts* (pp. 161–191). Clevedon: Multilingual Matters.

Minnis, J. R. (2006). First Nations education and rentier economics: Parallels with the Gulf States. *Canadian Journal of Education*, 29 (4), 975–997. http://doi.org/10.2307/20054207.

Nydell, M. K. (2012). *Understanding Arabs: A Guide for Modern Times*. Boston, MA: International Press.

O'Neill, G. T. (2016). Heritage, heteroglossia and home: Multilingualism in Emirati families. In L. Buckingham (Ed.), *Language, Identity and Education on the Arabian Peninsula* (pp. 13–38). Bristol: Multilingual Matters.

Onley, J. (2005). Britain's informal empire in the Gulf 1820–1971. *Journal of Social Affairs*, 22 (87), 29–45.

Pennington, R. (2015, March 25). ADEC reveals major changes to Abu Dhabi schools' curriculum. *The National*. Retrieved from: www.thenational.ae.uae/adec-reveals-major-changes-to-abu-dhabi-schools-curriculum.

Pieterse, J. N. (2010). Views from Dubai: Oriental globalization revisited. *Encounters*, 2, 15–37.

Piller, I. (2018). Dubai: Language in the ethnocratic, corporate and mobile city. In D. Smakman, & P. Heinrich (Eds.), *Urban Sociolinguistics* (pp. 77–94.). London: Routledge.

Randall, M., & Samimi, M. A. (2010). The status of English in Dubai. *English Today*, 26 (1), 43–50.

Reports and Statistics (2018). Retrieved from: www.moe.gov.ae/Ar/OpenData/Documents/2015-2016.pdf.

Ridge, N. (2011). The role of curriculum in creation of a knowledge-based economy in the UAE. In the Emirates Center for Strategic Studies and Research (ECSSR). *Education in the UAE Current Status and Future Developments*, 55–81.

Shaaban, A. (2012, July 15). The marriage Puzzle. *The National*. Retrieved from: www.khaleejtimes.com/kt-article-display-1.asp?xfile=data/nationgeneral/2012/July/nationgeneral_July185.xml&section=nationgeneral.

Smakman, D., & Heinrich, P. (Eds.) (2018). *Urban Sociolinguistics*. London: Routledge.

Solloway, A. (2016). English in the United Arab Emirates: Innocuous lingua franca or insidious cultural Trojan horse? In L. Buckingham (Ed.), *Language, Identity and Education on the Arabian Peninsula* (pp. 176–196). Bristol: Multilingual Matters.

Statistics Canada (2008). *Immigration and Ethnocultural Diversity in Canada*. Retrieved from: https://www12.statcan.gc.ca/nhs-enm/2011/as-sa/99-010-x/99-010-x2011001eng.cfm.

Taha-Thomure, H. (2008). The status of Arabic language teaching today. *Education, Business and Society: Contemporary Middle Eastern Issues*, 1 (3), 186–192.

TANMIA (2006). *Human Resource Report 2005*. Dubai: TANMIA.

Thorne, C. (2011). The impact of educational reform on the work of the school principal in the United Arab Emirates. *Educational Management Administration and Leadership*, 39 (2), 175–185.

Tollefson, J., & Tsui, A. (2004). *Medium of Instruction Policies: Which Agenda? Whose Agenda?* Mahwah, NJ: Lawrence Erlbaum Associates.

UAE Yearbook (2013). Retrieved from: www.mofa.gov.ae/EN/Documents/3556.pdf.

United Nations Development Program (UNDP). (2018). *United Arab Emirates*. Retrieved from: www.ae.undp.org/content/united_arab_emirates/en/home.ttml.

Winslow, W., Honein, G., & Elzubeir, M. (2002). Seeking Emirati women's voices: The use of focus groups with an Arab Population. *Qualitative Health Research*, 12 (4), 566–575.

Yang, M. (2018). Trumpism: A disfigured Americanism. *Palgrave Communications*. doi:10.1057/s41599-018-0170-0.

Zhu, H. (2010). Language socialization and interculturality: Address terms in intergenerational talk in Chinese diasporic families. *Language and Intercultural Communication*, 10 (3), 189–205.

3   Responses to Feelings of Linguistic and Cultural Fragility in the Gulf

I was tired of the acute embarrassment I felt whenever I tried to reserve a hotel room, or was invited to dinner at a restaurant. In my own country! My Arab country, where restaurants, hospitals and hotels all announced that 'only English is spoken here'.

Abdulla (Character in Al-Harthi's novel 'Celestial Bodies', 2018)

Nothing is softer or more flexible than water, yet nothing can resist it.

– Lao Tzu

The opening quotes in this chapter reflect common responses to English in the Gulf. In the first, Abdulla from Jokha Al-Harthi's award-winning novel 'Celestial Bodies' expresses his dismay at needing English for survival in his native Oman. His response is to take English lessons from American teacher, Bill, despite resentment over the necessity of having to do so. In the second quote, if we take water as analogy for English, it slowly seeps or rapidly flows into many societies making resistance difficult. In the UAE, there is a marked feeling of English being 'wanted not welcome' due to it being pushed forward in an era of neoliberalism, and at the same time pushed back against due to its dominance and perceived effects on the Arabic language and local cultural identities.

Neoliberal ideologies are currently being pushed forward by leaders in the UAE, whereby individuals are encouraged to 'build themselves up by acquiring soft skills such as communicative competence to compete in the global market' (Kubota, 2019). Global communicative competence is seen to be connected with English proficiency, which in turn equates to modernity and development. Hence, English is very much a part of the UAE government's 'Vision 2021' strategic plan, which marks the golden jubilee of the formation of the nation. The 2021 Vision, which was launched by H.H. Sheikh Mohammed bin Rashid Al Maktoum (the Prime Minister of the UAE and Ruler of Dubai) in 2010, has the overarching goal of 'making the UAE among the best countries in the world'

(Vision2021.ae). Within Vision 2021, six pillars have been mapped into six national priorities: 1) sustainable environment and infrastructure, 2) world-class healthcare, 3) first-rate education system, 4) competitive knowledge economy, 5) safe public and fair judiciary, 6) cohesive society and preserved identity. For all six of the previous priorities, English plays a major role, although it is not mentioned explicitly in the wording of the pillars. Within education, the specific goals include greater use of Smart technologies, increasing preschool enrollment, having Emirati students rank amongst the best globally for reading, mathematics and science, and hiring internationally accredited teaching staff. Without mentioning 'English', these goals are all closely connected with proficiency in the language. A further goal stated which relates to education is that Emiratis 'have a strong knowledge of the Arabic language' (Vision2021.ae). It is interesting that there is a need to state this explicitly, as if knowledge of English is assumed or taken for granted, but knowledge of the nation's first language needs to be stated as a 'goal'.

Within the final pillar of Vision 2021, which is the priority of developing a 'cohesive society and preserved identity', there is recognition of the challenges that accompany the UAE's remarkable pace of development. One such challenge is 'national identity'. Here, it is the goal to 'respond proactively to challenges' and 'to preserve a cohesive society proud of its identity and sense of belonging' by promoting an 'inclusive environment that integrates all segments of society while preserving the UAE's unique culture, heritage, and traditions' (Vision2021.ae). Again, the need to actively 'preserve' national identities reveals unease with the effects of cultural and linguistic superdiversity in the nation. Although English implicitly plays a major role in the strategic goals of the UAE, and it is a language which is pragmatically exciting and even liberating for increasingly confident speakers to learn and use, in recent years, notable resistance to the effects of global English has been evident across the Gulf. Feelings of cultural fragility or 'superfluous vulnerability' (Al-Khouri, 2012, p. 5) have led the UAE, and other GCC countries, to construct new forms of legislative structures to preserve local identity (Al-Khouri, 2012, p. 5). Forms of resistance include both top-down government-directed initiatives and bottom-up grassroots or 'peopled ground' (Lugones, 2010) movements.

3.1 Emiratization

The UAE government's 'Emiratization' initiative, which encourages Emiratis to enter the workforce with the aim of reducing its reliance on so many foreign workers (Kirk, 2010, p. 11), is perhaps the most prominent sign of counteraction. In Abu Dhabi, a local Emiratization council (Tawteen) has been established to support and develop Emiratization strategies with the aim of increasing the percentage of Emiratis working in the private sector (Al Shaiba, 2014, p. 78). Emiratization within the field of education has become significant with new teacher training colleges focusing on qualifying a generation of Emirati teachers (Sandiford, 2013, p. 2). It is hoped that these new Emirati teachers will be personally invested in the system, able to promote a 'sense of national awareness and indigenous culture' (Findlow, 2005, p. 298) and at the same time raise educational standards. Currently, there are very few Emirati teachers in schools and universities. Only 36% of teachers in state schools are Emirati, and in private schools a shockingly low number of 0.3% of teachers are national citizens (Statistics Center for Abu Dhabi, 2017). At the English Language Foundation Program department in the university where the study takes place, there are no Emirati teachers employed and only a handful who are Arabic-English bilinguals. Although cultural transmission is arguably an important part of any state school system, due to the imbalance in population between expatriates and Emiratis, fostering a strong sense of cultural identity through education has been identified as even more important in the context of the UAE (Gallagher, 2019a, p. 8).

However, the process of Emiratization, in education and in general, has been anything but smooth. A study by TANMIA, which is part of the Ministry of Labour, examined problems national graduates encountered when trying to find work in the private sector. The findings from the study showed these problems included a reluctance to accept what were seen as low wages and long working hours, not meeting the English proficiency level required, and lack of certain skills required (Al Shaiba, 2014, p. 78). In the field of education, according to Gallagher (2019b, p. 127), 'high-quality teacher education candidates can be elusive, and it is difficult to attract nationals to teaching, especially males'. Reasons for low levels of interest in teaching include comparatively low salaries compared to other sectors (Riddlebarger, 2015), lower status compared with other professions (Buckner, 2017), the 'psychocognitive challenge of turning previous learning on its head' (Gallagher, 2019b, p. 135) whereby students' experiences of being students themselves and observations of old-fashioned teaching methodologies clash with how they are trained to teach in university courses, as well as the strain and stress of frequent policy changes (Thorne, 2015). In Dickson's study (2013) surveying 500 Emirati school leavers on career choices, it was found that only 3% planned to choose teaching as a career. It was perceived as being a demanding, tiring, difficult, and underappreciated field. It is especially unpopular with male Emiratis to the point that in 2018 there were no initial teacher education candidates in any of the teacher training institutions in the UAE (Gallagher, 2019b, p. 136). There is, therefore, a desire to lessen the reliance on foreign workers but at the same time a reluctance to enter private sector work under the same conditions, which leads back to the 'wanted but not welcomed' feeling regarding expatriate workers discussed previously.

3.2 Cultural Identity Themed Conferences and Symposia

Naming Arabic the official language of all federal authorities and establishments in 2008, coupled with the fact that the same year was declared 'the year of national identity' (Al Baik, 2008, as cited in Badry, 2011, p. 91), highlights a need, in the eyes of the leaders, for bolstering cultural and linguistic security in the UAE. The need to preserve national identity was highlighted as the most prominent challenge to Emirati society by Sheikh Khalifa bin Zayed in his 2008 National Day address to the nation, where it was stated 'openness has had its cost' (Habboush, 2008).

Furthermore, multiple conferences have recently been organized to discuss ways to reaffirm cultural security, such as the 2008 UAE National Identity Conference, held at the Emirates Palace, Abu Dhabi, the 2012 Qatar University conference on Arabic and identity, the Sharjah 2013 conference on 'The Role of Museums and Cultural Institutions in Strengthening Identity', Dubai's 2013 'Second International Conference on Arabic Language', and the 2014 Gulf Comparative Education Society (GCES) symposium 'Locating the National in the International'. In addition to this, the Gulf's largest annual English Language Teaching (ELT) conference, TESOL Arabia, chose the theme of 'language, culture and communication' for its March 2016 conference with plenaries focusing on the issue of culture, language, identity, and globalization. Plenary speakers discussing these areas included Claire Kramsch (*Which culture should we teach in an era of globalization?*), Salah Troudi (*Teaching though culture: What culture? Whose culture?*), Peter Stanfield (*Language and Culture: The possibility of teaching*), and Neil McBeath (*Cultural change in the Arab Gulf: Natural progression or imperialist plot?*), to name just a few. Later in the same year, Oman's most prestigious university, Sultan Qaboos University, Muscat organized an international conference on 'Connecting the dots in a glocalized world' (November 2016) with plenary speakers Jan Blommaert and Rani Rubdy speaking on the topic of cultural globalization. The same conference four years later in 2020 also centres around cultural issues with the theme of 'Exploring Cultural Intersections'. It is clear, therefore, that globalization and cultural identity are recognized as highly relevant areas of discussion in the region and rather than there being a general feeling of content with the status quo, there are divided reactions to the pace and direction of English in the Gulf.

3.3 Arabic Language Drive

Concerns over the dominance of English and loss of Arabic have also led to a marked Arabic language drive at multiple levels. This relates primarily to improving the quality of Arabic teaching in schools, as well as encouraging the use of Arabic in society via reading, writing, and social media. On a panoptic scale, the Arabic Language Charter, which was introduced in 2012, concentrates on 13 items, ranging from ensuring Arabic is used as the official language of UAE government services as well as for formal written communication, laws, and decrees, to encouraging private schools and language centres to offer Arabic classes for non-native learners (Taha-Thomure, 2019, p. 20). In May 2014, the 'Mohammed bin Rashid Arabic Language Award' was launched, which aimed to 'nourish Arabic' (Taha-Thomure, 2019, p. 20) by rewarding 'exceptional contributions in serving the Arabic language' (Al Allaq, 2014, p. 120).

Reading

Specifically, for reading, the 'Arabic Reading Challenge' was introduced in 2015. In its second year of running, 35,000,000 participants from 15 Arab countries and 11 foreign countries participated and a total of 50,000,000 books were read in Arabic as part of the challenge. Further efforts to promote reading in Arabic include the 'Reading Law' which was passed in 2016. This involves every Emirati newborn receiving a 'knowledge briefcase' (Al-Qasimi, 2017, p. 38) that includes books which target the child's reading needs from birth to four years. The following year, in 2017, the 'National Arabic Language Strategy' was launched which dedicated $30 million in funding to 30 national initiatives (Al-Qasimi, 2017) including projects aimed at strengthening reading in Arabic through a literature-based approach in schools and establishing 'reading corners' and workshops. Programs such as 'Made in the UAE' and 'Qalam' (which means 'calligraphy pen') aim to increase the diversity of Arabic children's books and materials. In addition, 2016 was made the 'Year of Reading' with efforts to encourage reading in Arabic, being strengthened further with the introduction of library programs and author support programs such as '1001 Titles' being introduced to support local talent (Al-Qasimi, 2017, p. 39). Finally, the Abu Dhabi Authority for Culture and Heritage has recently launched several projects to uplift the Arabic Language such as the 'Kalima' Project (meaning 'word' project) which aims to translate hundreds of foreign books into Arabic to overcome the 'translation draught in the Arab world' (Kalima, n.d., para.1).

Promoting Arabic in Schools

In relation to the teaching of Arabic in schools, Arabic as a subject in schools has a tarnished reputation in the UAE due to predominant negative perceptions and experiences, especially in private schools. Partly this is due to old-fashioned teaching methodologies for the subject of Arabic, with an emphasis on grammar, drilling, and rote learning. This becomes especially evident when compared with the innovative pedagogical approaches often employed in the teaching of English and the teaching of other subjects, such as mathematics and science through the medium of English. English-speaking and Western-trained teachers most often use student-centred approaches to teach English such as task-based learning (Ellis, 2003) as well as employing digital resources as part of a blended learning approach. Such approaches encourage students to actively participate in learning through problem-solving and critical thinking. Mobile technology, which is much more accessible in the medium of English, allows digital natives to learn in a way which matches their everyday experiences. Using technology also encourages flexibility with language use in terms of embracing a range of registers and semiotic resources. A further factor influencing negative perceptions of Arabic teaching is dominant ideologies of linguistic purism surrounding MSA where it is viewed as 'an untouchable body of rules and syntax that cannot be modernized, and cannot by flexible, fun, or evolving' (Taha-Thomure, 2019, p. 7) thus making the language daunting or unfriendly. Such negative perceptions of Arabic lessons are reflected in annual ratings in private schools which are posted on the 'Knowledge and Human Development Authority' (KHDA) website. In 2016, 15 out of 149 private schools inspected were rated 'outstanding' overall. However, when looking at ratings for individual subjects, the Arabic language (being taught both as a first language and a second) was rated as weak or acceptable, with the occasional 'good' in schools rated 'outstanding' (Taha-Thomure, 2019, p. 9). This demonstrates the discrepancy between Arabic and English, or other subjects taught through the medium of English. In response to such a reality, numerous initiatives, as previously mentioned, have recently been introduced with the aim of promoting and preserving Arabic.

Promoting Arabic Through Social Media and Art

On social media, the Bil-Arabi (meaning 'In Arabic') initiative has had a marked presence since its creation in 2013. Initially the idea was proposed by a group of UAE university students, and it was then adopted by the Mohammed Bin Rashid Al Maktoum Foundation. It has the aim of enhancing the image of the Arabic language and promoting it as an international language which connects people. It encourages people to post and share updates on social media websites such as Facebook, Twitter, and Instagram solely in Arabic. This initiative is especially pushed forward on 'UN Arabic Language Day' on the 18th of December each year. Nation-wide Arabic language activities, both on the ground and on social media, are also supported by the Bil-Arabi initiative. On the ground activities include booths in malls which allow people to complete tasks and games using the Arabic language, and reading clubs and poetry readings at public schools. Those participating in activities are encouraged to share their photographs and videos online with the hashtag #bilarabi. Harnessing the power of social media has proved successful in promoting Arabic as the Bil-Arabi movement has been reported as 'getting stronger by the year' (" Bil Arabi Initiative", 2017).

An example of how individuals are promoting the Arabic language in the UAE through art and projects attached to the social media hashtag 'bilarabi' can be seen in Figure 3.1. Lebanese-born Nadine Kanso, who lives in Dubai, promotes the Arabic language through jewellery which symbolizes Arab identity and expressing oneself in Arabic. It is interesting to note, however, that English still features prominently in the Twitter posts advertising these products. In Figure 3.1.2, behind an image of 'Arabic letter' earrings, is a message in English. In Figure 3.1.1, however, English is less prominent in the posting (apart from some of the hashtags such as 'fine jewellery' and 'made in the UAE'). Furthermore, the necklace in Figure 3.1.1 symbolizes both the Arabic language and Emirati identity, as in the UAE mothers often introduce themselves or are referred to as 'Umm' (Mother of) and their eldest son's name (Notzon & Nesom, 2005, p. 20). For example, I would be 'Umm Thomas' or 'Mother of Thomas' rather than 'Sarah'. This is more common amongst older generations but such a practice is still very much part of Emirati society. When meeting a new person, an Emirati woman might be asked, 'what should I call you, 'Umm (mother of) . . .?', for instance.

The Arabic language jewellery in Figure 3.1 could be seen as a counter-discourse to the dominance of English. Due to globalization, the vast majority of shops in UAE malls are American or European chains which would typically use English for name-based products. Here I am reminded of a poignant moment early on in my UAE life. While shopping in the US furniture store, *Pottery Barn*, an Emirati woman with her newborn baby stopped and asked me the English spelling of her baby's name 'Saeed'. She was not sure how to spell it in English but wanted the store to embroider it

| *3.1.1:* 'Mother of Marzouk' necklace promoting Arabic with hashtag 'bilarabi' (In Arabic) | *3.1.2:* Arabic letter earrings promoting Arabic with hashtag 'bilarabi' (In Arabic) |

Figure 3.1 The Bil Arabi Movement in Action. Arabic Language Jewellery Promoted With '#bilarabi' Hashtag

Screen captures taken by author with permission of Nadine Kanso

onto a cushion. Having newly arrived, it struck me as ironic that this baby would grow up seeing his name in English on this cushion, not Arabic, and that I was needed for something so closely related to his identity. It should be noted, however, that *Pottery Barn* now offers their name embroidery service in both Arabic and English. It would be interesting to know which is the more popular choice amongst new Emirati parents though.

Grassroots Promotion of Arabic – Events and Institutions

At a more grassroots level, locally organized events to promote Arabic have also been held in Abu Dhabi, such as the 'Language of Happiness' event in Delma Park (Al Subaihi, 2016), which focused on boosting Arabic through engaging methods such as ventriloquists reading stories and quizzes with prizes. The project organizer, Ms. Alsabaaneh, stated that the purpose of events such as this was to promote Arabic within the family and 'encourage parents to engage with their children in Arabic and take them to events predominately in Arabic' (Al Subaihi, 2016). This was a response to observations Alsabaaneh made upon moving to Abu Dhabi from Palestine, regarding the feeling of being surrounded by English. A further example of community events promoting Arabic is the 'Neon Book Hunt' which was launched in Umm Al Emarat Park in November 2019. More than 1000 books, some of which were donated by the Kamila Translation Project, were hidden in the evening for children to find with neon lights. The children could keep the books once found ("Neon Book Hunt Beckons", 2019).

The promotion of Arabic over English can also be seen when walking along the corridors at the university in which the study takes place. Figure 3.2 shows one of many posters promoting the use of Arabic (the mother language) amongst Emiratis.

Figure 3.2 Sign of Resistance to English Posted in a Local University Corridor
Photograph by the author

Here, we can see a bold message directed at Emirati students studying in an EMI university, asking them to become acquainted or reacquainted with their mother language, Arabic. Such a message reflects growing concerns over the dominance of English and the fading of Arabic amongst young Emiratis. The need for Arabic to be pushed forward in such a way to its own speakers could be interpreted as a concrete sign of its fragility in the region. At the same university, efforts have recently been made to encourage foreign faculty and staff to learn Arabic. As seen in Figure 3.3.1, free Arabic classes at two different levels are offered twice a week during the teachers' common break. Although the advertisement for these lessons states 'back by popular demand' many faculty and staff complain that they struggle to find time to attend during the busy working week. At local international schools where English is the medium of instruction, Arabic often falls by the wayside as it is treated as a 'special subject' with just 45 minutes given to it any one time (Taha-Thomure, 2019, p. 10). Furthermore, non-Arabic-speaking parents (the majority) often find it difficult to support their children with the language. Perhaps as a result of this, Arabic is also being promoted amongst parents. Figure 3.3.2 shows an 'Arabic club for parents' being offered free of charge once a week.

3.3.1: Advertisement for free Arabic classes for foreign faculty

3.3.2: Advertisement for free Arabic classes for parents at an international school.

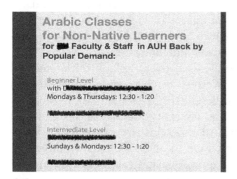

Figure 3.3 Free Arabic Lessons Offered at Universities and Schools
Screen captures taken by the author

3.4 Resistance to EMI Language Policy

In addition to Arabic language initiatives in schools and universities, there has been a large body of resistance to educational reforms, which brought in Western educational models, increased EMI, and increased the hiring of Western teachers. This resistance can be seen across the Gulf and in other nations. One of the strongest forms of resistance in the region, which Belhiah and Elhami (2015, p. 4) describe as a 'watershed moment in the history of higher education in the GCC', was the decision of the Supreme Education Council in Qatar in 2012 to abandon EMI and instead make Arabic the language of instruction (AMI) at its most prestigious university, Qatar University. This momentous decision served to open dialogue on this possibility in other GCC nations, especially as concerns about recent reforms involving EMI were mounting. Further afield, in Indonesia, which has the largest Muslim population worldwide, pedagogical and ideological concerns relating to EMI policies have led to significant resistance. Due to a legal battle launched by teachers, parents, and other educational stakeholders, federal courts ruled against the implementation of EMI in public schools arguing that this policy seriously threatens local languages and cultural identity (Louber, 2019, p. 62).

Concerns in the UAE over imported Western education models and curricula centre around the lack of inclusion of local culture and the denigration of Arabic. Aydarova (2012) explains how even when attempts are made to indigenize or localize Western imported models, they are often unsuccessful, as rather than blending Emirati culture into the mix, often teachers use their own interpretation of Emirati culture as 'a filter through which they sift the curriculum, eliminating features that they think do not belong' (p. 291). This leads to a watered-down version of a Western model, where they get 'little of "best of the West" and even less of "local culture and heritage"' (Aydarova, 2012, p. 291). Lootah (2011) argues that hiring foreign expertise at the levels of consultation, setting programs, determining curriculum content, and supervising teaching, as seen in the Madares Al Ghad project, NSM, and the institutions of higher education, creates subordination to Western culture, which 'undermines the chances of equipping students with knowledge, creativity and innovative ability' (p. 49).

Further concerns have also been raised over the appropriateness of hiring Western educators due to Western teachers embodying Western cultural values which are vastly different to the students they teach. As Karmani (2005, p. 95) states, in the university foundation programs in particular, teachers consist primarily of 'an exclusive corps of Anglo-Western TESOL practitioners, most of whom . . . lack the most rudimentary knowledge about "Islam" or . . . the most basic structures of the Arabic language'. These teachers and managers, Hudson (2019, p. 245) states, 'bring with them not only their expertise in English language instruction, but also their own views about society, culture, and ethics; views that may be considerably at odds with those of the society in which they are now living'. Burkett's study (2016) with 120 Emirati university student participants and five university teachers investigated Emirati students' cultural norms and university teachers' sociocultural awareness, looking at whether there was a gap between the two. Findings revealed that there was 'seemingly more of a cultural gap between expatriate teachers and their Emirati students than in other contexts – and in some cases, this gap can be quite large' (p. 6). This is consistent with James and Shammas (2013) theory of 'cultural apartheid' in the region, which is affected by social stratification at a macro-level as outlined in Chapter 2 of this book. Here, there is a distinct feeling of 'us and them' experienced by both students (all Emirati with Arabic as their first language) and teachers (all expatriate with mainly English as their first language).

As well as criticisms over the hiring of Western teachers and the importation of foreign curricula, the gatekeeper status of EMI has also been contested. As Ryan (2010, p. 3) states, 'the system (EMI) equates intelligence with knowledge of English, which is quite arbitrary'. It is true to say that many Emiratis with skills in areas other than languages are often 'held back' by not being able to master English to the required level needed to pursue their major. Ryan (2010) blames such a situation partly on English-speaking teachers, stating, 'We (English teachers) put up a stop sign, and we stop them in their tracks. They can't pursue their dream any longer until they get English . . . we teachers are the gatekeepers' (2010, p. 2). Unlike other countries where EMI is a choice, in the UAE such a choice is not available, thus making the stakes higher in terms of the level of English proficiency needed for academic success. As Al Ameri (2013) states, 'to hook success on the ability to speak a specific language rather than intellectual capability is just plain wrong'; however, he goes on to say, 'but this is the reality of the world we live in'. This comment, sums up the circular nature of EMI in that it is resented for its gatekeeper status but at the same time wanted and needed. It is not an easy issue to resolve.

3.5 Translingual Practice for Social Justice

A further form of resistance to the dominance of English in the region is the use of 'translingual practice' (Canagarajah, 2013) rather than 'standard or inner-circle' English. Translingual practice involves the mixing of languages, often in creative ways. Here young Emiratis are straying from traditional notions of multilingualism (fluency in two or more 'pure' and separate languages or 'two solitudes'; Cummins, 2007) and are actively reshaping language use through many forms of fluid and creative linguistic hybridity. Unlike organized forms of resistance, translingual practice is generally organic in nature in that for most multilinguals linguistic hybridity is commonplace and unconscious.

As briefly explained in Chapter 1 of this book, four main types of linguistic hybridity exist in the UAE context (Table 3.1). While *code-switching* and *translanguaging* can apply to all languages, *white dialects* and *Arabizi* relate specifically to the mixing of Arabic and English. Through various modes of linguistic hybridity, Emiratis are moving away from inner-circle models of English and thereby reshaping the use of English and Arabic in today's UAE. Table 3.1 shows the types of linguistic hybridity that occur in the UAE.

Table 3.1 Types of Linguistic Hybridity Occurring in the UAE Context

Form of Hybridity	Definition	Languages Involved
Code-Switching	'Reserving different languages for different purposes' (Canagarajah & Dovchin, 2019, p. 14)	Two or more distinct language systems
Translanguaging	'The savvy interweaving of different languages by the same speaker in the course of the same utterance as if they were one language' (Kramsch, 2018, p. 21)	Linguistic and semiotic resources
White Dialect	'Hybridity within the Arabic language rather than between languages. (Hopkyns et al., 2018, p. 9)	Dialects of Arabic language
Arabizi	'The use of English letters to represent Arabic sounds and English numbers to represent Arabic sounds with no spelling equivalent in English (Al Fardan & Al Kaabi, 2015)	Arabic & English

The power and agency involved in such practice could be seen as a resistance strategy against monolingual ideologies underlying 'English only' educational policies in English medium universities. Moreover, *white dialects* in particular could be very much seen as a resistance strategy aimed to contribute to the protection of the Arabic language by way of being an alternative to combining Arabic with English. However, in many cases, since translingual practice is 'intuitive and/or habituated, the interlocutors do not have a theorized position on the politics of their communication' (Canagarajah & Dovchin, 2019). In other words, Emiratis using translingual English may be unaware that they are resisting 'English only' policies in some domains, simply because this is the most natural way of communicating.

While such multilingualism and translingualism is quite ordinary in superdiverse contexts, in recent years there has been a paradigm shift from 'natural multilingualism' to 'multilingualism for social justice' which Kramsch (2018) calls 'the invention of multilingualism'. While multilingualism has always been a reality, the meaning of what being multilingual involves has changed or been 'reinvented' in the age of globalization and in the age of superdiversity. Kramsch (2018, p. 22) argues that multilingualism in today's postmodern age is 'an ideology of diversity, plurality, flexibility, adaptability' which has, therefore, lost its traditional meaning of multiple monolingualisms (the ability to speak several languages like monolingual speakers of those languages). The postmodern meaning of 'multilingual' denotes the ability to use various linguistic repertoires and other semiotic resources to effectively aid communication. In this sense, multilingual speakers using translingual Englishes are, consciously or unconsciously, resisting monolingual or double monolingual policies and ideologies. In the UAE, such translingual practice can be frequently observed in conversation, in texting, and on social media communication.

Talking T-Shirts – Wearing a Message

Translingual practice is not only present in daily conversations and on social media, but the mixing of English and Arabic also appears in local pop culture such as on T-shirt designs which target teenagers and young adults. For example, youth-orientated Spanish fashion brand 'Pull & Bear', which has eight stores in the UAE, (Figure 3.4) use both English and Arabic in one sentence or in one phrase on many of their T-shirt designs. Here, linguistic hybridity is used playfully and creatively to create amusing or clever messages which only those with knowledge of both English and Arabic would understand. With slogan T-shirts or 'Talking-Ts' being a large part of their line, the aim of the brand is to combine the latest international trends with influences that are seen on the street, by watching out for new social movements and reflecting this in the clothing (Pull & Bear.com). Clearly, translingual practice in the Emirates is viewed as one such social movement. Young UAE residents, Emirati or otherwise, choosing to wear this clothing are perhaps making a statement about themselves as multilingual or translingual speakers. In this sense, the clothing reflects the sociolinguistic reality 'on the street' rather than policies which present English and Modern Standard Arabic as two pure languages placed side-by-side.

In Figure 3.4, we see translanguaging through a combination of English and Arabic words written in their respective scripts. In the case of 3.4.1, 3.4.4, and 3.4.6, Arabic transliteration of English words are used. These messages only make sense if one has knowledge of both English and Arabic. For 3.4.2, 'ya عربي' means an Arab person. 'Ya' is used as a way of calling people in Arabic to attract their attention and it precedes their names. For example, one would hear a friend calling 'Ya Sarah', while in English it would just be 'Sarah'. Ya can also be used with affectionate nicknames such as 'sugar (sukkar) or honey (asak)' as well as names which indicate family position such as aunt or uncle. In 3.4.3, the Arabic reads 'who is my beloved?'. It takes the form of a question but it is a statement more than a question, so means 'my beloved'. The messages reflect bilingual or translingual identities and insider groups.

3.4.1: No pain, no gain   *3.4.2:* Be easy, Arab   *3.4.3:* Good afternoon
                              person   my beloved

3.4.4: Ha Ha, so funny   *3.4.5:* It's not you, it's me   *3.4.6:* When I saw you,
                                                               I was like wow

Figure 3.4 Examples of Linguistic Hybridity on Clothing Designs

Photographs by the author

Such examples (Figure 3.4) also illustrate the discrepancy between 'language on the ground' and language policies which promote two 'pure' languages (standard English and MSA). Not only in the UAE but in other global contexts too there is often a disjunction between top-down bilingual policies and translingual practice. Such countries include Tanzania (Higgins, 2009), Korea (Lee, 2006), Mongolia (Dovchin, 2019), and South Africa (Makoni, 2003), to name only a few. In such contexts, translingual practices can act as a resistance to the dominant language. For instance, in Dovchin's (2019) study investigating the translingual practice of Mongolian-Kazakhs living in Australia, translingualism was used as a resistance strategy to English native-speaker norms. As Dovchin (2019) states,

Kazakh-Mongolian immigrants 'strategically adopt these languages, which are not necessarily perceived as desirable by the dominant society within their in-group interactions, since they are exclusive to outside audiences, strengthening the sense of ownership of language and distancing it from outsiders' (p. 11). Scott (1985) names such grassroots resistance strategies 'infrapolitics' or 'weapons of the weak' where the everyday resistance of subalterns, or in the case of the UAE a demographic and linguistic minority, shows that they have not consented to dominance.

3.6 Questioning the Effectiveness of Responses to the Dominance of English

We can see that responses to feelings of cultural and linguistic fragility in the region are varied. These responses range from top-down government programs such as 'Emiratization' and national laws or initiatives aimed at safeguarding Arabic, to the bottom-up resistance from communities, students, schools, universities, artists, and clothing brands. Despite the various responses to feelings of linguistic and cultural fragility outlined previously, the effectiveness of such resistance is questionable. There are three main reasons why cultural and linguistic identities in the UAE remain fragile despite both top-down and bottom-up efforts made to resist the dominance of English in the region. Firstly, English continues to grow in importance globally at a rapid pace making it, in the eyes of many, 'too powerful to fight'. Secondly, many of the Arabic language initiatives, discussed previously, have a tendency to focus on preserving Arabic as a 'pure language' or promoting 'Arabic only' or 'Arabic as a replacement for English', which is arguably unrealistic and undesirable in multilingual contexts. Finally, although translingual practice as a form of resistance to 'English only' policies has the potential to be effective by making both English and Arabic relevant and alive, the effectiveness of translingual practice is lessened in the face of fortified or institutionalized monolingualism. In addition, translingual practices are given little credibility in formal domains with many believing that they symbolize 'English interfering with Arabic' thus an additional way in which English is dominating. These issues will be discussed further in the following sections.

English – Too Powerful to Fight

Suleiman (2004, p. 35) describes Arabic as 'a small island in danger of being submerged by the foreign linguistic flood' and by far the largest part of such a flood is English. Just as a flood cannot easily be contained, English cannot be ignored or sectioned off. In fact, its presence is growing. As English continues to grow, its importance seems to overshadow various forms of resistance. Lootah (2011, p. 47) effectively calls into question the contradictory forces at play regarding English's role in the UAE.

How can we interpret the fact that the political leadership has sensed this danger and declared 2008 the year of national identity while education institutions continue reinforcing the English language and marginalizing the Arabic language as the first language of instruction? How can the Ministry of Education set about Emiratizing the educational cadre as a strategic goal while there is a foreign presence in all educational institutions which is still growing? How do we expect to reinforce students' confidence in themselves and in their identity while we are reducing their confidence in Arab teachers and their conviction that their language is one of knowledge? The English language is being reinforced as a language of science and knowledge and foreign teachers are presented as exemplars.

Lootah's (2011) series of questions highlight how the various efforts to strengthen Emirati identity, such as naming 2008 the Year of National Identity, Emiratization, and Arabic learning drives, are arguably ineffective against the backdrop of strident and thriving EMI educational policies and the hiring of foreigners as exemplars of knowledge.

Such contradictory forces are not unique to the UAE, but, as Kramsch (2018, p. 18) states, today's postmodern era is 'marked by various contradictions'. This includes 'increased diversity but also growing homogeneity, increased multilingualism but also growing monolingual mentalities, increased breakdown of national and linguistic boundaries but also increased control' (Kramsch, 2018, p. 18).

The Impracticalities of 'Preserving' a Language

Often as a response to the increased linguistic and cultural diversity globalization brings, governments attempt to regain control over what is perceived to have been lost. There are attempts to hold globalization and its accompanying language, English, at arm's length, and to channel resources into preserving or protecting the national tongue. However, the word 'preserve' conjures up images of the 'Lenin Lab' where the deceased communist revolutionary and founder of the Soviet Union has painstakingly been kept in pristine condition by 200 embalming experts (Litvinova, 2016) for 149 years. While preserving a corpse or a historic building may be achievable, 'preserving' anything as characteristically fluid and flexible as language is a very difficult task. Part of what drives a desire to 'preserve' local languages, as part of language purity missions, are feelings of lack of control due to the rapid pace of globalization which affects the Gulf region more dramatically than many other global contexts. Barney (2004) associates the discourse of globalization with 'post-nationalism' which is 'the diminishing ability of states to protect and nurture domestic, indigenous cultural industries in the context of global, liberalized market conditions'. This 'diminishing ability to protect' the Arabic language results in overt attempts to control and police language use.

Despite scholarly recognition of the need to reinvent the term multilingualism to suit the way languages are used in today's globalized and superdiverse world, there is a 'persistent old nation-based monolingualism' (Kramsch, 2018, p. 23) which exists in many contexts. As Gramling (2019) states, despite the cognitive, social, political, cultural, moral, and commercial arguments against monolingualism, it has been 'reelected'. Here, perhaps as a reaction to not being able to control the parameters of this new more complex and messier multilingualism, there has been a resurgence of the 'one language, one culture' mentality, where languages are seen to represent different cultures and do not mix comfortably without the respective languages being in some way polluted or distorted. We can most definitely see this in the context of the UAE with local media presenting the languages English and Arabic as competitors, where the acquisition of one equates to the loss of another. Monolingual mentalities fuel many organized forms of resistance which have a focus on replacing English with Arabic or promoting only Arabic. 'Arabic only' movements can be seen as a direct counterargument to 'English only' policies in education. This is not only apparent in the UAE but also in other global contexts such as the USA, where the growth of 'English only movements' by right-wing conservatives can be observed as a reaction to Latino immigrants speaking Spanish (Romero, 2017). As a response to this, 'home language only campaigns' are a common form of resistance to the dominance of English.

While 'Arabic only' initiatives may encourage some Emiratis to make a conscious effort to use only Arabic on social media for example, other multilinguals will use the language/languages which come naturally at the time, whether it be English or more often a mix of English and Arabic. In this sense, it is difficult to police a language. Moreover, when a language is given a 'hard sell', it often becomes less attractive. When one is told 'don't use English, use Arabic', English often becomes more appealing still.

Institutionalized Monolingualism

Other less organized forms of resistance to the dominance of English in the region, such as translingual practice, also face certain challenges. Although translingual practice allows many languages or linguistic repertoires to be used and is a natural phenomenon in multilingual contexts, such practice is often rejected in formal contexts not only due to ideological monolingualism or 'linguaphobia' (Gramling, 2019) but also as a result of fortified or institutional monolingualism where policies support the use of one language. In the context of the UAE, English Medium Instruction policies would be an example of this. In many other contexts such as the USA, Gramling (2019, p. 3) argues that 'monolingualism as a political and economic structure is just now really getting going in earnest'. Rather than monolingual ideologies being reserved for cultural conservatives or nationalists, they have become multi-partisan 'big-tent' affairs which are impenetrable. This 'ideological thinning, administrative thickening' (Gramling, 2019, p. 3) means that despite grassroots movements, institutional monolingualism is stronger. This is especially the case in the post-2016 age of Trump in the USA, UKIP and Brexit in the UK, AfD in Germany, and ÖVP in Austria (Gramling, 2019, p. 4).

Especially in societies which tend to respect authority and official policies uncritically, institutionalized monolingualism may have an impact on how multilingual speakers view their own language practices. Feelings of shame or guilt when mixing languages may result due to the lack of credibility awarded to translingual practice in formal contexts such as in education. Although translanguaging may be viewed as fashionable, cool, or creative (as reflected in the T-shirt designs seen earlier in this chapter), institutional or commercial multilingualism supports two pure forms over translingual practice (Gramling, 2019, p. 10). For example, test scores on a CV would reflect proficiency in separate 'pure' languages rather than an individual's full linguistic repertoire used to aid communication.

Furthermore, translanguaging is politically complicated. Kraidy (2002) explains, 'while some see hybridity as a site of democratic struggle and resistance against empire, others have attacked it as a neocolonial discourse complicit with transnational capitalism, cloaked in the hip garb of cultural theory' (p. 316). From the latter group's point of view, using English in multilingual contexts through translingual practice essentially feeds into the growing power of global English (Skutnabb-Kangas, 2000). After all, instead of the local language being used all the time, English replaces some of what might once have been said in the local language. Values and cultural practices also pass through language, thereby 'giving English more life' (Canagarajah & Dovchin, 2019, p. 15). Therefore, some argue that forms of linguistic hybridity, such as Arabizi, threaten not only the Arabic language but also Muslim and Arab identity, considering the deeply rooted connection between the Arabic language, including its script, and the Quran (Esmael, 2016). It is true to say that by adopting a translingual orientation where English is mixed with other languages and semiotic resources using linguistic hybridity and repertoire building, individuals are inadvertently developing neoliberal practices and dispositions (Canagarajah, 2017) even as they are resisting and negotiating English in local contexts for their own purposes (Canagarajah & Dovchin, 2019, p. 16). Here we see the complexities and conflicting positions involved in both cultural and linguistic hybridity.

Wanted Not Welcome

We can summarize by identifying a distinct conflict of desires in relation to English. On the one hand, the goals of the UAE's leaders, and in turn the goal of many individuals, centre around neoliberal ideologies and competing on a global stage. To do this, English is seen as a necessary skill and is promoted heavily, especially in the nation's education system. On the other hand, there is a concern that by embracing English so fully, citizens are relinquishing Arabic. This chapter began by highlighting various forms of resistance to the effects of global English in the Gulf region, from government-driven initiatives to grassroots activism. The effectiveness of such resistance was called into question due to the overpowering importance placed on English in multiple domains as well as the nature of various forms of resistance being somewhat flawed. It was further argued that top-down attempts to strengthen Arabic generally focus on boosting Arabic alone, rather than embracing how English and Arabic are often used in combination. Bottom-up resistance in the form of linguistic hybridity as seen on local clothing designs and as used naturally by Emirati youth, while having the potential to be effective, is not given enough credibility in many domains such as in university classrooms, partly due to dominant ideologies of language purity in the region. Here we see a push-pull relationship surrounding English, where it is wanted for its enabling qualities but resisted due to the effects of its dominance. This notion of English being wanted but not welcome is central to the study which will be explained in Chapter 4 of this book.

References

Al Allaq, W. (2014). Arabic Language in a globalized world: Observations from the United Arab Emirates. *Arab World English Journal, 5* (3), 113–123.

Al Ameri, K. (2013, May 2). Arabic is precious, but the English language is essential. *The National*. Retrieved from: www.thenational.ae/thenationalconversation/comment/arabic-is-precious-but-the-english-language-is-essential.

Al Fardan, H., & Al Kaabi, A. (2015). *Spoken Emirati Phrasebook*. Abu Dhabi: Cultural Programs and Heritage Festivals Committee, Abu Dhabi.

Al-Harthi, J. (2018). *Celestial Bodies*. Inverness, Scotland: Sandstone Press Ltd.

Al-Khouri, A. M. (2012). Population growth and government modernization efforts: The case of GCC countries. *International Journal of Research in Management and Technology, 2* (1), 1–8.

Al-Qasimi, B. (2017). UAE's publishing industry: A vision of an avant-garde nation. *Publishing Research Quarterly, 33* (1), 37–40. http://dx.doi.org/10.1007/s12109-016-9494-z

Al-Shaiba, A. (2014). Key perspectives on preparing UAE nationals for employment. In the Emirates Center for Strategic Studies and Research (ECSSR). *The Future of Education in the UAE Innovation and Knowledge Production*, 67–95.

Al-Subaihi, T. (2016, March 23). Abu Dhabi park event encourages children to exercise their Arabic. *The National*. Retrieved from: www.thenational.ae/uae/education/abu-dhabi-park-event-encourages-children-to-exercise-their-arabic.

Aydarova, O. (2012). If not "the best of the West," then "look East": Imported teacher education curricula in the Arabian Gulf. *Journal of Studies in International Education, 17* (3), 284–302.

Badry, F. (2011). Appropriating English: Language in identity construction in the United Arab Emirates. In A. Al-Issa, & L. S. Dahan (Eds.), *Global English and Arabic* (pp. 81–122). Bern: Peter Lang.

Barney, D. (2004). *The Network Society*. Cambridge: Polity Press.

Belhiah, H., & Elhami, M. (2015). English as a medium of instruction in the Gulf: When students and teachers speak. *Language Policy*, 14, 2–23.

Bil Arabi initiative gets stronger by the year (2017, December 16). *Gulf News*. Retrieved from: https://gulfnews.com/opinion/editorials/bil-arabi-initiative-gets-stronger-by-the-year-1.2141866.

Buckner, E. (2017). *The Status of Teaching and Teacher Professional Satisfaction in the UAE*. Ras Al Khaimah: UAE. Retrieved from: www.alqasimifoundation. com/admin/Content/File-562017233517.pdf.

Burkett, T. (2016). Emirati students' cultural norms and university teachers' awareness: A socio-cultural gap? *Perspectives*, 24 (1), 5–11.

Canagarajah, S. (2013). *Translingual Practice: Global Englishes and Cosmopolitan Relations*. New York: Routledge.

Canagarajah, S. (2017). *Translingual Practices and Neoliberal Policies: Attitudes and Strategies of African Skilled Migrants in Anglophone Workplaces*. Switzerland: Springer.

Canagarajah, S., & Dovchin, S. (2019). The everyday politics of translingualism as a resistant practice. *International Journal of Multilingualism*. https://doi.org/ 10.1080/14790718.2019.1575833.

Cummins, J. (2007). Rethinking monolingual instructional strategies in multilingual classrooms. *Canadian Journal of Applied Linguistics*, 10, 221–240.

Dickson, M. (2013). School improvements in Abu Dhabi, United Arab Emirates: Asking the 'expert witnesses'. *Improving Schools*, 16 (3), 272–284.

Dovchin, S. (2019). Language crossing and linguistic racism: Mongolian immigrant women in Australia. *Journal of Multicultural Discourses*. https://doi.org /10.1080/17447143.2019.1566345.

Ellis, R. (2003). *Task-Based Language Learning and Teaching*. Oxford: Oxford University Press.

Esmael, A. (2016). *The Effect of the Empowerment of the 'White Dialect' on Enhancing Standard Arabic*. Paper Presented at the 5th International Arabic Conference, Dubai, United Arab Emirates.

Findlow, S. (2005). International networking in the United Arab Emirates higher education: Global-local tension. *Compare*, 35 (3), 285–302.

Gallagher, K. (2019a). Introduction: Education in the UAE – context and themes. In K. Gallagher (Ed.), *Education in the UAE: Innovation and Transformation* (pp. 1–18). Singapore: Springer.

Gallagher, K. (2019b). Challenges and opportunities in sourcing, preparing and developing a teacher force for the UAE. In K. Gallagher (Ed.), *Education in the UAE: Innovation and Transformation* (pp. 127–145). Singapore: Springer.

Gramling, D. (2019). On reelecting monolingualism: Fortification, fragility, and stamina. *Applied Linguistics Review*, 1–18. https://doi.org/10.1515/ applirev-2019-0039.

Habboush, M. (2008, December 2). Khalifa stresses national identity. *The National*. Retrieved from: www.thenational.ae/uae/khalifa-stresses-national-identity-1.562584.

Higgins, C. (2009). *English as a Local Language*. Bristol, UK: Multilingual Matters.

Hopkyns, S., Zoghbor, W., & Hassall, P. (2018). Creative hybridity over linguistic purity: The status of English in the United Arab Emirates. *Asian Englishes*, 20 (2), 158–169.

Hudson, P. (2019). A gin and tonic and a window seat: Critical pedagogy in Arabia. In M. E. Lopez-Gopar (Ed.), *International Perspectives on Critical Pedagogies in ELT* (pp. 241–263). New York: Palgrave Macmillan. http://doi.org/10.1007/978-3-319-95621-3_12.

James, A., & Shammas, N. M. (2013). Developing intercultural intelligence: Dubai style. *Journal of International Education in Business*, 6 (2), 148–164.

Kalima (n.d.). *Why Kalima Was Created*. Retrieved from: www.kalima.ae/en.

Karmani, S. (2005). Petro-linguistics: The emerging nexus between oil, English, and Islam. *Journal of Language, Identity, and Education*, 4 (2), 87–102.

Kirk, D. (2010). *The Development of Higher Education in the United Arab Emirates*. Abu Dhabi, UAE: The Emirates Center for Strategic Studies and Research.

Knowledge and Human Authority (KHDA). Retrieved from: www.khda.gov.ae/en/Website.

Kraidy, M. M. (2002). Hybridity in cultural globalization. *Communication Theory*, 12 (3), 316–339.

Kramsch, C. (2018). Is there still a place for culture in a multilingual FL education? *Language Education and Multilingualism*, 1, 16–33.

Kubota, R. (2019). *Two Faces of Neoliberal Communicative Competence: A Call for Transformation*. Plenary talk at Languaging in Times of Change Conference, University of Stirling, Scotland, September 26–27.

Lee, J. S. (2006). Linguistic construction of modernity: English mixing in Korean television commercials. *Language in Society*, 35, 59–91.

Litvinova, D. (2016, May 9). Lenin lab: The team keeping the first Soviet. *The Guardian*. Retrieved from: www.theguardian.com/world/2016/may/09/lenin-lab-team-keeping-first-soviet-leader-embalmed-moscow.

Lootah, M. S. (2011). Assessing educational policies in the UAE. In the Emirates Center for Strategic Studies and Research (ECSSR). *Education in the UAE Current Status and Future Developments*, 27–52.

Louber, I., & Troudi, S. (2019). "Most of the teaching is in Arabic anyway", English as a medium of instruction in Saudi Arabia, between de facto and official language policy. *International Journal of Bias, Identity and Diversities in Education*, 4 (2), 59–73.

Lugones, M. (2010). Toward a decolonial feminism. *Hypatia*, 25 (4), 742–759.

Makoni, S. (2003). From misinvention to disinvention of language: Multilingualism and the South African Constitution. In S. Makoni, G. Smitherman, A. F. Ball, & A. K Spears (Eds.), *Black Linguistics; Language, Society, and Politics in Africa and the Americas* (pp. 132–152). London: Routledge.

Neon Book Hunt Beckons in the Capital (2019, October 20). *The Gulf News*. Retrieved from: https://gulfnews.com/uae/neon-book-hunt-beckons-in-the-capital-1.67263914.

Notzon, B., & Nesom, G. (2005). The Arabic naming system. *Science Editor*, 28 (1), 20–21.

Pull & Bear Company Concept: An Ever-Young Community. Retrieved from: www.pullandbear.com/ae/page/company.html.

Riddlebarger, J. (2015). *English Instruction in Abu Dhabi*. Retrieved from: http://newsmanager.commpartners.com/tesoleflis/issues/2014-12-22/l.html.

Romero, S. (2017, August 24). Use of Spanish grows in U.S., despite politics. *New York Times*, p. 1.

Ryan, P. (2010). *Don't Insist on English!* Retrieved from: www.ted.com/talks/patricia_ryan_ideas_in_all_languages_not_just_english/transcript?language=en.

Sandiford, C. (2013). The enculturation of pre-service Emirati English language teachers. *Education, Business and Society: Contemporary Middle Eastern Issues*, 7 (1), 2–16.

Scott, J. C. (1985). *Weapons of the Weak: Everyday Forms of Resistance*. New Haven: Yale University Press.

Skutnabb-Kangas, T. (2000). *Linguistic Genocide in Education or Worldwide Diversity and Human Rights?* Mahwah, NJ: Lawrence Erlbaum Associates.

Statistics Center of Abu Dhabi (2017). *Education Statistics 2016–2017*. Retrieved January 4, 2019 from: www.scad.ae/Release%20Documents/Education%20Statistics%202016-17%20-%20EN.pdf

Suleiman, Y. (2004). *A War of Words: Language and Conflict in the Middle East*. Cambridge: Cambridge University Press.

Taha-Thomure, H. (2019). Arabic language education in the UAE: Choosing the right drivers. In K. Gallagher (Ed.), *Education in the UAE: Innovation and Transformation* (pp. 75–93). Singapore: Springer. doi:10.1007/978-978-981-13-7736-5_5.

Thorne, C. (2015). *An Investigation of the Professional Identity of Teacher Educators in the UAE*. PhD thesis, Exeter, UK.

Vision2021.ae. Retrieved from: www.vision2021.ae/en/uae-vision.

4 The Study – Multiple Perspectives

Truth is often a multiplicity of perspectives . . . the more viewpoints and versions of events there are, the closer the reader gets to an overarching truth.

– Susan Barker

If you are not going to swim deep with me, then get out of my waters.

– Bridget Devoue

4.1 University Setting: A Microcosm of Society

A gigantic, modern, futuristic spaceship-shaped campus on the outskirts of Abu Dhabi was the scene of the study (Figure 4.1). While it is architecturally unique and stunning, it is literally located in the middle of the desert with very little surrounding it that one could walk to. As Pieterse (2010) states, such a setting for a university is typical of 'petro-urbanism' found in the Gulf states, where oil cities are 'characterized by rapid development organized around car transport, with broad multi-lane roads that barely have sidewalks' (p. 23). As a result of its location, once at the university, students and faculty are generally there for the whole day. Breaks are spent in offices or meeting rooms, the library, sports centre, or many campus cafes, including the very popular Starbucks chain. This makes it an extremely convenient place for scheduling research time with participants.

The university is one of three government-sponsored institutions and it has a sister campus in Dubai. As explained in Chapter 2 of this book, although English Medium Instruction (EMI) is growing globally (Dearden, 2015; Macaro, 2018), it is especially dominant in higher education in the UAE. While the university in which the study takes place aims to produce bilingual graduates in English and Arabic, all majors except Arabic and Islamic Studies are taught through the medium of English. When one walks into a classroom it is English one hears teachers speaking and English course materials one sees being used. Outside the classrooms, although multilingual and translingual practice is common, English books dominate the library shelves and the university library

Figure 4.1 University in Which the Study Took Place
Photograph by the author

database operates primarily in English. English is the language of assessments, assignments, and presentations. In the university foundation program, which is the more specific context of the study, English-speaking faculty members outnumber Arabic-speaking teachers. Therefore, as with UAE society outside the university, multilingualism is ordinary but English dominates, especially in its written form.

The university could be viewed as a microcosm of UAE society due to the diversity of nationalities and linguistic backgrounds of people working there, as well as the university's strong 'culture of change', which reflects the fast-paced change seen in greater UAE society, as outlined in Chapter 2 of this book. In terms of diversity, although English is the medium of instruction, in hallways and cafes at the university, one will hear many languages spoken as well as translingual practice being commonplace. For example, Emirati students use multiple languages such as colloquial Arabic with friends and English with their multinational teachers. Translingual practice includes using both English and Arabic with the addition of other words from languages such as Tagalog and Amharic, which they may have picked up from Filipino and Ethiopian domestic helpers, or Turkish and Korean from popular dramas. In the university's many coffee shops, salons, and book stores, additional languages can be heard due to the multinational makeup of the staff.

In terms of a 'culture of change', one semester is rarely a copy of the previous one. Routines cannot be settled into for long before a major change is implemented. Examples of changes made to the English foundation program include a move from general English to English for general academic purposes. This has accompanied name changes to the levels within the program as well as changes made to content of courses to reflect the new academic English curriculum. Further changes have included the reduction in length of the English foundation program from two years to one year, and then to the program morphing into a language development program to be taken side-by-side credit-bearing courses. A further change, which had a more dramatic effect on the student sample for the study, was the difference in female/male student numbers at the university. While there have always been more females than males, this gender imbalance was exacerbated in the months leading up to the main data collection period, by the Cabinet's relatively new requirement for Emirati men between the ages of 18 and 30 to serve between nine months to two years military service (Salem, 2014). Most high school graduates choose to do this before enrolling in higher education. This requirement dramatically reduced the number of male students in the program during the study period. The decision for the undergraduate student sample to be 80% female and 20% male, although not as balanced as was hoped, is representative of the current number of students at the university. Overall, we can see that due to levels of diversity and change, the university in which the study takes place could be seen as a microcosm of UAE society.

Although the university has features which are unique to the region, such as gender-segregated classrooms and facilities, there are many elements of the study context which share similarities with EMI universities in other settings. Here we see that the concept of 'small cultures', as mentioned in Chapter 1 of this book, come into play, where those studying in EMI settings may share certain practices which transcend national borders. For example, Hong Kong and Singapore predominantly hire foreign teachers with Western degrees to teach mainly national students in the medium of English. Similarly, many countries in Europe hire EMI teachers from abroad to teach both local and international students (Daryai-Hansen et al., 2017). Having looked at the study setting, we will move to look the study approach.

4.2 Approach: Making the Invisible Visible

When navigating the methodological maze, one is bombarded with possible approaches to take. Although one approach may be a perfect fit for some studies, in many cases elements of more than one approach are appropriate. With this in mind, I adopted an innovative hybrid approach

Table 4.1 Research Questions

	Research Questions
RQ1	What do the languages, English and Arabic, represent to Emirati undergraduates, Emirati primary school teachers, and expatriate university English teachers?
RQ2	In the participants' view, how does English affect layers of cultural identity in the UAE?
RQ3	In the participants' view, what are the English teaching preferences amongst Emirati undergraduates and Emirati primary school teachers with regard to teacher nationality, course content, and medium of instruction?

through combining phenomenology with a multiple case study design to produce a phenomenological case study.

The study aimed to understand the sociolinguistic realities and attitudes of the three groups of participants by exploring opinions, insights, and perceptions on the impact of global English on Emirati cultural identities. This was achieved by exploring the issues from multiple angles and by using multiple data collection methods (Keddie, 2006, p. 20) as a trademark feature of the case study approach. The key research questions can be seen in Table 4.1.

The 'bounded nature' (Creswell, 2007, p. 61) of the case study approach fits the study as participants are bounded by both time and place, due to living in Abu Dhabi and, more specifically, working or studying at the university. As the study looks at the perspectives of three groups of participants: Emirati undergraduate students, Emirati primary school teachers, and expatriate university English teachers, it can be described as a 'multiple case study' which is descriptive in nature, as the aim is to present a complete description of the phenomenon within its context (Yin, 2003, p. 5). In this study, the phenomenon being investigated is 'English in the UAE and its impact on cultural identities' and the cases or units of analysis are the three groups of participants. As the study investigates how these three groups of individuals (three cases) understand and perceive their experiences of a particular phenomenon, it was also appropriate to use the phenomenological approach. Phenomenology, which was founded in the early twentieth century by Edmund Husserl and was later furthered by Berger and Luckmann (1966) in *The Social Construction of Reality* (Kvale, 1996, p. 52), deals with 'people's perceptions or meanings; people's attitudes and beliefs; people's feelings and emotions' (Denscombe, 2010, p. 93), making it ideally suited to addressing the research questions in this study. Another feature of phenomenology is its emphasis on the existence of multiple realities. As Denscombe (2010, p. 97) states,

Phenomenology rejects the notion that there is one universal reality and accepts, instead, that things can be seen in different ways by different people at different times in different circumstances, and that each alternative version needs to be recognized as being valid in its own right.

This exemplifies my epistemological and ontological beliefs that centre around interpretivism, subjectivity, relativism, and social constructivism. Phenomenological research essentially aims to 'to make the invisible visible' (Kvale, 1996, p. 53) and focuses on the life world of participants with an openness to their experiences.

One of the distinctive features of a phenomenological case study is the use of multiple research tools in order to provide a rigorous account which investigates the attitudes and experiences of the participants in depth. For this reason, three distinct and complimentary research instruments were used to provide three different angles by which to approach the research questions. The research instruments included focus groups, open-response questionnaires, and a researcher journal for the practice of reflexivity. Figure 4.2 provides a visual representation of the study approach.

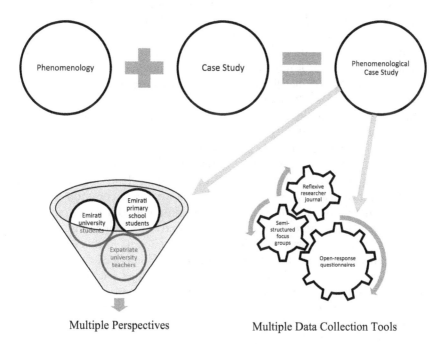

Multiple Perspectives   Multiple Data Collection Tools

Figure 4.2 Study Approach

The following sections will explore these choices further by discussing the importance of using multiple data collection tools and gaining multiple perspectives.

Angle 1: Focus Groups

Focus groups, which are 'group discussions exploring different sets of issues' (Kitzinger & Barbour, 1999, p. 4), are not synonymous with group interviews. Rather than the discussion being only between the researcher and group members, discussion also takes place amongst the group members themselves (Kitzinger & Barbour, 1999; Parker & Tritter, 2006; Wilson, 1997). The group is 'focused' as it involves some kind of collective activity such as debating a set of questions. Although focus groups are not as common as interviews in everyday life (Edley & Litosseliti, 2010, p. 156), in academia, focus groups or group interviews have grown in popularity (Cohen et al., 2007, p. 373; Farquhar & Das, 1999, p. 47; Kitzinger & Barbour, 1999, p. 1; Wilson, 1997, p. 209) to the point where they are now considered to be 'at the heart of qualitative research' (Stephens, 2009, p. 93).

As a data collection tool, focus groups were chosen for two main reasons. Firstly, focus groups allow for different perspectives in an informal discussion and are, therefore, 'ideal for exploring people's experiences, opinions, wishes and concerns' (Kitzinger & Barbour, 1999, p. 5). They also challenge the power dynamics often found in standard interviews by giving the participants greater control and turning the interviewer into more of a facilitator or moderator. This power is achieved by participants shaping the flow of the discussion and co-constructing knowledge as a group. As Thomas (2008, p. 78), points out, 'focus group discussions emphasize participation, supportive environments, discussion, depth and interaction between all members'.

Secondly, focus groups are particularly recommended for Gulf Arabs (Thomas, 2008; van den Hoven, 2014; Winslow et al., 2002) as they replicate a culturally familiar form of discussion. Traditionally, social, religious, political, or business meetings amongst common interest groups take place in 'majlis' (place of sitting). This is a public space in houses or offices where guests are received and entertained. Due to a tradition of discussing issues in this fashion, participants in this study most likely felt comfortable in a focus group setting. Stephens (2009, p. 94) emphasizes this point when stating that focus groups are 'well suited to cultural contexts that privilege the communal over the individual'. In a supportive group environment, a level of candour and spontaneity from members tends to be evoked that is not achieved in one-to-one interviews (Winslow et al., 2002, p. 566).

Although, for the previous reasons, focus groups were an appropriate data collection tool, it is important to recognize potential problems with the method. Firstly, with increased power for the participants comes less control for the facilitator. There is the possibility of 'losing control', although as Kitzinger and Barbour (1999, p. 13) point out, 'the "freer" and more dynamic situation of a focus group may actually access "better data" than a more subdued and formal encounter'. Secondly, peer interaction may result in 'group think' (Dreachslin, 1999, as cited in Thomas, 2008, p. 8), where one or two dominant members of the group lead the discussion and other members tend to agree or stay silent, perhaps not having the chance to make themselves heard. Finally, a further concern was whether or not some issues were too sensitive to discuss in a group. As previously noted, the influence of English as a global language on culture and identity may be regarded as a sensitive issue in the Arab world nowadays. In focus groups, the speakers may feel inhibited by others' perceptions of their opinions. This is especially true if there is a dominant and religiously conservative character in the group who prevents participants from openly expressing their opinions 'in deference to perceived righteousness and singular religious interpretations of culture' (James & Shammas, 2013, p. 155), which is not uncommon. However, the literature shows that sensitive topics can be discussed in groups and people may be more, rather than less, likely to self-disclose or share personal experiences in group rather than dyadic settings (Carey, 1994; Morgan & Krueger, 1993; Winslow et al., 2002). Indeed, Morgan and Krueger (1993) even refer to 'a certain thrill in the open discussion of taboo topics'. In the Gulf countries, open group discussions tend to be lively rather than inducing group members to feel awkward or shy. To conclude, the benefits of focus groups outweigh the negatives in this setting.

Angle 2: Open-Response Questionnaires

To counter some of the disadvantages of focus groups, provide a fuller picture, and increase the rigour of the study in line with a case study approach, a second research tool was used: the open-response questionnaire.

Open-response questionnaires were used for four main reasons. Firstly, a large amount of data (152 questionnaires in total) could be collected in a relatively short amount of time. Secondly, using questionnaires assures complete anonymity which most other techniques do not provide. This means that students and teachers may be more likely to disclose true opinions without any fear of being judged, and this may counter 'group think', which was identified as a potential flaw in focus group data. Thirdly, the rate of return is generally high, as it is not so much of a commitment in terms of time and energy. Finally, using questionnaires means that the questions are identical for each participant and no facilitator comes between the participant and the question, perhaps influencing responses. As the questionnaires were self-administered (without the presence of the researcher) (Cohen et al., 2007, p. 344), respondents were able to complete them in familiar surroundings and did not, therefore, feel under any pressure from the researcher.

Disadvantages of using questionnaires, such as participants not always giving as much detail as one might like, were countered by the complementary use of focus groups. Both questionnaire and focus data may be influenced by 'self-flattery'. As Skehan (1989, p. 61) points out, 'the approval motive (or the social desirability factor) is a danger for any sort of introspective or self-report data'. Teachers and students, in this case, may want to show themselves in a positive light. In this sense, 'responses are often coloured by what respondents assume is desired by the investigator or by what is socially acceptable' (Gass & Selinker, 1994, p. 254). Questions relating to emotionally sensitive areas such as 'identity' may attract less-than-honest answers in order to avoid embarrassment or disloyalty. It was hoped, however, that the anonymity of the questionnaires and the supportive atmosphere of the focus groups would counter these potential problems.

Angle 3: Reflexivity Through a Researcher Journal

The third method used was a researcher journal. The value of keeping a research journal is affirmed in the literature (Borg, 2001; Dornyei, 2007; Engin, 2011). Researcher journals help with the process of researching (Borg, 2001, pp. 162–169) and facilitate the development of 'thick description', which is relevant to a phenomenological approach. Geertz's (1973, p. 3) notion of 'thick description', borrowed from Gilbert Ryle, focuses on recording not only what the participants say but also their tone of voice, gestures, facial expressions, and circumstances to provide fuller and richer data.

Researcher journals also give the opportunity for reflexive research. Reflexivity can be defined as 'critical reflection on the research process and on one's own role as a researcher' (Findlay, 2002) or, in other words, 'bending back or turning back one's awareness on oneself' (McLeod, 2001, p. 195). As Bensa (2010, p. 39, as cited in Risager & Dervin, 2015, p. 14) states, data collection is often, mistakenly, thought of as simply picking 'mushrooms in a forest'. Instead, it is important to recognize the process of negotiations and encounters that take place and to distinctly 'hear' rather than 'listen to' the study's social players. As Risager and Dervin (2015, p. 14) state, 'leaving out this reflexive work exoticises the research participants, whereas our interlocutors should be "co-authors" instead'. Flood (1999, p. 35) further stresses the importance of reflective research by stating, 'without some degree of reflexivity any research is blind and without purpose'. It is generally agreed upon in the literature that reflexivity is an important part of qualitative data (Denscombe,

2010; Findlay, 2002; Kramsch, 2012; Lockwood Harris, 2016; Mann, 2016; Pillow, 2003; Roegman et al., 2016).

Pillow (2003, p. 181) names reflexivity as *recognition of self* and reflexivity as *recognition of other* as useful reflexive strategies. These strategies were used in varying degrees throughout the data collection and data analysis stages of the study. Firstly, reflexivity was used as *recognition of self* by observing myself through the use of reflective notes. It is true to say that, 'Embedded within the research process are relationships of power that all researchers must face' (Pillow, 2003, p. 182). Facing these power relationships involved recognizing the 'insider' and 'outsider' roles I had as a researcher and how these roles could be affecting the research. As Roegman et al. (2016, p. 45) explain, 'outsider' describes researchers who work with participants who are different from themselves, whereas the 'insider' researcher shares significant identities with the participants. For this study, my role as researcher was far from simple but rather multifaceted and frequently changing according to the participant group. As Braun and Clarke (2013, p. 10) point out, for any research, we are likely to have multiple insider and outsider positions. Such insider/outside roles have been discussed and problematized from a variety of perspectives in the literature (Dwyer & Buckle, 2009; Irvine et al., 2008; Knowles, 2019; Kusow, 2003). In the case of this study, as a woman I had an insider role with most of the participants (the majority of Emirati university students, all the Emirati primary school teachers, and around half of the expatriate teachers). This similarity between us may have helped the Emirati participants to feel more comfortable and open, especially in a society in which the sexes are often polarized. However, I had a greater number of outsider roles with the Emirati undergraduate students in particular, such as nationality, age, religion, race, dress, language, and level of education. Although being an 'outsider' is often seen as an advantage due to presumed objectivity (Roegman et al., 2016, p. 45), I was aware that my outside status may have caused participants to be more wary and less candid, and in some cases this could have affected responses. For example, being a white female non-Muslim British PhD candidate in my 30s dressed in Western business clothes distinguished me as a clear 'outsider'. When asked questions about attitudes towards English, therefore, it was hard to ignore the fact that due to English being my first language, participants were perhaps reluctant to be critical out of kindness or sensitivity. They were perhaps more likely to answer in an 'English-friendly' way, so as not to offend what I clearly represented if merely by appearance.

As a decision was made to use two translators for bilingual support during the focus groups, it is also important to recognize the impact the translators may have had on the participants. Both translators were female, giving them an 'insider role' with the majority of the participants. One translator was in her 40s, born in Syria but a citizen of the United

States. The other translator was in her 50s, a British and Sudanese citizen. They both had friendly demeanours and were helpful when needed for translating Arabic, but quietly listened when English was being spoken, which was most of the time in all focus groups, except amongst the male university student focus group members who used Arabic for a greater part. It was hoped that the presence of an Arabic-speaker may have made participants more relaxed and able to use both languages, which seemed to be the case.

Finally, the importance of self-monitoring and self-censoring was recognized. I was careful not to voice my own opinions on the culturally sensitive topics being discussed. Guillemin and Gillam (2004) stress the need for researches to consider 'micro-ethical dimensions of research practice' (p. 265), in that it is necessary to be alert and prepared for ethical issues surrounding sensitive topics. Not only was this important as a researcher not wanting to influence the data, but in addition, as James and Shammas (2013, p. 155) state, it is particularly important due to 'the current political climate where criticism of UAE society can result in extreme consequences'. For example, in numerous cases, voicing a critical opinion of the UAE government or 'transgressing unwritten rules' (James & Shammas, 2013, p. 155) has resulted in academics having contracts immediately terminated (Hudson, 2019).

As well as reflecting on my role as a researcher, I also used reflexivity to gain a deeper understanding of the participants (reflexivity as *recognition of other*). Making notes on focus group participants such as their ways of dressing, ways of sitting, gestures, and manners created a more accurate picture of not only what was said but also feelings surrounding thoughts and comments. Braun and Clarke (2013, p. 9) highlight the importance in being able to 'reflect on, and step outside your cultural membership, to become a cultural commentator, so that you can see, and question, the shared values and assumptions that make up being a member of a particular society'. This involved identifying my own assumptions and putting them aside ('bracketing' them off) so that the research was not automatically shaped by my identity as a researcher (Fischer, 2009). For example, whereas I had expected Emirati participants to be in favour of Arabic medium instruction (AMI) over EMI, due partly to how I might feel if I were in the same situation and media attention on the need to protect Arabic from fading, often participants were wholeheartedly in favour of EMI, as will be seen in Chapter 7 of this book, seeing it as the only way forward. At points in the focus group sessions, I had to fight my instinct to become involved in the discussion personally, giving the counterargument. As Braun and Clarke (2013, p. 9) state, bracketing off one's own assumptions is 'hard to do, but vitally important for being able to get "deep" into qualitative data', as well as being, 'a continuing mode of self-analysis and political awareness' (Callaway, 1992, p. 33).

4.3 Participants: Multiple Realities

As befitting to a multiple phenomenological case study, it was essential to investigate the phenomenon of global English and cultural identities through the eyes of a diverse range of participants. Gaining the insights of different nationalities, ages, professions, and genders aimed to provide a full picture of the phenomenon under investigation. Thus, three groups of participants were selected for this study due to the varied perspectives they brought to the research questions. These groups included Emirati university students (both male and female), Emirati primary school teachers (female), and expatriate university teachers (both male and female and from a range of 11 countries). We will now look at these participant groups in more detail.

Group 1: Emirati University Students

The first group included 100 Emirati university students (80 female and 20 male) studying in the university's English foundation program. Their perspectives were valuable as their future education depends on their English level, in that they are attending an English medium university and had not yet met the entrance requirements (IELTS 5.5). All named Arabic as their first language. The participants' ages ranged from 18 to 30, with most being aged between 18 and 20. The majority of the students (80%) had been learning English for between 12 and 15 years, meaning they started learning English in Kindergarten (KG) or Grade 1. They planned to major in a range of 17 different subjects with the most popular choices being Information Technology (16%), Media (12%), Business (10%), and Art/Design (7%). Due to the range of chosen majors, it could be said that the participants represent a wide range of university students. However, as all the students in this group required time in the foundation program and all attended state schools rather than private schools, they cannot be said to represent Emirati university students in general.

Group 2: Emirati Primary School Teachers

The second group included 12 female Emirati primary school teachers aged between mid-20s and late 40s. They had been studying English between 9 and 21 years and had been teaching for the local educational council, teaching a range of STEM (Science, Technology, Engineering, and Mathematics) subjects. Their views were pivotal to the research as they had been affected by English in education in multiple ways. Firstly, they were on sabbatical at the university to improve their English proficiency level due to the new requirements (teaching core subjects in English from kindergarten) imposed by the New School Model (NSM), as mentioned in Chapter 2. When this model was introduced in 2010, teachers whose English was below the level of IELTS 6.5 were granted a sabbatical for up to two years in order to achieve the language proficiency needed to deliver the curriculum in English and continue their teaching careers. The fact that their future careers depended on their level of English made them extremely important stakeholders. They also had the benefit of being older than the Emirati university students (first group of participants) and therefore had seen more of the changes discussed in Chapter 2. Finally, ten (83%) were mothers and had a vested interest in the topic not only from their own points of view but also for the next generation including their own children. Most of their children were of school age with one teacher having a daughter studying at university in the UK. As well as being in frequent contact with the Emirati primary school students they taught, having families of their own gave this group additional, and highly personal, perspectives on the effects of English on the next generation, a subject that they mentioned frequently and spoke about at length.

Group 3: Expatriate University English Teachers

The 52 expatriate university English teachers who made up the third group all taught in the university foundation program. In this group, 29 (56%) were male and 23 (44%) were female, which reflects the gender balance in the program. The teachers were born and raised in a range of countries with most coming from English-speaking countries such as the UK (38%), USA (29%), Australia (9%), Canada (7%), New Zealand (6%), and Ireland (2%). Teachers from non-English-speaking countries (Romania, Turkey, Belgium, Mexico, and Tunisia) comprised 9%. Three of the teachers had dual nationality, so named both countries. The largest portion of teachers were aged between 41 and 50 (44%), with 35% aged between 51 and 60, 11% aged over 61 and 10% aged 31 and 40. The teachers all held master's degrees and some had doctorates. They had between 3 and 18 years teaching experience in the Gulf. They had also previously taught in 52 other countries, ranging from Finland to Pakistan, from Hong Kong to Mozambique, and from Japan to Germany, just to name a few. The most common countries of former teaching positions were the UK (18), Japan (14), Korea (8), Spain (8), and USA (8). The English teachers were therefore experienced teachers not only in the Gulf but also internationally, making their perspectives well-informed and diverse.

The views of the participants in each stakeholder group are important because the issues under investigation involve and surround them on a daily basis. The careers and livelihoods of the primary school teachers, in particular, are dependent upon their success in English as the continuation of their teaching careers are at risk if they cannot gain IELTS 6.5 by the end of their sabbatical period studying at the university. The expatriate English university teacher views were deemed important and relevant as they are part of the majority expatriate population in the UAE, also with a vested interest in the topic. They have a wealth of experience teaching in the Gulf and have witnessed the fast-paced change which has taken place in the UAE. Some had lived in the Gulf region longer than the Emirati students in the first group had been alive. They too are directly affected by educational policies centring around English as a medium of instruction (EMI). The university students are the nation's millennials whose views are fundamental in shaping the future.

4.4 Data Collection and Analysis: Emergent Themes

As mentioned at the start of this chapter, the university was an ideal setting for the collection of data due to its campus being removed from the city centre of Abu Dhabi and the extreme heat making most want to stay inside. The university also has a strict attendance policy meaning that few students are absent from classes, especially as data collection took place towards the end of the semester where attendance tends to be higher due to lessons focusing on final exam preparation. These factors meant that scheduling focus groups and visiting classes was easily achieved without typical problems of missing focus group members or absent students in class. This section will briefly outline how the data was collected and analyzed to present a clear picture of the procedures and approaches taken.

Data Collection

When collecting the data, the questionnaires were given to the university students and primary school teachers in their classrooms with the permission of their teachers, who acted as gatekeepers. The focus groups took place in a reserved meeting room, which provided a quiet and comfortable setting during the daily two-hour lunch break. Table 4.2 provides an overview of the participant numbers and how they contributed to the study.

Table 4.2 Participant Numbers and Ways of Contributing

Participant Groups	Total Number of Participants	Questionnaire Respondents	Focus Group Respondents
Emirati University Students	100	100 (80 females, 20 males)	18 (2 female groups of 6, 1 male group of 6)
Emirati Primary School Teachers	12	12 (all female)	12 (2 groups of 6 females)
Expatriate University Teachers	52	40 (22 males, 18 females)	12 (2 mixed-gender groups of 7 males and 5 females)

Sampling – Selecting the Participants

For the student questionnaires, 'cluster sampling' (Kelly, 2006, p. 29) was used as the research population (all the Level 4 (highest level) foundation students in the university) had been divided into random classes or 'clusters' at the start of the semester. From a total of 14 classes (clusters), nine were used as the university student participant sample (7 female and 2 male classes). As these classes (clusters) were already in existence at the start of the data collection period, the sample represented a random cross-section of the program's students. The sample of nine classes contained 122 students in total. A total of 104 students attended classes on the data collection days. From this number, two students chose not to participate in the research. A further two students only completed one or two questions and could therefore not be included in the data set. As a result, from a possible 104 participants, 100 fully completed the questionnaires. This was a high return rate of 96%, which had been anticipated due to the research tool chosen as explained earlier in this chapter. The classes (clusters) were selected based on whether the teacher of the class was willing to sacrifice around 20 minutes of class time for the students to complete the questionnaires. The questionnaires were given to the participants over the course of a week. Participants were given a project information sheet and consent form in both English and Arabic. Following best ethical practice, it was made clear to the participants that pseudonyms would replace real names, they would be participating on a voluntary basis and could leave at any time, and their information would be private and confidential.

For the student focus groups, 'purposive sampling' was used which involved participants being 'hand-picked' (Denscombe, 2010, p. 35) to get the best information from those who were more likely to provide detailed and valuable insights into the research topic. To ensure this was the case, the classroom teachers were asked to recommend students from their classes who they felt would participate fully in a focus group setting; these tended to include confident speakers or students who had shown interest in the topic. Focus group sign-up sheets were left with the teachers upon collection of the completed questionnaires. It was explained to the students that the focus groups would be taking place the following week. As the sign-up sheets were given to all nine classes, there were over 20 volunteers. The first 18 on the lists were included in the focus groups due to wanting to restrict the groups to three groups of six (two female groups and one male group). As a result, the groups partly consisted of students who knew each other and also strangers. The focus group sessions took place during the students' two-hour lunch break in a reserved meeting room on campus.

Sampling for the primary school teachers was less complex. They were a group of 12 already in existence. As well as their teacher allowing me access to the group, all members were present on the data collection day and all agreed to participate in the research. For the expatriate teacher sample, purposive sampling was used for the focus group members (two groups of six) as teachers were specifically selected in order to include a range of nationalities and experiences in the Gulf. Once the 12 focus group members had agreed to participate, the remaining 50 teachers in the program were contacted. From this research population of 50, 40 teachers completed the questionnaires, which represented a return rate of 80%.

Data Collection Tool Design and Bilingual Support

The design of the data collection tools and the choice of language/languages to use for data collection were major considerations. I chose to use mostly open-response questions for the questionnaires. Although fully closed-answer or multiple-choice survey would have made for more easily quantifiable results, I wanted the participants to give thought to the questions and to express their opinions in their own words, which is in line with an interpretivist paradigm. Ultimately a fuller picture and richer data can be obtained this way, as participants are treated as 'real people rather than theoretical abstractions' (Ushioda, 2009, p. 220). As Cohen et al. (2007, p. 331) correctly point out, 'the space provided for an open-ended response is a window of opportunity for the respondent to shed light on an issue'. As the topic of English and cultural identity is potentially controversial or sensitive, special attention was paid in avoiding 'loaded' questions which may be emotionally charged, or overly positive or negative. Although the university is pro-technology and, in fact, every student is provided with an iPad on enrolling at the university, there are often hitches with using electronic questionnaires such as students coming to class without their iPad, having no charge, or intermittent Wi-Fi issues. It was, therefore, decided that the questionnaires would be paper-based.

The same considerations regarding question choice, noted previously, were given to the design of the semi-structured focus group questions. As with the questionnaires, focus group questions were organized thematically to systematically cover the research questions. In the context of the UAE, particular attention needed to be paid to group composition in terms of gender, group size, and identity. The Emirati university student and Emirati primary school teacher focus groups were single-sex groups due to the culture and the religion of the UAE requiring strict segregation of the sexes (Winslow et al., 2002, p. 572). The expatriate teacher focus groups, on the other hand, were mixed to add variety to the groups and to allow me to distinguish individual voices in the recorded data more effectively. Another consideration with focus groups is whether to work with people who already know each other or whether to work with strangers. Kitzinger and Barbour (1999, p. 8) point out that many social science researchers prefer to work with pre-existing groups. This was the case for the expatriate teachers who were colleagues and the primary school teachers who were classmates. This was partly true for the student focus groups as some members were classmates and some were not.

The focus groups varied in length, with the average time being 46 minutes. All seven focus groups were recorded using a digital recorder as well as the 'Sound Note' app. The recorder and iPad were placed in an unobtrusive position to minimize nervousness. Recording the focus group discussions allowed me to have an accurate record of the conversations with pauses, hesitations, intonation patterns, etc. as well as allowing me to note down non-verbal signals. Although video data of the focus groups would have been preferable, it is a strict cultural and religious taboo to video Emirati women and was therefore not permissible in this study. As Gokalp (2019, p. 4) recognizes, it is the responsibility of researchers to modify methods in ways that allow participants to feel at ease. With this in mind, video recordings were not used. Each focus group contained six members which allowed for a range of opinions to be heard without being 'out of control' or having several simultaneous conversations taking place. The role of the researcher was also vital to consider, as previously discussed. As Winslow et al. (2002, p. 567) state, 'A skilled facilitator is the key to success'. I was careful not to present myself as an expert on the subjects under discussion which may have ended lines of discussion prematurely.

A final consideration relevant to the collection of focus group data was language and bilingual support. On the one hand, one could argue that richer data would emerge if participants were able to use their first language, Arabic. As Kosny et al. (2014) recognize, not having enough lexical knowledge in a second language may make participants hesitant to speak up. However, there are also many arguments for using the medium of English. Firstly, Twinn (1998, as cited in Winslow et al., 2002, p. 572) describes the importance of undertaking data analysis in the language of the interview. This is due to meanings being lost in translation or some Arabic expressions having no direct equivalent in English. It was also felt that if the focus groups were conducted solely or mostly in Arabic, it would remove my involvement as a facilitator. The spontaneity and naturalness of focus groups, which is a key strength of the method, would be taken away if a research assistant needed to translate everything for me after each person had spoken. It was, therefore, decided to have 'bilingual support' in the form of an Arabic-speaking research assistant but that this assistant would only be used in situations where it was necessary. Such decisions to include bilingual support or 'language brokers' have proved successful in other contexts such as in Duran's (2019) study where Thai refugees were able to voice complicated ideas through language brokers. I therefore hired two translators, as mentioned previously, who spoke fluent Arabic and English. Both translators were female colleagues who taught English at the university and also worked in assessment and student support. They were in their 40s and 50s. One of the translators was from Sudan and the other from Syria. Both were fully bilingual, holding British and American passports respectively.

Data Analysis

Holliday (2002, p. 101) aptly calls the data analysis process the 'dark night of the soul' in that the task is often unruly and daunting. Analyzing data is far from simple and straightforward and even less so if the data is qualitative. As Marshall and Rossman (1999, p. 150) state, qualitative data analysis is 'a messy, ambiguous, time-consuming, creative, and fascinating process. It does not proceed in a linear fashion: it is not neat'. This section will explain the approach used to analyze the data.

In total, data from 152 open-response questionnaires and seven focus group recordings, together with notes in the researcher journal, were analyzed. As the questionnaire and focus group questions were organized around the three research questions (Table 4.1), thematic analysis (TA), which involves identifying, analyzing, and reporting patterns in the data, was an appropriate choice (Holliday, 2002, p. 100). As Savin-Baden and Howell Major (2013, p. 440) point out, 'What is unique about thematic analysis is that it acknowledges that analysis happens at an intuitive level'. In this sense, it is less about hard statistics but rather *interpreting* the mass of data collected, falling in line with the interpretive paradigm. The strengths of the approach are its flexibility in terms of research questions, theoretical framework, methods of data collection, and sample size. Also, the findings from thematic analysis are generally accessible to a wide range of readers due to the organization of the findings under distinct themes, making for a more reader-friendly experience. Figure 4.3 provides a visual representation of the study's data analysis.

Stage 1: Quantitizing Questionnaire Data

Although almost all the questionnaire data was qualitative, I was able to analyze some questionnaire responses by 'quantitizing' (Dornyei, 2007, p. 270) the data as a first step. As Kirk and Miller (1986, p. 10) point out, 'qualitative research does not imply a commitment to innumeracy'. In this sense, gathering the percentage of expatriate English teachers who spoke Arabic or other languages, for example, helped to build a picture of the group's linguistic background. Likewise, gathering statistics on the number of years the undergraduate students had been studying English was revealing and relevant to the student group composition. A further easily quantifiable part of questionnaire data related to the first research question which explored what English and Arabic represented. Here,

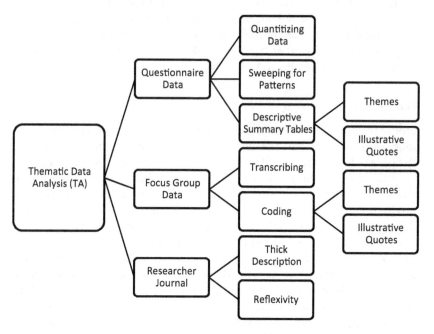

Figure 4.3 Data Analysis

participants were asked to name five words they associated with the languages English and Arabic. For the data these questions produced, 'code
landscaping' was used. As Saldana (2013, p. 199) explains, 'code landscaping is based on the visual technique of "tags" in which the most frequent word or phrase from a text appears larger than the others. As the
frequency of words or phrases decrease, so does the visual size'. This was
achieved through word clouds formulated through the online software
'Wordle'. There were initially some minor setbacks. For example, when
I entered the raw data into the online software, the resulting word clouds
were a little misleading. This was due to the software being unable to
perform *stemming* (understand different words as variations of the same
root or stem). For example, it was not able to recognize *talks, talking,*
and *talked* as variants of the stem *talk.* In the case of my data, if 70%
of the participants said the word 'religion' and 30% said 'religious' in
association with the Arabic language, these two words would be shown
separately and smaller than they would if they were combined (100%).
I therefore decided to do the stemming manually and enter 'religious'
and 'religion' as only 'religion'. This resulted in a more accurate representation of the number of participants who had chosen this concept.
Although time-consuming, I also decided to manually change punctua-
tion differences (e.g., some participants used a capital letter and others did
not), which would also be recognized as a different word by the software

and therefore be misleading. A final change to the raw data was to use a hyphen for two-word answers if both words were important to ensure the words remained together in the word cloud (for example, 'Mother-tongue'). Despite the minor shortcomings of the software, the word clouds proved to be a highly effective way of analyzing and displaying the data.

Stage 2: Sweeping the Data

As the questionnaires were written in both English and Arabic, some participants chose to respond in Arabic. All students' Arabic questionnaire answers were translated into English by the two translators (as mentioned previously). From the Emirati university students' group, 14% chose to use Arabic for all or some of their questionnaire responses. The Emirati primary school teachers and expatriate university teachers only used English.

Coding the open-response answers in the questionnaires was a multistep process. As the questionnaires were paper-based, I started by numbering them and entering the data per question into spreadsheets. For initial coding, it was possible to divide responses into broad groups. For the second coding, it was necessary to delve more deeply into the data and look at the most common reasons for these general positions. This involved sweeping the data for patterns and themes, which I did manually by using printed copies of the spreadsheets and highlighter pens. This allowed me to feel particularly connected and close to the data. As Savin-Baden and Howell Major (2013, p. 431) point out:

> sorting by hand allows researchers to be 'hands on' during the process. They work with the data enough to know it extensively and to develop an intuitive sense of its essential features and elements. It allows them to begin to feel the patterns in the data and to physically shift and sort until findings emerge from the chaos.

With the printed open-response questionnaire data in front of me, I read the answers for each question systematically and noted down all the reasons participants had given for their responses. The same or similar reasons could be seen in the data repeatedly and usually around 15 to 17 categories could be identified for each question. I then looked at the categories and combined similar ones together to reduce the number of categories. Using colours to identify patterns allowed me to clearly see similar themes and content within the data.

Stage 3: Use of Descriptive Summary Tables

After each questionnaire question data set had been coded in this way for each of the three participant groups, descriptive summary tables (Savin-Baden & Howell Major, 2013, p. 428) were created for the main themes (which corresponded with the research questions) for each of the three participant groups. This visual representation of the data or 'data display' (Miles & Huberman, 1994) was useful in allowing me to quickly and efficiently summarize a general overview of the findings and easily compare participant groups.

As I wanted participants' voices to be heard in their own words, in the descriptive summary tables as well as providing a summary of the data for each theme, I selected a number of representative quotes for the most mentioned categories to support points being made. As Denscombe (2010, p. 296) states, extracts give 'the reader a flavor of the data and let the reader "hear" the points as stated by the informants'. This also allows readers to make up their own minds about what the data says rather than having only to trust the interpretation of the researcher.

Stage 4: Transcribing and Coding the Focus Group Data

The focus group interviews covered the same themes in the same order as the questionnaires. Despite the many similarities with regard to the content of the data, the process of data analysis for the focus groups was more complex and messier still. Several factors contributed to the 'messiness' of the focus group data. Firstly, the nature of focus groups meant greater freedom for the participants in terms of shaping the discussion. For this reason, at times the discussions veered from my questions. At other times focus group members would comment on a topic relating to questions scheduled for later in the session. As the focus groups were semi-structured in nature, some flexibility was given with the order of topics.

I started my data analysis of the focus group recordings by 'characterizing' the data (Savin-Baden & Howell Major, 2013, p. 419) where I transcribed the recorded speech 'verbatim', in that exactly the same words were used. However, as Savin-Baden and Howell Major (2013, p. 419) point out, 'verbatim' is somewhat of a 'slippery term' as the process still requires analysis, interpretation and close observation, which can lead to 'noticing unanticipated phenomena' (Bailey, 2008, p. 130). For example, one researcher may transcribe the social talk at the beginning of a focus group session or include the content of an interrupting telephone call, whereas another may decide it is not important. For this study, due to the mass of data collected (5 hours and 25 minutes of recorded data), rather than using overly complex transcription codes, I decided that the primary focus would be on the content of what was being said. After characterizing the data, I was able to immerse myself in it further by reading and viewing it over and over again. The purpose of this was to understand it at 'both a gut level and as a whole' (Savin-Baden & Howell Major, 2013, p. 420) before beginning to analyze it or break it apart. Once the focus group data had been divided into the three major themes, further coding began in the same fashion as the thematic analysis for the open-response questionnaire data. Little attempt to quantify the data was made in this case though due to the fact that not all participants responded to every question, or if they did, it was not in a linear fashion. Instead the main sub-themes were noted and colour-coded.

Stage 5: Thick Description and Reflexivity

I also made detailed notes in my researcher journal before, during, and after the focus groups. These notes included descriptions of what the participants were wearing, facial expressions, and gestures. For example, for the Emirati students and Emirati primary school teachers, comments on dress were seen as relevant because, especially for the male under-graduate focus group, dress varied greatly. Some of the students wore the traditional 'Kandoura' (long white traditional robe) and 'Ghutra' (white headscarf held on the head by a black cotton ring) and others were dressed in jeans and T-shirts with English slogans on them. Such choices may have indicated attitudes towards English as well as cultural identity. The following picture (Figure 4.4) shows a digital version of a sketch made in the researcher journal at the start of the Emirati undergraduate male focus group. The sketch indicates details such as the position of the participants and dress.

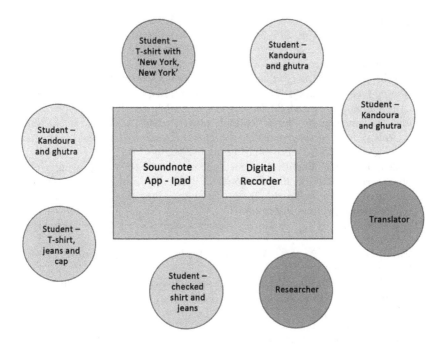

Figure 4.4 Digital Representation of Sketch in Researcher Journal During the Male Emirati University Student Focus Group Session

Emerging Themes

As the questionnaire and focus group questions were organized around the three research questions, responses were divided into three main categories which form the chapter headings of the next three chapters of the book: *Language and symbolism, English and cultural identity,* and *English Medium Instruction: sociolinguistic implications.* Within each main category, data has been divided into key themes, as can be seen in the subsequent chapters.

References

Bailey, J. (2008). First steps in qualitative data analysis analysis: Transcribing. *Family Practice,* 25 (2), 127–131.

Berger, P. L., & Luckmann, T. (1966). *The Social Construction of Reality.* London: Penguin.

Borg, S. (2001). The research journal: A tool for promoting and understanding researcher development. *Language Teaching Research,* 5 (2), 156–177.

Braun, V., & Clarke, V. (2013). *Successful Qualitative Research: A Practical Guide for Beginners.* London: Sage Publications.

Callaway, H. (1992). Ethnography and experience: Gender implications in fieldwork and texts. In J. Okely, & H. Callaway (Eds.), *Anthropology and Autobiography* (pp. 29–49). New York: Routledge.

Carey, M. A. (1994). The group effect in focus groups: Planning, implementing, and interpreting focus group research. In J. M. Morse (Ed.), *Qualitative Research Methods* (pp. 225–241). London: Sage Publication.

Cohen, L., Manion, L., & Morrison, K. (2007). *Research Methods in Education.* London: Routledge.

Creswell, J. W. (2007). *Qualitative Inquiry and Research Designs: Choosing Among Five Approaches* (2nd ed.). Thousand Oaks, CA: Sage Publications.

Daryai-Hansen, P., Barfod, S., & Schwarz, L. (2017). A call for (trans)languaging: The language profiles at Roskilde university. In C. M. Mazak, & K. S. Carroll (Eds.), *Translanguaging in Higher Education: Beyond Monolingual Ideologies* (pp. 29–49). Bristol: Multilingual Matters.

Dearden, J. (2015). English as a medium of instruction – a growing global phenomenon. *Report: British Council.* Retrieved from: www.britishcouncil.org/education/ihe/knowledge-centre/english-language-higher-education/report-english-medium-instruction.

Denscombe, M. (2010). *The Good Research Guide* (4th ed.). New York: Open University Press.

Dornyei, D. (2007). *Research Methods in Applied Linguistics.* Oxford: Oxford University Press.

Dreachslin, J. (1999). Focus groups as a quality improvement technique: A case example from health administration education. *Quality Assurance in Education,* 7 (4), 224–32.

Duran, C. S. (2019). 'I have so many things to tell you, but I don't know English': Linguistic challenges and language brokering. In D. S. Warriner, & M. Bigelow (Eds.), *Critical Reflections on Research Methods* (pp. 13–30). Bristol: Multilingual Matters.

Dwyer, S. C., & Buckle, J. L. (2009). The space between: On being an insider-outsider in qualitative research. *International Journal of Qualitative Methods*, 8 (1), 54–63.

Edley, N., & Litosseliti, L. (2010). Contemplating interviews and focus groups. In L. Litosseliti (Ed.), *Research Methods in Linguistics* (pp. 155–179). London: Continuum.

Engin, M. (2011). Research diary: A tool for scaffolding. *International Journal of Qualitative Methods*, 10 (3), 296–306.

Farquhar, C., & Das, R. (1999). Are focus groups suitable for 'sensitive' topics? In R. S. Barbour, & J. Kitzinger (Eds.), *Developing Focus Group Research* (pp. 47–63). London: Sage Publications.

Findlay, L. (2002). Negotiating the swamp: The opportunity and challenge of reflexivity in research practice. *Qualitative Research*, 2, 209–230.

Fischer, C. T. (2009). Bracketing in qualitative research: Conceptual and practical matters. *Psychotherapy Research*, 19 (4–5), 583–590.

Flood, G. (1999). *Beyond Phenomenology: Rethinking the Study of Religion*. London: Cassell.

Gass, S. M., & Selinker, L. (1994). *Second Language Acquisition*. Mahwah, NJ, London: Lawrence Erlbaum Associates.

Geertz, C. (1973). Thick description: Toward an interpretive theory of culture. In C. Geertz (Ed.), *The Interpretation of Cultures* (pp. 3–30). New York: Basic Books.

Gokalp, A. (2019). Revisiting our understandings in ethnographic research. In D. S. Warriner, & M. Bigelow (Eds.), *Critical Reflections on Research Methods* (pp. 31–42). Bristol: Multilingual Matters.

Guillemin, M., & Gillam, L. (2004). Ethics, reflexivity, and 'ethically important moments' in research. *Qualitative Inquiry*, 10 (2), 261–280.

Holliday, A. (2002). *Qualitative Research*. London: Sage Publications.

Hudson, P. (2019). A gin and tonic and a window seat: Critical pedagogy in Arabia. In M. E. Lopez-Gopar (Ed.), *International Perspectives on Critical Pedagogies in ELT* (pp. 241–263). New York: Palgrave Macmillan. http://doi.org/10.1007/978-3-319-95621-3_12.

Irvine, F., Roberts, C., & Bradbury-Jones, C. (2008). The researcher as insider versus the researcher as outsider: Enhancing rigour through language and cultural sensitivity. In P. Liamputtong (Ed.), *Doing Cross-cultural Research: Ethical and Methodological Perspectives* (pp. 35–48). Dordrecht: Springer.

James, A., & Shammas, N. M. (2013). Developing intercultural intelligence: Dubai style. *Journal of International Education in Business*, 6 (2), 148–164.

Keddie, V. (2006). Case study method. In V. Jupp (Ed.), *The SAGE Dictionary of Social Research Methods* (pp. 20–21). London: Sage Publications.

Kelly, A. (2006). Cluster sampling. In V. Jupp (Ed.), *The SAGE Dictionary of Social Research Methods* (pp. 20–21). London: Sage Publications.

Kirk, J., & Miller, M. L. (1986). *Reliability and Validity in Qualitative Research*. London: Sage Publications.

Kitzinger, J., & Barbour, R. S. (1999). Introduction: The challenge and promise of focus groups. In R. S. Barbour, & J. Kitzinger (Eds.), *Developing Focus Group Research* (pp. 1–20). London: Sage Publications.

Knowles, S. Y. (2019). Researcher-participant relationships in cross-language research: Becoming cultural and linguistic insiders. In D. S. Warriner, & M.

Bigelow (Eds.), *Critical Reflections on Research Methods* (pp. 85–97). Bristol: Multilingual Matters.

Kosny, A., MacEachen, E., Lifshen, M., & Smith, P. (2014). Another person in the room: Using interpreters during interviews with immigrant workers. *Qualitative Health Research*, 24 (6), 837–845. doi:10.1177/1049732314535666.

Kramsch, C. (2012). Subjectivity. In C. A. Chapelle (Ed.), *The Encyclopedia of Applied Linguistics*. http://onlinelibrary.wiley.com/book/10.1002/9781405198431.

Kusow, A. M. (2003). Beyond indigenous authenticity: Reflections on the insider/outsider debate in immigration research. *Symbolic Interaction*, 26 (4), 591–599.

Kvale, S. (1996). *InterViews*. London, CA, New Delhi: Sage Publications.

Lockwood Harris, K. (2016). Reflexive voicing: A communicative approach to intersectional writing. *Qualitative Research*, 16 (1), 111–127.

Macaro, E. (2018). *English Medium Instruction*. Oxford: Oxford University Press.

Mann, S. (2016). *The Research Interview: Reflective Practice and Reflexivity in Research Processes*. Houndmills, New York: Palgrave Macmillan.

Marshall, C., & Rossman, G. B. (1999). *Designing Qualitative Research*. Thousand Oaks, CA: Sage Publications.

McLeod, J. (2001). *Qualitative Research in Counseling and Psychology*. London: Sage Publications.

Miles, M. B., & Huberman, A. M. (1994). *Qualitative Data Analysis: An Expanded Sourcebook*. London: Sage Publications.

Morgan, D. L., & Krueger, R. A. (1993). When to use focus groups and why. In D. L. Morgan (Ed.), *Successful Focus Groups* (pp. 3–19). London: Sage Publications.

Parker, A., & Tritter, J. (2006). Focus group and methodology: Current practice and recent debate. *International Journal of Research and Method in Education*, 29 (1), 23–37.

Pieterse, J. N. (2010). Views from Dubai: Oriental globalization revisited. *Encounters*, 2, 15–37.

Pillow, W. S. (2003). Confession, catharsis, or cure? Rethinking the uses of reflexivity as methodological power in qualitative research. *International Journal of Qualitative Studies in Education*, 16 (2), 175–196.

Risager, K., & Dervin, F. (2015). Introduction. In K. Risager, & F. Dervin (Eds.), *Researching Identity and Interculturality* (pp. 1–24). New York: Routledge.

Roegman, R., Knight, M. G., Taylor, A. M., & Watson, V. W. M. (2016). From microscope to mirror: Doctoral students' evolving positionalities through engagement with culturally sensitive research. *International Journal of Qualitative Studies in Education*, 29 (1), 44–65.

Saldana, J. (2013). *The Coding Manual for Qualitative Researchers* (2nd ed.). London: Sage Publications.

Salem, O. (2014, January 2014). UAE Cabinet introduces mandatory military service for Emirati males. *The National*. Retrieved from: www.thenational.ae/uae/government/uae-cabinet-introduces-mandatory-military-service-for-emirati-males-1.685784.

Savin-Baden, M., & Howell Major, C. (2013). *Qualitative Research: The Essential Guide to Theory and Practice*. New York: Routledge.

Skehan, P. (1989). *Individual Differences in Language Learning.* London: Arnold.

Stephens, D. (2009). *Qualitative Research in International Settings.* New York: Routledge.

Thomas, A. (2008). Focus groups in qualitative research: Culturally sensitive methodology for the Arabian Gulf? *International Journal of Research and Method in Education*, 31 (1), 77–88.

Twinn, S. (1998). An analysis of the effectiveness of focus groups as a method of qualitative data collection with Chinese populations in nursing research. *Journal of Advanced Nursing*, 28 (3), 654–661.

Ushioda, E. (2009). *A Person-in-context Relational View of Emergent Motivation, Self and Identity.* In Z. Dornyei, & E. Ushioda (Eds.), *Motivation, Language Identity and the L2 Self* (pp. 215–228). Bristol: Multilingual Matters.

Van den Hoven, M. (2014). The use of English for education in the Arab world: An ethnographic investigation of female Emirati pre-service teachers' conceptions of English as a medium of instruction. In. K. M. Bailey, & R. M. Damerow (Eds.), *Teaching and Learning English in the Arabic-Speaking World* (pp. 65–82). New York: Routledge.

Wilson, V. (1997). Focus groups: A useful qualitative method for educational research? *British Educational Research Journal*, 23 (2), 209–224.

Winslow, W., Honein, G., & Elzubeir, M. (2002). Seeking Emirati women's voices: The use of focus groups with an Arab population. *Qualitative Health Research*, 12 (4), 566–575.

Yin, R. K. (2003). *Applications of Case Study Research.* London, Thousand Oaks, New Delhi: Sage Publications.

5   Language and Symbolism

Branding is a deliberate differentiation.

– Debbie Millman

5.1 Language Use and Ideologies

Just as language, culture, and identity are interrelated concepts which do not exist independently of each other, *language use* and *language ideologies* are also closely intertwined. This chapter begins by exploring the concepts of language use and language ideologies, which were touched upon in Chapter 1, in greater depth. The language use of the Emiratis and expatriates in the study will then be examined before turning to look at symbolism surrounding the UAE's two dominant languages English and Arabic and the implications of resulting ideologies.

Defining Language Use and Language Ideologies

Language use can refer to the languages one uses naturally or chooses to use. Language use may vary according to social context, space, interaction patterns, and domain, amongst other factors. A language could be acquired as a child, used with one parent, or in a classroom, or as a lingua franca, for example. Language may be used out of necessity, ease, by choice, or, even, in some cases, as a form of resistance. Increasingly, in multilingual contexts boarders between languages are blurring and rather than languages being used as distinct entities, 'linguistic repertoires' (Blommaert, 2005) are employed as a natural way of communicating effectively. Here, rather than the importance being placed on the number of individual languages a person speaks, priority is placed on how individuals use their linguistic resources to aid communication. Linguistic repertoires involve 'the totality of linguistic resources, knowledge about their function and about their condition of use in an individual or community' (Blommaert, 2005, p. 254). In this sense, 'conventional understandings of boundaries between culturally and politically distinct languages are challenged' (Li, 2018). Here we see, from a translanguaging perspective, language is an ongoing process rather than an entity and it is a 'verb rather than a noun' (Becker, 1988, p. 25). However, despite the tendency for fluid linguistic repertoires to be used over isolated languages, in many cases language ideologies support the latter. In other words, despite the mixing of languages taking place on the ground, firm ideas of what languages represent result in languages being ideologically separate.

Ideologies can be defined as 'conceptual schemes' (Davidson, 2013, p. 209) or systems of concepts which shape our thoughts and perceptions. Irvine and Gal (2000) open their chapter on 'Language Ideology and Linguistic Differentiation' with the famous quote 'A language is simply a dialect that has an army and a navy'. Here, the army represents an outside force to be opposed and the navy represents protection of the internal. The very act of identifying languages creates opposition to other languages with which they contrast in some larger sociolinguistic field (Irvine & Gal, 2000, p. 35). As seen in the quote at the start of this chapter by American writer, Debbie Millman, by attaching labels of meaning to various languages is to brand them in one sense, and 'branding is deliberate differentiation' which separates rather than unites. Irvine and Gal (2000, p. 36) identify three semiotic processes by which people usually form language ideologies. The first process is 'iconization', where linguistic features that index social groups appear to be iconic representations of them, thus representing a group's inherent nature or essence. Such connections between linguistic features and social groups may be historical, contingent, or conventional (Irvine & Gal, 2000, p. 37). For example, English is often viewed as the 'icon of the contemporary age' (Guilherme, 2007, p. 74) but within the language are varieties which present different associations in people's minds.

A second process influencing language ideology is 'fractal recursivity' which involves the projection of an opposition, salient at some level of relationship, onto some other level (Irvine & Gal, 2000, p. 38). Here, an image of a large group may be applied to an individual associated with that group and vice versa. For example, an idea about one Emirati might be generalized to all Emiratis and then to all Arabs or, conversely, an idea about Arabic-speakers in general might be applied to an individual Emirati.

A third process contributing to language ideologies is 'erasure' where facts that are inconsistent with the ideological scheme may either be ignored or get explained away. In this sense, a social group or a language may be seen as homogeneous with its internal variation disregarded. For example, an Emirati who has a Spanish parent or does not wear traditional dress might be dismissed or brushed aside due to not fitting the language or cultural norm or ideology associated with Arabic-speaking Emiratis.

Essentialism in Language Ideologies and Polarization of Languages

When identifying languages, there is a tendency to define the self against some imagined 'other'. As Irvine and Gal (2000, p. 39) point out, in the process of identity formation, the 'other', or the contrast, is often essentialized and imagined as homogeneous. In lockstep with 'othering' comes generalization where there is a tendency to want to place people and languages into neat boxes. Seeing one country as having one culture and one language is part of this notion. As Irvine and Gal (2000, p. 73) state, 'It has become commonplace in sociolinguistics that linguistic forms, including whole languages, can index social groups'. The ideology of societal monolingualism and linguistic homogeneity often imagines languages as corresponding with essentialized representations of social groups (Irvine & Gal, 2000, p. 77) and, as Anderson (1983, p. 38) states, societal monolingualism provides fertile ground for linguistic nationalism, whereby we return to the image of a language possessing its own army and navy. Rather than languages being purely functional, they are deeply embedded in the politics of a region and those observing them. Language, in this sense, is more than a language; it becomes symbolic of lives, cultures, and identities.

Language Ideologies – No View From Nowhere

Language ideologies are often below our awareness in the sense that we may be unsure of why we have certain beliefs about languages. Often the sources of ideologies are societal, historical, and media-related. As Irvine and Gal (2000) state, 'there is no view from nowhere: no gaze that is not positioned'. Positions come to us through multiple sources. The colonial period or 'unofficial colonialism' in the case of the UAE, for example, 'forged ideas that have remained deeply embedded in (many people's) analytical frameworks' (Irvine & Gal, 2000, p. 72) in terms of power related to colonial languages and injustices surrounding the treatment of local languages. Equally, mass migration and increasing diversity may affect language ideologies in terms of 'insider/outsider' positions. This can be seen in instances of *racial micro-aggressions* (Kubota, 2019) which can be defined as 'brief and commonplace daily verbal, behavioural, and environmental indignities, whether intentional or unintentional, that communicate hostile, derogatory, or negative racial slights and insults' (Sue et al., 2007, p. 273). An example of a racial micro-aggression can be seen in Lee and Simon-Maeda's (2006) study where Asian-Canadian English teachers were frequently asked 'where are you really from?'. This reflects monolingual ideologies, racism, and the belief in uniformity in any one country. In addition to historical and societal influences on language ideologies, folk theories can also act as conduits of beliefs which shape young minds through hierarchical, moral, and aesthetic properties within broader cultural systems. In the UAE, Gallagher (2019) gives the example of storybooks mainly being written in English, and the few existing bilingual storybooks separating the languages, thus sending out a message that languages do not mix. Monolingual ideologies are thus encouraged in storybooks resulting in children growing up thinking that translingual practice is taboo. It could be argued that children's literature is the most influential type of publication in terms of the formation of ideologies or systems of beliefs through a 'catch them young' (Dixon, 1980) strategy. In media too, representations of languages and the social groups attached to them greatly influence language ideologies. For example, Republican USA-based 'Fox News' has political motives for pushing forward the image of Arabic-speaking terrorists and exaggerating negative associations with Arabic. As will be seen later in this chapter, many of the expatriate university teacher participants grew up surrounded by such voices in the media, which affected their language ideologies in relation to Arabic.

Emiratis' and Expatriates' Language Use

In a country with Arabic as the official language and English as a lingua franca and medium of instruction, one would expect both languages to be used by the country's residents. However, as outlined in Chapter 2 of this book, this is often not the case. While the country's two main languages are used by Emiratis, the study's findings revealed that expatriate teachers mainly rely on English, feeling they have no pressing need for Arabic. While 'choosing' not to learn or use Arabic might be a viable option for the expatriates, the reverse is not an option for Emiratis. Emiratis cannot elect to ignore English. Furthermore, the need for English as a second language, as with other places in the world, seems to have pushed out the learning of a third language in most cases, unless a third language is spoken by a parent. The following sections will explore the Emirati and expatriates' language use in more detail.

Emiratis' Language Use

For Emiratis, both Arabic and English are used. All the undergraduate university students named Arabic as their first language and 96% named English as their second. Only 13% of the undergraduate students spoke an additional language as can be seen from Table 5.1. Only four of the male undergraduate students stated they did not have a second or other language. Similar to the Emirati university students, all the Emirati primary school teachers named Arabic as their first language and English as their second with no mention of third languages, which testifies to the dominance of English as the main additional language in the region.

Table 5.1 Second or Other Languages Spoken by Emiratis

Language Used Other Than Arabic	Emirati University Students	Emirati Primary School Teachers
English	96%	100%
Turkish	4%	0%
Indian/Hindi	4%	0%
Korean	3%	0%
Spanish	1%	0%
French	1%	0%

Given the UAE's multilingual environment, one might expect a wider range of languages to be mentioned. Van den Hoven and Carroll (2016) speak of Abu Dhabi's 'rich linguistic context' (p. 37) stating that the Emirati pre-service teacher participants in their study recognized English and Arabic as the primary languages but also spoke of using four peripheral languages: 'Indian', 'Persian', 'Filipino', and 'Korean'. In the present study, however, only 13% of the university students mentioned a language other than English as a 'second or other' language (Turkish, Indian/Hindi, Korean, Spanish, French), demonstrating the wide gap in terms of scope and power between English and the 'peripheral languages'.

Expatriates' Language Use

As could be expected due to the university's hiring practices favouring English teachers from Western English-speaking countries, 90% of the expatriate university teachers named English as their first language, with the exception of the five teachers from Tunisia, Belgium, Romania, Turkey, and Mexico, who named Arabic, Flemish, Romanian, Turkish, and Spanish as their first languages, respectively. Languages spoken as a second or other language included a range of 20 (Table 5.2). The six most common second languages were European languages (French, Spanish, German, and Italian) and Asian languages (Japanese and Korean).

The multilingual composition of the teachers compared to the Emiratis is perhaps not surprising due to the fact they are language teachers (have

Table 5.2 Second or Other Languages Spoken by Expatriate Teachers

1	French (40%)	6	Korean (10%)
2	Spanish (37%)	7	Turkish (8%)
3	German (17%)	8	Arabic (8%)
4	Japanese (15%)	9	**Other:** English, Greek, Russian, Portuguese,
5	Italian (12%)		Swahili, Loa, Hebrew, Mandarin, Cantonese, Chinese, Dutch, Polish, Thai (each language between 2% and 6%)

an interest in languages), chose to live abroad, and are mainly older than the Emiratis in the study, giving them more life experience. However, what is surprising is that despite their multilingual nature as a group, Arabic was only mentioned as a second or other language by 8% of the teachers, despite a combined total of 508.5 years living in the Gulf (an average of just under 10 years per teacher). A reason contributing to this could be that in the university's 'English only' classrooms the use of Arabic is neither expected nor encouraged. Burkett's study (2016, p. 10) supports these findings as low levels or nonexistent Arabic language skills were also found in his expatriate university English teacher participants.

Expatriate university teachers spoke of the difficulties they experienced when learning Arabic due to diglossia and lack of access. For example, Thomas (UK/Canada) described a lack of motivation for learning Arabic which he had not experienced as a language learner previously. As local spoken Arabic, Khaleeji, is quite different from written Arabic (Modern Standard Arabic), to the point where one could consider them almost different languages (Yorkey, 1974), the diglossic nature of Arabic can act as a barrier to learning. In Thomas' case, the MSA he had learnt in textbooks did not match the Arabic his students spoke, causing him to be an object of fun in their eyes. Emily (New Zealand) also explained her low level of motivation for learning Arabic compared with other languages, partly due to lack of accessibility. Consequently, the word she most associated with Arabic was 'failure' as seen in Example 5.1.

Example 5.1

> *I actually tried learning Arabic but was put off by all the different versions, and the fact my students laughed at me when I used Egyptian Arabic. After that I put the books down.*
>
> (Thomas, UK/Canada)

> *Failure! This is the first language I've given up on. I've learnt loads of languages over the years and enjoyed the access to the cultures I've lived in that the language gave me. For some reason, I couldn't master any enthusiasm for Arabic at all. I find this strange and a bit distressing.*
>
> (Emily, New Zealand)

> *Pseudonyms used for all participant names

Others shared frustrating experiences when trying to learn Arabic or use Arabic in the Gulf due to lack of opportunities to use it or practice it. This was in part due to the amount of English found in the region, as seen in Example 5.2.

Example 5.2

When I first moved to Oman, I had studied Arabic at university and had never got fluent at speaking because I had never spent time abroad, I dropped out before that, but I thought 'oh great I'm going to Oman I'm finally going to be able to speak Arabic and use all the knowledge that I had from before', and you just can't, in the Gulf, it's just impossible.

(Tabitha, UK)

I'm actually thinking of going to an Arab country like Egypt next summer to learn the language. It's interesting that I cannot learn the language here, it's so frustrating.

(Yonka, Turkey)

Tabitha and Yonka's comments in Example 5.2. indicate that to learn Arabic in the Gulf is a near-impossible task. There are certainly limited opportunities to learn Arabic in terms of 'naturally picking it up' or formally attending language classes. One needs to be quite proactive, determined, and resourceful to effectively learn Arabic in the Gulf, where English is the lingua franca and Arabic language schools are few and far between. As Randall and Samimi (2010) confirm, 'Professional institutions specializing in teaching Arabic to adult non-native speakers of Arabic are a rarity' (p. 45). An article in a recent issue of *Time Out Abu Dhabi* (August 10–16, 2016) entitled 'Me, myself and Abu Dhabi' recognizes the extremely low or nonexistent levels of Arabic many expatriates have when stating, 'Let's face it, many people in Abu Dhabi can barely even garble a "marhaba" (hello)' (Neveling & Wilson, 2016, p. 17). The article goes on to suggest expatriates try and find Arabic-speaking language buddies. This is far from easy, however, due to rigid social stratification as well as the dominance of English in public domains. Al-Shamsi (2009) confirms that due to the dominance of English in the Gulf, 'an attempt to speak proper Arabic is futile since most of the workers who work in various stores and companies and the domestic workers either speak English or flawed Arabic' (p. 2).

Although not mentioned explicitly during the focus group sessions, anecdotally speaking, expatriate teachers often blame their lack of Arabic on being busy at work as well as lack of commitment to the UAE as a long-term home. Many are in the Gulf to make money, which they funnel into savings accounts and properties back home. This 'work to live' phenomenon is well known throughout the country to the point where it is probably the most common form of small talk. Certainly, taxi drivers are fond of saying 'people are here to work – that's it' (in English). It is true that as soon as the university spring semester ends (in May), the teachers return to their countries in droves. Despite the positive aspects of living in the UAE such as year-round sunshine and luxury, for many there is a sense of 'doing time' until the next holiday. Not until late August do the 'back to the sandpit' updates on social media start to appear. In this sense, there is a transient feeling and a lack of investment, which may result in a reluctance to learn Arabic. The unevenness between the use of English and Arabic undoubtedly affects attitudes and ideologies surrounding the languages, as well as further factors, as will be explored in the following sections.

5.2 Symbolic Language: English

To explore what English as a language symbolized to the study participants, all three groups were asked to name five words that they associated with English. They were then asked to do the same for Arabic. This provided a strong picture of what the languages represented. In the focus groups, symbolism of the languages and language ideologies were also discussed.

When asked to name five words associated with English, as can be seen in Table 5.3, there were several predominant and overlapping word associations across the groups. The most frequently mentioned words for each group represent a mixture of abstract associations (ideas and adjectives) and concrete or practical associations (areas English is needed/used). The most commonly associated words across the groups include *global /international, education /jobs, internet/entertainment, communication, travel, public life (hospitals, shops, restaurants), Western/British /American/Western places or artifacts*, and *useful/necessary/powerful*. Other common word associations for the Emirati cohort included *future/ development*, positive adjectives such as *easy/interesting/enjoyable*, and also *imposed/affect society/influence*. Perhaps to be expected, the expatriate university English teachers felt ownership of English with 33% associating English with *mother tongue/language*. Other common words mentioned by the expatriate teachers included *evolving/hybrid/dynamic/ varieties* as well as positive adjectives such as *trendy/lucky/exciting*.

In addition to the commonly mentioned word associations seen in Table 5.3, unique responses or word associations mentioned by smaller percentages of participants included: *disinterest, spelling mistakes, difficulties, ambition, dream, icons, independence, opinion, formal, extra, networking* (Emirati university students), *menu, coffee, non-Arabic Muslims* (Emirati primary school teachers) and *conquer, colonialism, spelling, irregular, rich, illogical, versatile*, and *achievement* (Expatriate university teachers).

A visual representation of all the English word associations can be seen in Figures 5.1, 5.2, and 5.3. The online software 'Wordle' allowed for the creation of these visual representations by showing each word's size in proportion to how often it was mentioned. Through this form of 'code

Table 5.3 Words Associated With English

	Emirati University Students	Emirati Primary School Teachers	Expatriate University Teachers
1	Education/university/ studying/teaching/ school (83%)	Internet (100%)	Global/international/ lingua-franca/ widespread/ everywhere (73%)
2	Global/international/ everywhere/ world (76%)	Jobs/career/studies/ teaching (92%)	Jobs/work/study/ business/teaching (68%)
3	Communication/ connection/ interaction (60%)	Travel (83%)	Western/UK/USA/ cultural artifacts associated with the West (tea, green fields) (58%)
4	Foreign/British/ American/blonde/ Christianity (45%)	Public life (hospitals, cafes, restaurants, shopping) (58%)	Useful/necessary/ flexible/powerful/ dominant/important/ needed (48%)
5	Public places (hospitals, malls, shopping, restaurants, daily life) (32%)	Entertainment (movies, books, emails, phone) (50%)	Entertainment (TV, Internet, books, literature) (48%)
Other Common Words	Future/development (27%), jobs/ careers (24%), positive adjectives (24%), affect/ imposed/ influence (17%)	Communication/ other cultures (42%), global/ international (17%)	Language/mother tongue (33%), evolving /hybrid/ varieties (28%) positive adjectives (28%)

landscaping' (Saldana, 2013) the dominant words become very clear as they almost leap out from the page. As the word clouds show every word stated rather than only themes as seen in Table 5.3, the most prominent words in the word clouds may not match the most popular themes in Table 5.3. However, together they clearly build a picture of what both languages represent to each participant group. We can summarize that for the Emirati university students, English is primarily associated with *global, international, communication, travel,* and *university.* For the Emirati primary school teachers, *Internet, travel,* and *studying* dominate. Finally, the expatriate university English teachers' word cloud supports the former two with *global, international, business,* and *communication* being amongst the most dominant words. English could therefore be said to encompass multiple major domains including the larger world (global business, travel, and communication), education, jobs, information, media, and entertainment.

Figure 5.1 Emirati University Students' Word Associations With English

Figure 5.2 Emirati Primary School Teachers' Word Associations With English

Figure 5.3 Expatriate University English Teachers' Word Associations With English

During the focus group sessions participants were also asked to name words they associated with 'English'. Focus group participants quickly moved from naming single words to delving deeper into the background and issues surrounding these words. This led to rich and revealing discussions. Key themes discussed included English as the language of communication, power, and prestige, English as a life skill, and the 'racialization of English language speakers' (Aneja, 2016, p. 581).

English as Important for Communication

In the focus groups when asked what English represented, its importance for communication both inside and outside the UAE was central to discussions. This strongly testifies to the power of the global nature of English. English was deemed important to progress in studies and careers, to help their children in the case of the primary teachers, and to enjoy various forms of entertainment in the case of the students, as well as for routine tasks such as shopping and medical appointments, as seen in Example 5.3. The variety of reasons given for the importance of English points to its all-encompassing nature in the region.

Example 5.3

For the products that we buy from the shop. All the products, most of them, the instructions are written in English. Sometimes we find them in English without Arabic.
(Lamya, Emirati university student)

For me, I find it in the hospitals, the latest research on different things, the medical maybe the education, and you find it in English, only English. If you want to work in Arabic it's rarely to have an article or study or survey in Arabic.
(Oshba, Emirati primary school teacher)

They use the English language for everything, even teaching. When we search for a worksheet or a video.
(Lubna, Emirati primary school teacher)

We can't complete our life without English, so it's important to interact and communicate with others.
(Shatha, Emirati university student)

English is a crucial language because I need it for work and communicating with others. Without English you may feel useless because

> *almost everywhere you need to talk English. For example, in hospitals or in shopping malls, you need to know the language to communicate.*
> (Iptisam, Emirati primary school teacher)
>
> *It's usable everywhere and everything in our life.*
> (Bashayer, Emirati primary school teacher)
>
> *It (English) is definitely the language of the future.*
> (Atheya, Emirati university student)

For the Emirati primary teachers, especially, the very fact that keeping their jobs and future teaching careers rested on their ability to score Band 6.5 in the IELTS test further exemplifies the extreme power of English in the UAE. English was described as 'crucial', 'useable everywhere and for everything', and 'the language of the future'. This view of English is supported by findings from the pilot phase of the present study where similarly strongly-worded comments were seen in response to being asked about the importance of English, including the comment 'English is everything' (Hopkyns, 2016, p. 98). Findings from Al-Jarf's (2008) study with 470 Saudi Arabian undergraduates further support this view in that 96% of the participants considered English, 'a superior language, being an international language, and the language of science and technology, research, electronic databases and technical terminology' (p. 193). Further existing studies also testify to the view that Gulf nationals see English as both dominant and essential (Ahmed, 2011; Al Allaq, 2014; Al-Issa & Dahan, 2011; Al-Jarf, 2008; Badry & Willoughby, 2016; Hopkyns, 2014, 2015, 2016; Mahboob & Elyas, 2014; Sandiford, 2013; Solloway, 2016). The expatriate university English teachers' feelings supported the Emirati cohort's views with comments that English was 'undoubtedly' important 'in every area'.

English as a Language of Power and Prestige

English was associated with power, prestige, and future success in the eyes of both Emiratis and expatriate university English teachers. Hamdan's powerful comment, 'I don't think you can develop without English' (Example 5.4) reflects a 'progressive politico-pragmatic' (Baker, 2017, p. 283) view of English acquisition which embraces a 'discourse of opportunity' (Tollefson & Tsui, 2004). Expatriate teacher, Joe (Canada), also voices this notion in Example 5.4.

Many expatriate teachers felt they had directly benefitted from the prestige attached to English. Some expressed feelings of being born lucky due to being English-speakers and benefitting from its status without the

---

Example 5.4

I don't think you can develop without English.
(Hamdan, Emirati university student)

English is . . . an ideology and a position, a privileged position in the world, that evolved historically and is still maintained today and that's why we can make money off it because it has a value that's attached to a certain position.

(Joe, Canada)

---

struggle of having to learn it. This feeling of luck, and perhaps smugness, is not uncommon in native English speakers with many feeling relieved to be spared the time, effort, and expense of endless hours of language-learning and exams. There was, however, also an awareness of global English promoting a sense of linguistic superiority amongst native speakers and expatriate teachers commented on being 'lazier in terms of learning local languages', which seemed to arouse feelings of guilt and unease.

Linguistic Passport vs. Linguistic Imperialism

The two focus group sessions with the expatriate university English teachers resulted in particularly rich and in-depth discussions over whether English was truly global (a life skill not attached to any particular country) or whether it was still associated with Britain, America, and other English-speaking countries. It was argued by some that English has become detached from countries and is now considered a life skill by most, as seen in Example 5.5.

Example 5.5

It's become a life-skill. It's still part of the identity of English native speakers but it's more than that.

(Tabitha, UK)

Most students have no interest whatsoever in England. They kind of follow maybe Manchester United but they couldn't find Manchester on a map because I've asked them to find Liverpool and different clubs that they said they were following (laughs) and they had great difficulty in just relating them to a place and it's the same with the language. It's all on the internet, they are all chatting to their own generation and they've got no clue about the actual cultural origins

> *of English and why should they? But it enables them to communicate and create new networks, new friends, new jobs, new possibilities.*
>
> (Richard, Ireland)

> *It's just the thing you need. It's like a passport in some respects. A linguistic passport.*
>
> (James, Australia)

In Example 5.5, we can see through Richard's (Ireland) comment that despite the global popularity of some English football clubs such as Manchester United, which has the biggest following of any football club in the world (Miall & Milsted, 2013), English for many has become detached from a place. Rather, it has been adopted to suit individual needs and contexts. Other focus group members, conversely, felt that English is still very much attached to the countries in which it originated. Word associations such as 'Anglo Saxon' (Graeme, UK), 'Imperialism' (Joe, Canada), 'still attached to countries' (Douglas, USA), and 'America or the UK' (Richard, Ireland) indicate that English is still not entirely neutral, in that it still connects, in the minds of many, to native English-speaking countries and even the race of the people traditionally from those countries (white). As Kubota and Lin (2009) acknowledge, there is an implicit assumption that 'native speakers' and 'standardized English speakers' are white people. As seen in Table 5.2, 45% of the Emirati university students felt this association too, when naming words such as 'Foreign/British/American/blonde and Christianity'. University teachers Yonka (Turkey) and Joe (Canada) explain the connection they make between English and Caucasians, in Example 5.6.

Example 5.6

> *White. Very white. . . . When I first started learning the language, that was the thing, I would look at the name of the author and that was always male to begin with and they were always white. Of course, it has changed a lot but still I cannot associate English with other races to this day. Even now.*
>
> (Yonka, Turkey)

> *This current era of globalization, capitalism grew out of imperialism and I mean that's a historical connection that is often not ignored but just not dealt with the current era and I think that whole white male Western privilege thing comes from imperialism. It's still very much embedded in the English language teaching and learning around the world I feel.*
>
> (Joe, Canada)

Here we can see the influence of history, and colonialism in particular, on language ideologies surrounding English. Rather than drawing a line under the past, the comments in Example 5.6 show the influence of imperialism and more recently globalization on the image of English.

5.3 Symbolic Language: Arabic

Just as they had done for 'English', questionnaire participants were asked to name five words they associated with 'Arabic'. Focus group participants were also asked to comment on word associations, which led to further more detailed discussions on what Arabic represented. The most common five word associations with Arabic were remarkably similar across the groups but very different indeed from the words connected with English, as can be seen in Table 5.4.

For all three groups, *Religion* was the strongest association with Arabic. All the Emirati university students and primary school teachers mentioned *religion* as at least one of the five words they connected with Arabic, with many mentioning multiple religious associations such as *'Religion, Quran, Islam, Muslim, pray, Mosque, Prophet Mohamed,*

Table 5.4 Words Associated With Arabic

	Emirati University Students	Emirati Primary School Teachers	Expatriate University Teachers
1	Religion/Quran/ Islam/ Muslim/ pray/mosque/ Prophet Mohamed (100%)	Religion/Quran/ Islam/ Prophet Mohamed (100%)	Islam/Quran/Religion/ Muslim/Mecca/ Prophet Mohamed/ prayer (85%)
2	Culture/tradition/ customs/heritage/ history/old (89%)	Communication with family/friends/home/ daily usage (83%)	Middle East/Gulf/ UAE/ Arabic speaking countries/ desert (60%)
3	Home/family/ community/ gathering/friends/ ancestors (64%)	Culture/tradition/ customs/heritage (58%)	Language/script/ calligraphy/poetry/ alphabet/regional dialect (58%)
4	First language/ mother tongue (51%)	Entertainment (music, poetry, reading, TV, apps) (50%)	Tradition/culture/ classical/ancient/ history (48%)
5	Gulf/UAE/Middle East/ nationality (20%)	My language/first language (33%)	Arabic words (e.g. haram, sushma) (40%)
Other Common Words	Grammar (8%), poetry (8%), beautiful (7%)	Teaching our kids (17%)	Difficult/complex (33%), positive adjectives (18%), guttural (13%), people/students (13%)

Mecca'. The second most common word connection across the groups was *culture/tradition/customs/history/heritage*. For Emiratis, Arabic was associated with *family/friends/home*, as well as a sense of ownership demonstrated by the responses '*my/first/mother tongue language*'. Arabic was also connected with the *Middle East* or *Gulf* as a region, or the *desert* in the case of expatriates. The expatriate English university teachers also reflected on Arabic as a language and associated it with common Arabic words (e.g., *haram*, meaning 'forbidden' or *sushma*, meaning 'what's it called?') as well as its script/calligraphy and local dialect, Khaleeji. Only one word association overlap between Arabic and English could be seen from the Emirati primary school teachers, who mentioned entertainment in connection with both languages. However, the forms of entertainment varied. Whereas English was connected with more modern forms of entertainment such as *movies* and *the Internet*, Arabic was associated with the more traditional *poetry* and *music*. Other unique or less common word associations (less than 4% of participants) included: *oil, easy life, scorching, disappearance, undeveloped, comfortable, has meaning, rich, special, honour, influence, adore, responsibility, power, elegant, civilization, wisdom*, and *proud* (Emirati university students), *like pearls in the sea* (Emirati primary school teachers), and *endangered, don't hear it enough, necessary, barrier* (Expatriate university teachers). The comparison between Arabic and 'pearls in the sea' conjures images of something precious or rare and an item to be treasured. Pearls also symbolize Emirati heritage as pearl diving is a tradition that goes back over 1000 years, before the Gulf was known for its oil. However, it has now all but completely died out (Butalia, 2015) and is very much associated with a bygone era. Figures 5.4, 5.5, and 5.6 allow all the word associations to be seen, and clearly the main words to jump out from the page are *religion, Quran, family, culture, tradition, mother tongue, difficult, Middle East, Islam*.

Figure 5.4 Emirati University Students' Word Associations With Arabic

Figure 5.5 Emirati Primary School Teachers' Word Associations With Arabic

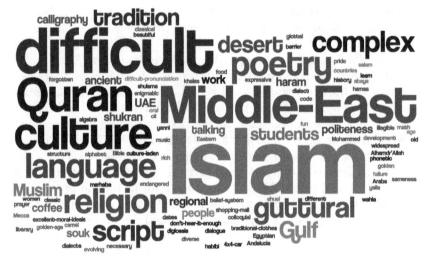

Figure 5.6 Expatriate University English Teachers' Word Associations With Arabic

Not surprisingly, similar associations were mentioned and discussed in the focus groups. The three main themes emerging from the focus groups were: religion, terrorism, and beauty.

Arabic as a Language of Religion

All Emirati participants felt that religion was implicitly tied to Arabic through the importance of the Holy Quran, as voiced in Example 5.7. Expatriate university teacher Rachel (UK) also stresses the connection between Arabic and religion when discussing the use of 'Allah Lexicon' (religious vocabulary containing the word 'Allah') (Morrow & Castleton, 2011) in everyday Emirati life. Words such as 'Inshallah' (God willing/maybe/we'll see), 'Mashalla' (God has willed it), 'Alhamdulillah' (Thank God), and 'Wallah' (I promise to God/I swear to God) are heard throughout the day in the UAE and it is almost impossible for expatriates not to adopt these expressions and use them subconsciously in their own conversations, as she explains in Example 5.8.

Example 5.7

Our culture, our customs. Also, the Holy Quran. All this keep us to encourage us to speak Arabic.

(Shaikha, Emirati university student)

Religion, Islam and home because all of us in our home talk in Arabic language.

(Lubna, Emirati primary school teacher)

Example 5.8

Arabic is so rooted in religion, so many people, and so many of the phrases that you pick up quickly as a foreigner living here are connected to religion. Insh 'allah, you know, in God's will. Ma'allah, may God protect you, you know this kind of thing.

(Rachel, UK)

Although religion is all-consuming in the Gulf and closely tied to Arabic, it is distinctly disassociated from English. As Hudson (2019, p. 246) points out, 'for a native-speaker ELT professional arriving in Arabia for the first time, the presence of religion is an immediate and palpable phenomenon'. Religion is visible in the way Gulf students dress, the changes to calendars during the holy month of Ramadan, daily calls for prayer which are broadcast from loudspeakers on mosques' minarets, as well as the frequent use of religiously loaded phrases. However, religion is viewed as a sensitive topic in the classroom and new teachers to the Gulf are advised to avoid it along with other culturally delicate topics such as politics, music, and dating before marriage. Religion is not a popular or neutral textbook topic and is notably missing from English teaching reference books too (Varghese & Johnson, 2007, p. 7). By separating Islam and English in this way, divisive language ideologies are exacerbated.

Arabic as a Language of Terrorism

A further association with Arabic in the minds of the expatriate participants was its connection to terrorism. Such a language ideology was ingrained in many through Western media growing up. Terrorism for many was only connected with Arabic or Muslim crimes rather than crimes in general. As Kundnani (2015, p. 21) states,

> the term 'terrorism' is never used to refer to the military violence of Western states, or to the daily reality of gender-based violence, for example, both of which ought also to be labeled terrorism according to the term's usual definition: violence against innocent civilians designed to advance a political cause.

The association between Arabic and terrorism is recognized in the literature to be an image pushed deeper into people's minds by the media (Hudson, 2019; Karmani, 2005; Kundnani, 2015). As Karmani (2005, p. 743) states, 'the relentless media imagery of Muslims and Arabs as blood-thirsty terrorists, hijackers, kidnappers, and suicide bombers only bolsters this symbolism'. Powerful voices in the West often push forward negative stereotypes and essentialist views of Muslims and, by default, the Arabic language (Herbert & Wolf, 2004) causing Muslims to be viewed through the lens of radicalism fuelled by 'Islamophobic' discourses (Kundnani, 2015). In both expatriate teacher focus groups, participants candidly discussed this association, as seen in Example 5.9.

The focus group members went on to say, however, that this connection was not as 'real' as some people believe it to be. For this reason, a keyword associated with Arabic, participants felt, was *misunderstood*. In Example 5.10, Joe (Canada) fully recognizes the source of the association (Western right-wing media) but did not question it at the time. Only later could he step back and analyze this initial emotional reaction as a misperception.

Example 5.9

Let's be really honest about it, terrorism. The reason why terrorism jumped into my head is that there has been that linking of a language and a religion and a culture that the West believes that Arabic is, they're all the same, they're all tarred with the same terrorist brush.

(James, Australia)

Any time an act of terrorism is committed, you hear an Arabic word, in praise of God, you know, there's that association.

(Richard, Ireland)

I suppose it could have very negative associations with many people because it's very politicized. Like Ahmed the terrorist, and also 'haram', we all know that word, don't we? . . . And all of the names of the terrorist groups are in Arabic. So, a lot of people, especially who don't live here, will have a very negative view of, if you just say Arabic, they go 'ughhhh' (gasp).

(Graeme, UK)

Example 5.10

In Canada and the US maybe there's Fox News, that's right-wing jour-nalism. It does create a negative perception, maybe not of the Ara-bic language but Middle Eastern culture in general. And I think it's a misperception or a myopic view of that, that they present on purpose but that's I think my first feeling of Arabic but then I mean that's an emotional reaction it's not a logical understanding. Once I actually think about it I know that that's a misperception but that media influ-ence has been salient for me. It's affected me.

(Joe, Canada)

Sebastian (UK) also stressed the effect Western media has had on the image of Arabic as a language associated with terrorism, by contrasting how Arabic was seen by children, in this case his 7-year-old son, who had not been influenced by such media. As he explains, for expatriate children growing up in the UAE with Arabic as a subject at school, it is like learning any other modern foreign language; they are often full of interest, curiosity and wonder, as voiced in Example 5.11. Sebastian's comment highlights the contrast between how a child can see Arabic as a foreign language from a fresh perspective as opposed to adults who may be influenced by negative political worldviews and media images.

Likewise, in Example 5.11, Richard (Ireland) contrasts images North Americans have of Arabs as pushed forward by negative stereotypes appearing in the news, with the reality of a very peaceful and pleasant life they saw when visiting the UAE.

Example 5.11

I just think of my son. He's seven and he's studying Arabic now and he loves, he loves everything about this place and he's interested in Arabic culture and he's interested in Arabic words and he sees it as a very pure thing he's learning and for us we've been affected by what we read in the media and your own experiences I guess but when I see my son and the way he always asks me questions about this region and he's only seven and that's the reality of it. I mean that's the context.

(Sebastian, UK)

I had a couple of Canadian friends here last week and we were wan-dering around the malls and they were saying 'oh my God, I wish the people back home could see this, they'd just shut their mouths about all the negative stuff that comes out, you know'. All the stereotypes disappear that they are fed by the media.

(Richard, Ireland)

Arabic as Mesmerizing, Classic, and Beautiful

Positive associations with Arabic were also put forward, by both Emirati and expatriate participants, including feelings from the Emirati participants of pride in Arabic in that it was seen as a valuable language with a great history. This was voiced by Hessa in Example 5.12. There is, however, a detectable note of nostalgia in Hessa's words, as if the image of Arabic she describes is one of the past rather than the present.

Example 5.12

(Arabic) looks like the pearls in the sea . . . because it's a valuable language and it's full of strong expressions and strong structures also. Reminds us with our great history and with the famous science too.

(Hessa, Emirati primary school teacher)

From the perspective of the expatriate university English teachers, Arabic was disassociated from key areas of modern life such as jobs, entertainment, technology, education, or global communication. Instead, the most common associations named were 'the region of the Middle East' rather than the world, a religion they did not share, a language/script the vast majority had not learnt, and tradition rather than modernity. Arabic was seen as abstract, 'distant', and 'otherworldly', perhaps due to associations made with the Arabian folk stories in 'Arabian nights' (translated by Burton, 1997), also known as 'One thousand and one nights' or 'Alf layla wa-layla' in Arabic. Participants in Example 5.13 romanticized Arabic as mesmerizingly beautiful, classic, pure, and poetic, but felt it was difficult to learn due to its guttural sounds and many forms (diglossia).

Example 5.13

Isn't Arabic well known as being a fantastic language to express poetry? It's beautiful-sounding. Like when you're on the Etihad flight and there's the . . . but if you don't understand, it does sound very mesmerizing and very beautiful. So, there's another side to Arabic as well.

(Graeme, UK)

I'm studying Arabic at the moment and I'm finding it really really, how can I say, amazing. I'm in love with Arabic . . . It's a beautiful-sounding language and a beautiful script.

(Christina, Mexico)

Graeme's (UK) comment conjures an image of drifting to sleep on an airplane seat to the rhythmic waves of the Arabic language. Christina (Mexico), too, emphasizes the beautiful sound and appearance of Arabic rather than anything practical. This regional and abstract view of Arabic by foreigners was also found in a previous study by Kramsch (2009), who investigated subjective representations of languages with various language learners. Those studying Arabic romantically described the language as 'beautiful', 'elegant', and 'distinguished'. It was also associated with the region and landscape of Arabia with participants naming words such as 'deserts, the sea, waves rolling and retreating, music, beautiful architecture, Arabian nights' (Kramsch, 2009, p. 59). Very few participants in the study, or in Kramsch's study for that matter, associated Arabic with the wider world.

5.4 Implications of Divisive Language Ideologies

The way languages are viewed by their speakers and others may well have implications for the future, which, once established, can be difficult to shift. From the data analyzed in this chapter, we can see there is currently a wide gap between English, Arabic, and other peripheral languages in the UAE in terms of power. While English is undoubtedly deemed important to Emiratis, Arabic is viewed as mainly unnecessary to expatriates living in the UAE. This reality is exacerbated by the current divisive way in which English and Arabic are symbolized, with English representing the wider world, education, and progression and Arabic representing religion, home life (friends and family), and tradition. This supports Findlow's theory (2006) that distinct worldviews exist with relation to the two languages, with Arabic representing 'cultural authenticity, localism, tradition, emotions and religion' and English representing 'modernity, internationalism, business, material status and secularism' (p. 25). Troudi and Jendli (2011, p. 26) also state in relation to their study, looking specifically at Emirati university students' attitudes towards EMI in HE, that English in education represents 'power and success, modernism, liberalism, freedom, and equality'. It could be said, therefore, that as summarized by Abdel-Jawad and Radwan (2011), 'Arabic is in the heart while English is in the mind' (p. 147). In this sense, the languages represent very different spheres.

This binary way of viewing the languages may have serious effects on the future, with Arabic being defined by what English is not, and vice versa. For instance, if English is viewed as the language of the future and of the world, Al-Issa and Dahan (2011) warn that Arabic, conversely, could be viewed as:

something old-fashioned which does not merit their attention because, after all, what they are taught and continually reminded of, by everything and everyone surrounding them, is that English is the global language. English is the language of technology, business, medicine, and education – therefore it must be more important than Arabic because it does so much more for them than Arabic ever has the opportunity to.

(p. 14)

This polarized way of viewing languages also occurs in other multilingual contexts. For instance, Selleck's (2016, p. 559) study at a Welsh bilingual school found that pupils associated the less dominant, Welsh language with 'old, local, rural, heritage culture' as opposed to the 'urban, new culture' they associated with English. This led pupils to contest their institutionally salient identities in favour of aligning 'themselves with "modern" media and its use of English' (p. 560). Similarly, in Hammine's (2019) study in the Ryukyu Islands near Okinawa, Japan, the local Ryukyuan languages were viewed as 'backward, uneducated, and ugly', whereas the language of instruction and dominating language, Japanese, was associated with the words 'civilized, and sophisticated' (p. 118). In the Gulf, Findlow (2006) warns of a similar predicament where Arabic is relegated as 'non-useful' and Arabic culture is cast as 'other'. It is true to say that when English is dominant in every public domain from business and education to hospitals, shopping, and technology, its importance and superiority as a language cannot help but be stressed. As Sperrazza (2012) states:

> The predominance of English in UAE schools, as well as in the overall workforce, has practically demoted Arabic to the role of a second-class citizen in its own country. Also, the predominance of guest workers from formally colonized countries adds to a colonial linguistic hierarchy that places English first, then Arabic, with all other languages tailing behind.
>
> (p. 299)

This was the dominant view in the findings with Emirati participants giving numerous examples of areas in which English dominates from hospital settings, to educational resources and research, and even to instructions on products in shops. A further polarizing factor apparent in the data is the separation of English and Islam. In TESOL, Karmani (2005) states:

> In the mainstream arena of TESOL – certainly in many Arab and Muslim contexts – we continue to peddle on the one hand the notion

of English as a purely neutral linguistic 'tool' that opens doors to vast riches (let alone closes others) and, on the other, of Islam as little more than an arcane series of beliefs, rituals, and behaviours whose sole orbit of relevance is in the mosque and family.

(p. 743)

It is true to say that at the region's main conference, TESOL Arabia, there is seldom mention of how English and Islam could interact.

To summarize, it is apparent that such ideological separation of the languages fuels belief systems such as 'parallel monolingualism' (Creese & Blackledge, 2010) in the case of Emiratis, where languages are seen as incompatible in the same space due to polarized values attached. As Calafato and Tang (2019, p. 135) state, often Emiratis believe that multilingualism should operate within a domain-specific framework, where English is used outside the home and Arabic is for inside the home. In the case of expatriates, while attempts have been made by some to learn Arabic, for a majority such efforts have been minimal and/or fruitless. It appears that Arabic is not viewed as essential to expatriates' lives and therefore it is ignored, rejected, excused, or guiltily avoided.

To conclude, we can see the three semiotic processes of *iconization, fractal recursivity*, and *erasure* (as identified by Irvine & Gal, 2000, at the start of this chapter) influencing the language ideologies of both Emiratis and expatriates in the study. In terms of iconization, Arabic is seen to symbolize religion, home life, and family for Emiratis, and for expatriates, Arabic has associations with terrorism, through imagery pushed forward by the media, as well as romanticism associated with the fantasy Arabia of '1001 Nights'. Expatriates recognized that there is 'no view from nowhere' (Irvine & Gal, 2000) when discussing the effects of Western news channels on their views of Arabic. English, on the other hand, was viewed similarly by both expatriates and Emiratis in that it was seen to be an icon of global communication, the wider world, and education. We can see specific examples of the process of fractal recursivity (generalizing outward or inward) in action with Yonka's experience growing up reading English textbooks which were always written by white authors. This led her to associate English with whiteness on a larger scale.

Finally, we see the presence of erasure in language ideologies through the languages being seen to represent homogeneous groups, especially in the case of Arabic. Here Arabic is very much associated with a region and a national culture rather than representing diversity. Many speakers of Arabic, for example, fall outside a specific region, religion, and cultural traditions but this was not evident in the word associations. Rather, diversity which exists amongst Arabic speakers was swept aside and stereotypical features dominated the word associations. We also see in the findings a tendency to define English by what Arabic is not and vice versa, as shown by very little overlap in the word associations provided by participants.

References

Abdel-Jawad, H., & Abu Radwan, A. S. (2011). The status of English in institutions of higher education in Oman: Sultan Qaboos university as a model. In A. Al-Issa, & L. S. Dahan (Eds.), *Global English and Arabic* (pp. 123–151). Bern, Switzerland: Peter Lang.

Ahmed, K. (2011). Casting Arabic culture as the 'other': Cultural issues in the English curriculum. In C. Gitsaki (Ed.), *Teaching and Learning in the Arab World* (pp. 119–137). Bern: Peter Lang.

Al Allaq, W. (2014). Arabic language in a globalized world: Observations from the United Arab Emirates. *Arab World English Journal, 5* (3), 113–123.

Al-Issa, A., & Dahan, L. S. (2011). Global English and endangered Arabic in the United Arab Emirates. In A. Al-Issa, & Dahan, L. S. (Eds.), *Global English and Arabic* (pp. 1–22). Bern, Switzerland: Peter Lang.

Al-Jarf, R. (2008). The impact of English as an International Language (EIL) upon Arabic in Saudi Arabia. *Asian EFL Journal, 10* (4), 193–210.

Al-Shamsi, N. A. (2009). Challenges to national identity in the UAE. *Emirates Center for Strategic Studies and Research.* Retrieved May 11, 2016.

Anderson, B. (1983). *Imagined Communities: Reflections on the Origin and Spread of Nationalism.* London: Verso.

Aneja, G. A. (2016). (Non) native speakered: Rethinking (non) nativeness and teacher identity in TESOL teacher education. *TESOL Quarterly, 50* (3), 572–596.

Badry, F., & Willoughby, J. (2016). *Higher Education Revolutions in the Gulf: Globalization and Institutional Viability.* New York: Routledge.

Baker, F. (2017). National pride and the New School Model: English language education in Abu Dhabi, UAE. In R. Kirkpatrick (Ed.), *English Language Educational Policy in the Middle East and North Africa* (pp. 279–300). Cham, Switzerland: Springer International Publishing.

Becker, A. L. (1988). Language in particular: A lecture. In D. Tannen (Ed.), *Linguistics in Context* (pp. 17–35). Norwood, NJ: Ablex.

Blommaert, J. (2005). *Discourse: A Critical Introduction.* Cambridge: Cambridge University Press.

Burkett, T. (2016). Emirati students' cultural norms and university teachers' awareness: A socio-cultural gap? *Perspectives, 24* (1), 5–11.

Burton, R. (Trans.) (1997). *Arabian Nights.* London: Penguin.

Butalia, N. (2015, December). 11 facts about pearl diving in the UAE. *Khaleej Times.* Retrieved from: https://www.khaleejtimes.com/nation/general/11-facts-about-pearl-diving-in-the-uae.

Calafato, R., & Tang, F. (2019). Multilingualism and gender in the UAE: A look at the motivational selves of Emirati teenagers. *System, 84,* 133–144.

Creese, A., & Blackledge, A. (2010). Translanguaging in the bilingual classroom: A pedagogy for learning and teaching? *The Modern Language Journal, 94,* 103–115.

Davidson, D. (2013). On the very idea of a conceptual scheme. *The American Philosophical Association Centennial Series*, 209–222. doi:10.5840/apapa2013236.

Dixon, B. (1980). *Catching Them Young: Sex, Race, and Class in Children's Fiction*. London: Pluto Press.

Findlow, S. (2006). Higher education and linguistic dualism in the Arab Gulf. *British Journal of Sociology of Education*, 27 (1), 19–36.

Gallagher, K. (2019). Introduction: Education in the UAE – context and themes. In K. Gallagher (Ed.), *Education in the UAE: Innovation and Transformation* (pp. 1–18). Singapore: Springer.

Guilherme, M. (2007). English as a global language and education for cosmopolitan citizenship. *Language and Intercultural Communication*, 7, 72–90.

Hammine, M. (2019). Our way of multilingualism: Translanguaging to break a chain of colonialism. In C. Seals, & V. L. Olsen-Reeder (Eds.), *Embracing Multilingualism Across Educational Contexts*. Wellington, New Zealand: Victoria University Press.

Herbert, D., & Wollfe, J. (2004). Religion and contemporary conflict in historical perspective. In J. Wollfe (Ed.), *Religion in History: Conflict Conversion and Coexistence* (pp. 286–320). Manchester: Manchester University Press.

Hopkyns, S. (2014). The effects of global English on culture and identity in the UAE: A double-edged sword. *Learning and Teaching in Higher Education: Gulf Perspectives*, 11 (2).

Hopkyns, S. (2015). A conflict of desires: English as a global language and its effects on cultural identity in the United Arab Emirates. In R. Al-Mahrooqi, & C. Denman (Eds.), *Issues in English Education in the Arab World* (pp. 6–36). Newcastle upon Tyne: Cambridge Scholars Publishing.

Hopkyns, S. (2016). Emirati cultural identity in the age of 'Englishization': Voices from an Abu Dhabi university. In L. Buckingham (Ed.), *Language, Identity and Education on the Arabian Peninsula* (pp. 87–115). Bristol: Multilingual Matters.

Hudson, P. (2019). A gin and tonic and a window seat: Critical pedagogy in Arabia. In M. E. Lopez-Gopar (Ed.), *International Perspectives on Critical Pedagogies in ELT* (pp. 241–263). New York: Palgrave Macmillan. http://doi.org/10.1007/978-3-319-95621-3_12.

Irvine, J. T., & Gal, S. (2000). Language ideology and linguistic differentiation. In P. V. Kroskrity (Ed.), *Regimes of Language: Ideologies, Polities, and Identities* (pp. 35–84). Santa Fe: School of American Research Press.

Karmani, S. (2005). TESOL in a time of terror: Toward an Islamic perspective on Applied Linguistics. *TESOL Quarterly*, 39 (4), 738–744.

Kramsch, C. (2009). *The Multilingual Subject*. Oxford: Oxford University Press.

Kubota, R. (2019). A critical examination of common beliefs about language teaching: From research insights to professional engagement. In F. Fang, & H. P. Widodo (Eds.), *Critical Perspectives on Global Englishes in Asia* (pp. 10–26). Bristol: Multilingual Matters.

Kubota, R., & Lin, A. (Eds.) (2009). *Race, Culture, and Identity in Second Language Education: Exploring Critically Engaged Practice*. New York: Routledge.

Kundnani, A. (2015). *The Muslims are Coming! Islamophobia, Extremism and the Domestic War on Terror*. London: Verso.

Lee, E., & Simon-Maeda, A. (2006). Racialized research identities in ESL/EFL research. *TESOL Quarterly*, 50, 66–85.

Li, W. (2018). Linguistic (super)diversity, post-multilingualism and translanguaging moments. In A. Creese, & A. Blackledge (Eds.), *The Routledge Handbook of Superdiversity* (pp. 16–29). London: Routledge.

Mahboob, A., & Elyas, T. (2014). English in the Kingdom of Saudi Arabia. *World Englishes*, 33 (1), 128–142.

Miall, A., & Milsted, D. (2013). *Xenophobe's Guide to the English*. London: Xenophobe's Guides Ltd.

Morrow, J. A., & Castleton, B. (2011). The impact of global English on the Arabic language: The loss of the Allah lexicon. In A. Al-Issa, & L. S. Dahan (Eds.), *Global English and Arabic* (pp. 307–334). Bern, Switzerland: Peter Lang.

Neveling, A., & Wilson, L. (2016, August 10–16). Me, myself and Abu Dhabi. *Time Out Abu Dhabi*, 13–19.

Randall, M., & Samimi, M. A. (2010). The status of English in Dubai. *English Today*, 26 (1), 43–50.

Saldana, J. (2013). *The Coding Manual for Qualitative Researchers* (2nd ed.). London: Sage Publications.

Sandiford, C. (2013). The enculturation of pre-service Emirati English language teachers. *Education, Business and Society: Contemporary Middle Eastern Issues*, 7 (1), 2–16.

Selleck, C. (2016). Re-negotiating ideologies of bilingualism on the margins of education. *Journal of Multilingual and Multicultural Development*, 37 (6), 551–563.

Solloway, A. (2016). English in the United Arab Emirates: Innocuous lingua franca or insidious cultural Trojan horse? In L. Buckingham (Ed.), *Language, Identity and Education on the Arabian Peninsula* (pp. 176–196). Bristol: Multilingual Matters.

Sperrazza, L. (2012). A clash of cultural identities in the UAE. *International Journal of Arts and Sciences*, 5, 297–306.

Sue, D. W., Capodilupo, C. M., Torino, G. C., Bucceri, J. M., Holder, A. M. B., Nadal, K. L., & Esquilin, M. (2007). Racial micro-aggressions in everyday life. *American Psychologist*, 62 (4), 271–286.

Tollefson, J., & Tsui, A. (2004). *Medium of Instruction Policies: Which Agenda? Whose Agenda?* Mahwah, NJ: Lawrence Erbaum Associates.

Troudi, S., & Jendli, A. (2011). Emirati Students' experiences of English as a medium of instruction. In A. Al-Issa, & L. S. Dahan (Eds.), *Global English and Arabic* (pp. 23–48). Bern, Switzerland: Peter Lang.

Van den Hoven, M., & Carroll, K. S. (2016). Emirati pre-service teachers' perspectives of Abu Dhabi's rich linguistic context. In L. Buckingham (Ed.), *Language, Identity and Education on the Arabian Peninsula* (pp. 39–58). Bristol: Multilingual Matters.

Varghese, M., & Johnson, K. A. (2007). Evangelical Christians and English language teaching. *TESOL Quarterly*, 41 (1), 5–13.

Yorkey, R. (1974). Practical EFL techniques for teaching Arabic slang. *Design Issues*, 24 (2), 39–52.

6 English and Cultural Identity – the Good, the Bad, and the Complex

Cultural analysis is intrinsically incomplete. And, worse than that, the more deeply it gets, the less complete it is.

– Clifford Geertz

As indicated by the opening quote in this chapter, analyzing cultural identities is never simple or linear. Rather the deeper one goes, the messier it gets. This was very much the case in the current study. While initially general positions could be identified, the more these positions were explored, the more intricately complex and multidimensional they became. However, rather than recording anything one could easily measure, the focus of this study was to identify key themes and to paint a picture of the many complexities involved in the relationship between English and cultural identities. As a starting point, layers within the concept of cultural identity were identified. These layers included *individual participants' lives*, *culture in the UAE*, and *identities or ways of thinking*. Figures 6.1 and 6.2 show the effects of global English on these layers of cultural

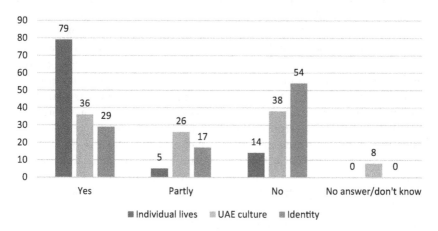

Figure 6.1 Emirati University Students' Views on the Effects of English on Cultural Identity (percentage)

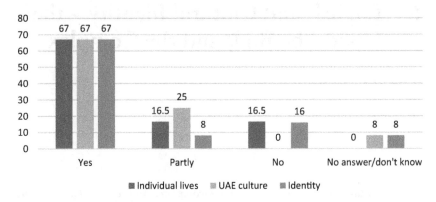

Figure 6.2 Emirati Primary School Teachers' Views on the Effects of English on Cultural Identity (percentage)

identity from the perspective of Emirati university students and Emirati primary school teachers, respectively.

For Emirati university students, English was seen to have affected individual lives most, followed by culture in the UAE, and then identities. Emirati primary school teachers' responses were more uniform across the categories with the majority feeling English had affected all layers of cultural identity evenly.

The mixed nature of responses with regard to the effects of English on culture and identity, both within the groups and between the groups, clearly support the concept of 'small culture formation' (Holliday, 2013) in that rather than a whole nation sharing one culture and members of that nationality thinking in the same way, smaller social groupings such as contemporaries, families, or work/study groups often form cultures of their own. As Holliday (2013) states, small culture formations happen all the time and are the 'basic essence of being human' (p. 3). We can see this, perhaps most glaringly, in the two groups' responses to how their identities are affected by English. The students, who were divided on the influence of English on their identities, chose to see language as either a major part of who they were or a minor part. This highlights that there are undoubtedly multiple factors which contribute to a person's notion of culture and identity. Almost all the Emirati primary school teachers, on the other hand, indicated that English had a major influence on identity. Being older, working in the field of education, being mothers, and playing a more prominent role in society are examples of small cultures to which the Emirati primary school teachers may belong. The existence of these small cultures could very well play a role in how the teachers feel their identities have been shaped with regard to the English language. Indeed, the fact that they are required to teach in English in order to keep their jobs, added to the possibility that they may feel a great responsibility for encouraging their children to use English, could explain the greater impact English has on their identities. It is certainly clear that ways of viewing global English and its effects on cultural identities in the UAE are far from homogeneous.

When going beyond general positions, there was considerable overlap and blurring of the categories and similar themes arose across the layers. As discussed in Chapter 1 of this book, cultural identity is a complex, multidimensional, and ever-changing concept, which is neither easy nor desirable to keep within rigid boundaries. For this reason, this section has been organized around common and reoccurring themes which were discussed across the layers.

As with the 1966 epic spaghetti Western film 'The Good, the Bad, and the Ugly', when exploring the effects of English on cultural identities, all the previous adjectives featured heavily. This chapter integrates these elements but substitutes 'ugly' with 'complex'. For each major theme, the good, the bad, and the complex were omnipresent. Figure 6.3 shows the four most prominent themes relating to the effects of global English on cultural identities.

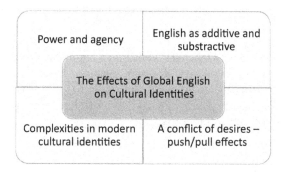

Figure 6.3 The Effects of English on Layers of Cultural Identity: An Overview of Main Themes

6.1 Power and Agency

The first major theme to emerge when looking beyond initial positions concerning the effects of English on cultural identities was the issue of power and agency. While some Emiratis felt they had control and agency over English and accompanying cultural aspects, others felt that due to the 'all powerful and far-reaching' nature of English, they had little control over its effects and were at its mercy. The expatriate teachers' perspectives, from an observer's angle, echoed such feelings surrounding power and agency.

Besieged Culture Mentality

It was voiced by some expatriate teachers that the diverse demographics of the UAE served to create a 'besieged culture mentality', similar to French-speaking Quebec in mainly English-speaking Canada, which made Emiratis more protective of traditional culture, serving to strengthen a distinct sense of cultural identity, as voiced in Example 6.1.

Example 6.1

They're living in a multilingual, multicultural society, which perhaps makes their own feeling of cultural identity stronger – a stronger need to reinforce their traditions and customs, to reinforce their cultural identity.
(Rose, UK)

I think because they are a minority as well. If you're a besieged culture you, most of us don't think about our identity from day to day, we are just who we are. But if you are a minority in your own country of course your cultural identity becomes even stronger because it's reactive.
(Richard, Ireland)

*Pseudonyms used for all participant names

Expatriate university teachers went on to comment on students resisting cultural change by openly drawing divisions between 'their culture' and outside influences, as voiced in Example 6.2. Here young Emiratis are reactive, in that they feel they have to work harder to maintain a traditional sense of cultural identity.

Example 6.2

I do (think there is resistance to cultural change) from things that students say for example, 'well, we, in our culture' you know bringing me back on track and reminding me that it's different in their culture or, that's at the forefront of their minds. That's the feeling I have. They are in a group and to that group they have to present a certain face and if they're stepping out of what is the expected norm in front of that group then that's quite a big message or statement.
(Tabitha, UK)

Emirati participants' comments very much reflected this notion of a besieged culture mentality. It was commented on that the government's many efforts to preserve Arabic culture and identity (as explained in Chapter 3 of this book) aimed to null the effects of English and keep local cultural identity 'strong' and 'unchangeable', as voiced in Example 6.3.

Example 6.3

Here in the UAE we do a lot of heritage about our traditions. We do here also for the festival, for the visitors to know more about our culture.

(Hamda, Emirati university student)

The UAE tries so hard to keep our culture and our identity more important than anything.

(Hafsa, Emirati university student)

Not only through government initiatives but also through strength of character and a love of Arabic, a strong sense of cultural identity was thought to exist. Here, local culture was said to be in Emiratis' hearts and minds, which negated the possible effects of English, as voiced in Example 6.4.

Example 6.4

We believe in our culture and it stays in our hearts and English developed us and didn't change our belonging or feeling of our culture.

(Amal, Emirati university student)

The Cultural Supermarket

Another form of reactivity to feelings of cultural fragility involved the utilization of Mathews' (2000) concept of the 'cultural supermarket', as explained in Chapter 1. It was felt that individuals could choose to use English for certain purposes, take 'the best of the West' and reject undesirable aspects of Western culture and English, thus having both power and agency over the effects of English. In a sense, by 'shopping in the cultural supermarket' or 'selective incorporation' (Tomlinson, 1999) individuals can 'pick and choose' certain parts of English, and Western culture, as explained by both Emiratis and expatriates in Example 6.5.

In Example 6.5, we can see that the cultural supermarket is not only a Western English-speaking one but also a global one. In addition, picking and choosing parts of mainly English-speaking cultures does not just refer to material aspects such as clothes, food, and popular culture. It can also refer to lifestyles, mindsets, and beliefs. For some, English allowed them to discover or explore aspects of their identities which they felt unable to explore through Arabic. Choosing value systems attached to Western English-speaking countries allowed some Emiratis to try out new identity options, which may not be supported in the local context.

Example 6.5

I think, as Emiratis, when we think there is something good, or we take the good thing from other as a kind of model, we will save our identity, but if we take it as a dress or hairstyle or something, it's something else. It will be something disturb or interfere our identity.
(Sheikha, Emirati primary school teacher)

I think they tend to 'pick and choose' in terms of what they take from the 'foreign culture'. Here there has been an explosion of global culture. This could be one of the most globalized places in the world.
(Douglas, USA)

English was described as liberating and an 'opening language' which allowed for new trains of thought which were restricted in Arabic due to its close attachment to religion, as voiced in Example 6.6.

Example 6.6

When I think about something in English it's opening and okay but in Arabic it's hard because our religion stop something that the English thing it's allowed.
(Shouq, Emirati university student)

You start thinking out of the circle and start knowing new stuff.
(Taif, Emirati university student)

Sometimes I stop thinking in traditional way and be flexible to let it go some of the old-fashioned behavior.
(Naeema, Emirati primary school teacher)

In Example 6.6, we see English being seen as instrumental for 'letting go' of old-fashioned behaviour associated with Arabic. This supports findings in Chapter 5 of this book where English is a language of the future and modernity, something to move towards, whereas Arabic is something old-fashioned and to be moved away from.

Expatriate university teachers also noticed English being used as a way to escape conventions with students who they described as 'out-layers'. For example, those not conforming to traditional images of gender or sexuality, those with mixed ethnicity parents, or those who had unusual interests tended to turn to English as a way of escaping Arabic conventions. They viewed their English-speaking selves as an alternative identity option and as an outlet for expressing hidden identities or differences not celebrated in the local context. The expatriate teachers spoke of students keeping diaries in English not as a way to practice the language but rather as a preferred means of language to record personal thoughts and feelings. English fitted their feelings and provided them with expressions matching their identities, which in some cases held negative connotations if translated into Arabic (Example 6.7).

Example 6.7

I had a student last semester who did not fit in with the other guys, so for him, English was far preferable than Arabic. Yes, he uses Arabic but you can see that it's kind of liberating to use English and he can access so many things online through English. I've known that before with other female students who perhaps have slightly strange interests or something like that.

(Tabitha, UK)

I've heard of students who keep diaries in English because it gives them privacy from other members of the family and it's a way that they can sort of note down their deeper feelings and maintain some sort of distance so it can liberate in that way, can't it?

(Rachel, UK)

Canagarajah and Dovchin (2019) state that in such situations, English can provide 'an alternative space to feel empowered' (p. 8). Here, the use of English over Arabic is strategic as English may be a 'better fit' for some aspects of their identities. Furthermore, writing in English often means that parents are not able to read what they have written due to their lack of proficiency in English.

If we expand the notion of the cultural supermarket further, Emiratis can choose not only to 'buy into or take' from other cultures but also 'sell or advertise' their own beliefs to others, through the medium of English. Here, the cultural supermarket works both ways and there is a sense of agency and control where English is used both as a tool for accessing other cultures as well as for promoting one's own. Rubdy and Alsagoff (2014) give examples of cultures moving in the opposite direction, that is from 'the rest to the West' (p. 5), such as Japanese manga magazines, Korean pop music and dramas, and Bollywood movies. Such 'reverse traffic' is often made accessible, at least partly through English. In the case of the UAE, Example 6.8 shows how English is used as a conduit for teaching others about aspects of local culture as well as religion.

Example 6.8

Nowadays UAE became a famous country. The Emirati culture now become known around the world. It didn't affect or change our culture but it helps to make UAE culture known.
(Kulaitham, Emirati university student)

Anyone from another country, I can explain my culture for them with English language. They will understand.
(Reem, Emirati university student)

The view in Example 6.8 has also been expressed in previous studies. For example, Clarke (2006, p. 229) found that English was seen as a tool for 'talking back'. His Emirati B.Ed. participants stated a reason for becoming English teachers was to teach their students to tell others that Emiratis are good human beings, and to communicate ideas and culture. As words linked to Arabic mentioned by the expatriate university English teachers in Chapter 5 of this book were 'terrorism' and 'misunderstood', this desire to use English as a way to 'talk back', 'defend one's self', or 'educate others' seems valid. As Janmohamed (2016) acknowledges in her book 'Generation M' on modern Muslim identities, fighting stereotypes of Muslims as terrorists is 'a constant battle' (p. 29).

A further form of agency or power over the effects of English on cultural identities was the mental separation of English and Arabic. Some Emirati participants stated that the Arabic language and culture could not be affected by English due to the strong connection between Arabic and Islam and the fact the Quran is, and will always be, accessible only in Arabic. A further separation of the languages was a private/public divide where Arabic was associated with the home and English with public domains, thus reflecting double-monolingual ideologies, where languages do not mix. Emirati university students Fatima and Alya voice such ideologies in Example 6.9.

Example 6.9

For me I separate my Arabic language from English. Everything has its own time.
(Fatima, Emirati university student)

In our family, we speak Arabic in home but also we speak English but we speak English outside, but in my home we should speak Arabic, only Arabic.
(Alya, Emirati university student)

Ironically, although double monolingual ideologies (the separation of languages) were voiced, young Emiratis frequently use both English and Arabic in the same sentence or conversation in many contexts. For example, in this study during the focus group discussions, translingual practice took place frequently, especially in the male Emirati university student focus group. Example 6.10 shows a sample of translingual practice on the topic of attitudes towards Western clothing. We can see how Hamdan uses a mixture of English and Arabic. In the first utterance he uses both languages in one sentence. His next sentence is in Arabic, and the next one in English.

Example 6.10

HAMDAN: Just *for comfort* (*Lel rah* للراحه).
TRANSLATOR: Only comfort. He is more comfortable, that's all. That's all he thinks about.
HAMDAN: *I also think I look more handsome in Western clothing* (Aydan, ana ahess annany ajmal bel thiyab al-gharbeyyah- أيضا، أنا أحس أنئ أجمل بالثياب الغربيه).
TRANSLATOR: He thinks he looks more handsome in Western clothes.
AUTHOR: Really?
TRANSLATOR: I don't think so by the way (laughter from the group). You should try it one day. You'd look great in a thobe (another word for kandoura or traditional white robe worn by men in the Arabian Gulf), I think.
HAMDAN: You don't want to see it.

Italic parts were spoken in Arabic (translation and transliteration provided in brackets).

While Example 6.10 shows extensive mixing of Arabic and English, in other parts of the focus groups, despite the presence of a translator, participants chose to use mainly English. Still, common words in the Khaleeji dialect punctuated this English instinctively such as the word 'Yani' which means 'how do you say it' or 'you know'.

English as the New Wasta

Despite the agency and power some felt with regard to shopping in the cultural supermarket and mentally putting English and Arabic in separate boxes, others expressed views which indicated a distinct lack of agency and power over language use and the effect of English on cultural identities. Both expatriate teachers and Emirati participants talked of the power outside influences and English held. It was recognized that the influence of both English-speaking cultures from the West and other global influences were heavily embedded in Emirati society. These influences affected cityscape, dress, traditions, and artifacts, all areas which are woven into

Emirati life. Expatriate teachers name a few ways in which Emiratis are Westernized in Example 6.11.

Example 6.11

It's very Americanized. I mean look at Dubai, it's a mini New York. You've got big skyscrapers and here you've got the grid system because of highways. Big cars.

(Graeme, UK)

The way they dress, a lot of them who come through IELTS, come with baseball caps. And you can see their attitudes are completely Westernized. And the way they dress and the way they talk to you is definitely influenced by Western music.

(Sebastian, UK)

The marching band, and there's bagpipes in the Emirati military marching band.

(Joe, Canada)

Joe's (Canada) mention of the obviously British tradition of bagpipes being part of the National Day parades can be seen in Figure 6.4 which shows a recent National Day event at the university in which the study takes place.

Figure 6.4 Bagpipes at an Emirati National Day Event

Photograph by the author

Some felt that the power of English was so great and its presence so overwhelming in daily life, resisting its influence on cultural identities was futile. It has acquired 'super power' status in the UAE which became especially apparent for participants after trips abroad as seen in Example 6.12.

Example 6.12

When I travel to China, they have Chinese words and English words. Here in the UAE, not Arabic. Just English, English, English. In all malls, hospitals everything. If they put both for foreign people and for Emirates people it would be good but they just put English. Some of them they have just English, English, English.

(Marwa, Emirati university student)

Some Emirati students spoke of the effects of English being almost something which had swallowed them or washed over them, something of which they had no control. We see in Example 6.13, Eiman's use of 'I find myself' indicating a lack of agency or control over her linguistic and cultural identity. Similarly, Hajar's statement sounds like a fact rather than a choice.

Example 6.13

I find myself more interested in English songs, shows, and movies. I have forgotten how to write Arabic and even how to use it in public places.

(Eiman, Emirati university student)

When I think now, I think in English.

(Hajar, Emirati university student)

The power of English was viewed as so great that it was even compared to *wasta*, which is a traditional form of social capital (as explained in Chapter 2 of this book) where, based on one's nationality and family name, certain advantages are granted. English, like *wasta*, is seen to hold a special inflated power that allows its speakers to access advantages over those who do not speak it or do not speak it well, as explained in Example 6.14.

Example 6.14

There are many people nowadays who forget Arabic. They all talk English. Now this world is all about English, especially universities. Students can't pass and graduate from universities or schools without learning English and have to get IELTS to pass levels and go to general or majors. And that's not fair. People stopped university because they didn't bring IELTS. Some of them go straight to get a job with wasta and some stay at home without job or continuing their education.

(Alanood, Emirati university student)

6.2 English as Additive and Subtractive

A second major theme centred around attitudes towards bilingualism. Arabic-English bilingualism, code-switching, and translanguaging were sometimes observed as being a source of pride, which is fast becoming part of young Emiratis' identities. On the other hand, there was concern over Arabic attrition due to the use of English.

Confident Bilinguals

Emirati university students spoke of 'feeling different from other people' due to being able to speak English. For instance, university student, Abdul, recalled a situation where he was called upon to translate for a customer in a restaurant who did not speak English and a waiter who did not speak Arabic. He felt confidence in his bilingualism and pride in being able to help others in his country. Emirati schoolteacher, Iptisam, also felt confident in herself as a bilingual speaker in multiple contexts (Example 6.15).

Example 6.15

I feel learning English makes me more confident, to be honest. Like, I feel more confident that I can go everywhere and talk and express myself freely but on the other hand if I didn't have the language, I'd be less confident and I would be really afraid of going to some places that didn't have Arabic.

(Iptisam, Emirati primary school teacher)

In these cases, it was felt that identities had changed for the better in terms of feeling more educated and competent. Pride was expressed in representing their country or Arabs in this way. The pride related to both reflective positioning (how one sees oneself) and interactive positioning (how one is viewed by others) as seen in Example 6.16.

Example 6.16

People will feel proud of me. They will say, she is Emirati but she can talk good in English.

(Reem, Emirati university student)

In the past, we travel in the past they don't know from where I am from and they think oh she is Arabic woman, they don't know an Emirati woman. But nowadays, they know I'm Emirati and I know how to speak English well.

(Ghareeba, Emirati university student)

Expatriate teachers also noticed pride and confidence Emiratis demonstrated when code-switching or translanguaging. In Example 6.17, Joe (Canada) observes a cafe conversation between two young Emirati friends who confidently switch between Arabic and English over the space of a conversation.

Example 6.17

I was at a coffee shop, a Tim Horton's, a Canadian restaurant, anyway, I only mention that because perhaps the people were there because it was Western, I don't know, but anyway, I think they were students, and they were switching between Arabic and English (clicks fingers three times) fluently and it seemed, I didn't understand what they were saying in Arabic but I wondered why they switched. Did they switch for certain topics or why did they switch? But it was very bilingual. They could easily communicate with each other in both languages and chose in the course of one dialogue, to use both languages.

(Joe, Canada)

Seeing English as bringing positive additional aspects to cultural identities as described previously, matches Garcia's (2009, p. 142) definition of additive bilingualism, where English adds (L1+L2=L1+L2) rather than takes away (L1 + L2 – L1 = L2).

A Generation of Non-Native Speakers

While English-Arabic bilingualism affects some individuals in a positive way, concerns were expressed by both Emiratis and expatriate university teachers as to the subtractive elements of bilingualism for some. For example, Rachel (UK) went so far as to state that there is now 'a whole generation of non-native speakers' in the UAE (Example 6.18), where they are neither fluent in English, nor Arabic. She may have been thinking of the students she teaches in the university foundation program who are struggling to achieve the IELTS 5.5 needed to be able to start their degree programs in the medium of English.

Example 6.18

I feel there is a whole generation of non-native speakers in this country now. They're not fluent in either language and I think that's such a danger . . . and it has real implications academically because how do you come across to people if you can't communicate effectively in either one of your languages?

(Rachel, UK)

While a few Emirati participants talked about their own loss of Arabic due to English (Hind in Example 6.19), most expressed concerns over the loss or demise of Arabic in society in general, distancing themselves from the issue and positioning themselves as disapproving observers (Sumeya in Example 6.19). Concerns were raised that Arabic was a 'dying' language which is slowly 'vanishing' or being 'deleted'.

Example 6.19

Nowadays more and more people can't speak the real Arabic and it's sad to me that the Arabic language is dying, even me, my Arabic now is really bad, it's like some Indian trying to speak Arabic!!

(Hind, Emirati university student)

In some people. They prefer English in everywhere. They delete Arabic language. They speak 24 hour English.

(Sumeya, Emirati university student)

When Hind comments on her Arabic being as bad as 'some Indian trying to speak Arabic' she reveals her attitude towards nationalities which are looked down upon (such as Indians) due to social stratification. Her comment also reveals a 'language purity' ideology, as discussed in Chapter 3 of this book, where there is a 'real Arabic' which must not be mixed with English or be spoken by anyone other than Gulf nationals.

In addition, there was a feeling of being 'hurt' or feeling 'pity' for Arabic as a language these days, as voiced in Example 6.20. Here, Khadiha wishes Arabic were the 'language of everything' rather than a language used to talk about traditions, especially in teaching. Hessa expresses sympathy for Arabic, from the stance of an uncomfortable observer.

Example 6.20

I sometimes feel sorry for when I hear the word Arabic nowadays, you know. I feel that Arabic, you know, become weak more and more because of many other aspects or, especially in the teaching, I feel that Arabic should not be the language of speaking of tradition or any other thing, it should be the language of everything.

(Khadija, Emirati primary school teacher)

To be honest, sometimes you feel negative in that I can't go anywhere without using English. In my country, I'm supposed to talk in my first language, which is Arabic. You know like, for example in hospitals sometimes when I see people they need translators and they need somebody to help them, I feel pity because it's our country. Everybody should be comfortable using their first language, not using their second language, which is English.

(Hessa, Emirati primary school teacher)

Different levels of disapproval with regard to the use of English over Arabic ranged from mild irritation to genuine fears for the survival of the language. On the side of mild irritation, university students commented on English being a language used to 'show off' or display superiority. Associating English with superiority is common in the Gulf, with the local nickname 'Bresteej boy' meaning 'prestigious guy' often given to Emirati men who speak English well or choose to speak it over Arabic (Seymour, 2016, p. 8). This is voiced by Fahad in Example 6.21.

Example 6.21

When a person uses English, his personality changes. He expresses different views, a different side of himself. Some people, when they start using English, think that anyone who only uses Arabic is ignorant.

(Fahad, Emirati university student)

Others felt much more than annoyance or irritation, going so far as to call English-speaking Emiratis 'freak people' or 'aliens', stating they found it difficult to recognize or relate to them. Partly they were viewed as aliens due to the amount of English they used and lack of Arabic, as voiced in Example 6.22.

Rather than seeing the emergence of the hybrid language 'Arabizi' as a form of resistance to 'English only' contexts, as discussed in Chapter 3, linguistic hybridity was mainly seen as a pollutant to Arabic. Emirati

---

Example 6.22

When I see them (younger Emiratis) I see like, freak people, like an alien. They look like Arabs but they talk a different language and they generate new language and you feel 'who are they?' And you feel that you don't want to communicate with them. I'll stay back, you know. It's not the way that I'm not inflexible to change or to accept the way that they live but it's not, I don't feel comfortable to see them or communicate with them.

(Oshba, Emirati primary school teacher)

---

university students described Arabizi as 'a new alphabet' and gave the example of the female name 'Marah', which is written 'ma3' (3 represents the Arabic letter ' ع ')'. When describing Arabizi, students often used the third person, as in 'they say. . .' instead of 'we say' (Example 6.23) to distance themselves from a practice they did not condone. In this sense, linguistic changes were seen negatively.

Example 6.23

The teenagers here in our culture create a new language. It's not exactly English. This language, nobody understands, not even they. They (Emiratis) understand the new words but native English speakers can't understand these words. So, it affects the Arabic language and English language. Like, 'delete'. They didn't say 'delete', they say 'deloot' or 'delooted', like that. New phrases. Something new. They know it, they understand. Also, they do it in chatting. Also, the message when they do broadcast, they send a message and they understand it but other people they can't understand it.

(Lubna, Emirati primary school teacher)

Example 6.23 demonstrates feelings of concern over loss of 'pure' Arabic and resulting feelings of alienation from the younger generation. Similar feelings of alienation from younger generations choosing to use English, over their L1, can be seen in Giampapa's (2004, p. 199) study, set in the multilingual context of Toronto, Canada, where Italian-Canadian teenagers using predominantly English or frequently code-switching are nicknamed the 'Armani generation' (Chianello, 1995) or 'cakerized' (Giampapa, 2004) as they are seen to have undergone the process of 'ethnic dilution'. While in the Canadian context this was an identity position that in the past was imposed through assimilating forces of the centre, it had become a contested position and a way of marking *italianita* (Italian character) through its denial. Similarly, the use of English and Arabizi can be seen as a conscious identity choice for young Emiratis in certain spaces, despite some disapproval from older generations.

The Domino Effect – Oshba's Stairs

Emphasis was placed on the interrelated nature of language, culture, and identity in that if one element is affected, the others in turn are affected as with a line of dominoes. In Example 6.24, Oshba uses the analogy of stairs to describe this 'domino effect' (Hopkyns, 2014).

Oshba's analogy of 'stairs' is depicted in Figure 6.5. It demonstrates the process of language changing one's cultural identity step by step.

Example 6.24

Learning the language, I saw it as stairs. The first step is to have the vocabulary of the language. Then you said, 'I will change my way of wearing my clothes to be like the foreign people' or the stereotype that you have about the same language that you are learning. So, you will change your clothes, then you will change your lifestyle, then you will change your attitude towards your old language because you see the new life. Then you will change step by step and you will lose your identity and your language in general, and you will not be able to go back to it because you will feel strange about your main identity. And what hurts nowadays is we saw our, not me, I mean in general, I mean the teenagers, the flexible people who are able to acquire a new language and lifestyle, they saw it as a shame to stay in their culture and their identity. They would like to change.

(Oshba, Emirati primary school teacher)

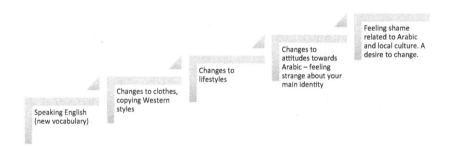

Figure 6.5 Emirati Primary School Teacher, Oshba's, Stairs Analogy Depicting Changes to Cultural Identity

We can see in the final two stairs that low self-esteem, embarrassment, and shame are connected to the main language. As Hammine (2019, p. 118) states, 'when a language is endangered, there are much bigger things at stake than the language itself'. This includes inequality, discrimination, differing life chances, depending on which language people speak (Romaine, 2008). Feelings of shame around one's first language can lead speakers to start rejecting their home (or heritage) culture and language because their desire to assimilate into the target language and culture are so strong. This phenomenon has been named 'ethnic ambivalence' (Dovchin, 2019, p. 6) or 'ethnic evasion' (Tse, 1998, p. 21) whereby speakers have little or no interest in their first language/heritage language which leads them to avoid using it. Ethnic evasion exists in many global contexts such as with Mongolian immigrants living in Australia avoiding other Mongolians and choosing not to teach their children the language (Dovchin, 2019), Chinese youth opting to speak English with parents in front of visitors (Tse, 1998), and Mexicans in the USA avoiding speaking Spanish so as not to be identified as Mexican (Orellana et al., 1999). In the UAE, this resonates with Ahmed's (2014, p. 105) claim that 'many fear the loss of Arabic language and by extension the Arabic culture'.

Parallels can also be drawn between Oshba's stairs analogy (Figure 6.5) and Kramsch's (1993) description of cultures being reduced to 'surface cultures' portrayed merely by 'the four F's: *food, festivals, fashion* and *folklore*' (Rubdy, 2016) and celebrated superficially on a country's 'national' or 'international day' before everything returns to normal. Although the prospect of Emirati culture being celebrated only as a novelty on National Day and the Arabic language morphing into a heritage language may seem extreme, this has happened historically in numerous regions at different points in time around the world. For example, worldwide, numerous cultures have lost a distinct identity originating from an ancestral language as a result of English, such as the Celtic languages which were once thriving but are now 'little more, in most places, than a curiosity' (Modiano, 2001, p. 343). In the early 1900s, for example, Breton children were forced to wear a piece of wood around their neck as a punishment if caught speaking Breton inside the school gates. Similarly, Welsh children caught speaking Welsh, faced a similar punishment (Jones & Singh, 2005, p. 83). Jones and Singh (2005, p. 83) point out that these 'target language only' policies portrayed a strong message that these children's mother tongue languages were inadequate for learning purposes, for communicating, understanding the world or expressing identity. In Wales now, 'less than 20 percent of the population can speak Welsh in addition to English' (Crystal, 1997, p. 40). There is a genuine fear from some participants that a similar outcome could become a reality for Arabic.

Although many concerns were voiced regarding Arabic loss and linguistic changes leading to semilingualism and cultural estrangement, the expatriate participants observed a reluctance from Emiratis to actively address such concerns. It was felt that although students at the university are often aware of their low Arabic proficiency, as indicated by the posters around campus reading 'Meet the mother language, Arabic' (Chapter 3, Figure 3.2), little action is taken and English continues to be prioritized, as voiced by Rachel (UK) in Example 6.25.

Example 6.25

These posters are up all over campus now, aren't they? Saying 'preserve your first language, preserve Arabic. Arabic is endangered'. They (my students) were saying 'yes, yes', a couple of people were saying, 'Yes. Yes. We do need to work harder'. But so many students on this campus don't. We hear them in the coffee shops, they're speaking English to each other out of choice.

(Rachel, UK)

6.3 Complexities in Modern Cultural Identities

In contrast to seeing the effects of English as purely additive (increasing confidence and pride) or purely subtractive (damaging and changing Arabic language, culture, and identity), some participants stressed that modern Emirati cultural identities were highly complex in that they often involved a mix of 'old and new'. While some viewed the formation of 'glocal identities' as a source of pride, others felt the mix of global and local influences was often lopsided in favour of English and Western culture.

Owning 'Glocal' Identities With Pride

Expatriate university teachers stressed that Emirati cultural identities are transitioning into a mix of traditional and modern, and this mix is often something which is embraced and 'owned', as voiced by James (Australia) in Example 6.26.

Example 6.26

(They are) no less Emirati but new young Emiratis. 'We do speak English and we do use Instagram . . . and women are starting to drive cars and that's because that's what we're making our country'. I think there is a real sense of 'we are really proud of Sheikh Zayed and the opportunities that he gave us' and I think that they are really kind of thrilled in a way, certainly the ones we teach anyway, are excited about the country and what they are becoming. They are very proud of themselves.

(James, Australia)

Some saw the UAE as 'forward-looking' and viewed Emiratis who embraced cultural changes as gaining access to greater freedom, work opportunities and new ways of behaving, as seen in Example 6.27.

Other expatriates gave distinct examples of Emiratis mixing old and new through observing traditional practices through new mediums.

Example 6.27

Here they are pretty much open to (change), there are eighteen-year-old girls getting a driver's license, being independent, making their own choices about all kinds of things they never made before like a husband sometimes.

(Richard, Ireland)

In Example 6.28, Richard (Ireland) speaks of Emiratis driving modern cars rather than riding camels, as they would have done in the past, but keeping the tradition of coffee-drinking in the desert rather than drinking alcohol in clubs, as many teenagers do in the West. Similarly, Rachel (UK) talks of her students being addicted to Snapchat, as many teenagers are globally, but posting pictures of traditions such as Henna (traditional designs painted onto hands and feet at weddings) as they drink their

---

Example 6.28

I remember driving back late at night from Ras Al Khaima to Abu Dhabi and on the side of the road, on the Emirates road which is very deserty up around there you know there's miles and miles of absolutely nothing except sand. These guys had driven out in their Nissan Patrols or whatever, their huge big cars, you know, and they'd parked them on the side of the road, built a fire and were sitting around doing things that probably their grandfathers had done. I mean they had arrived there in a completely different way and they were dressed in a completely different way but they were still like dudes their age in another country and they all had coffee pots by the way. Not whiskey, not beer, not wine. They weren't getting plastered out of their mind in the city center on a Saturday night. They were doing things culturally right.

(Richard, Ireland)

When you look at what they (students) are posting (on Snapchat), they're things that celebrate their culture. It's campfires in the desert with the relatives. It's like, I don't know, it's a bit of a cliché but a hennaed hand. But it is that kind of thing, yes there might be a Starbucks coffee in there but it's their daily experiences and often that's very reflective of Emirati culture, I think. If you look at that.

(Rachel, UK)

Yes, they seem very proud of their culture and religion. Most wear traditional dress, they are respectful of their leaders and their history. However, some of them are blending their culture with modern global culture. They like western movies (and Korean) and buy Western clothes to wear under their abayas.

(Zoe, USA)

Starbucks coffee. Zoe (USA) adds that under Emirati women's abayas are often Western clothes such as leggings and T-shirts.

It was argued that this mixing of old and new to create a modern sense of cultural identity did not make locals 'less Emirati' but rather 'new young Emiratis' who were excited about the country and what they were becoming. Figure 6.6 shows ways in which a modern 'glocal' Emirati identity is portrayed in Instagram posts.

6.6.1: Instagram posting of a trip to a family farm. Mix of tradition and modernity.

6.6.2: Instagram posting of 'glocal culture'. Italian coffee, modern smartphone and Shellac manicured-hand. Traditional image of Sheikh and falcon as screensaver. The picture is a Gulf-style 'selfie' which only shows the hand, not a face.

6.6.3: Instagram posting of Emirati student in the traditional Abaya reading in her EMI university library.

6.6.4: An Emirati university student's grandmother in traditional clothes which the student chose to share with her British teacher though Instagram.

Figure 6.6 Emirati University Students' Instagram Posts Representing a Mix of Old and New (Photographs are part of the 'Instagram Identity Project' which is an action research project conducted by the author. Consent forms were signed by participants for the publishing of these pictures).

The Instagram posts in Figure 6.6 demonstrate how tradition is often blended with modernity to create something unique and new which represents modern Emirati cultural identities. A further, more general, example of this can be seen though the adoption of the British blackberry-flavoured soft drink 'Vimto' as a symbol of Ramadan. Since Vimto was first exported to the Arab region in 1928, it has been adopted as a core part of Muslim culture and traditions, in somewhat of a cult fashion. It has been named the 'Ramadan Drink' as its high sugar content makes it perfect for breaking fasts. It is also marketed in the region as representing family togetherness during the Holy month, using the hashtag '#Vimtocometogether' on social media. As Lawrence (2015) states, in the Gulf, 'drinking a glass of *Vimto* at Iftar (the breaking of the fast) is now a tradition as strongly associated with Ramadan as stockings are with Christmas'. The purple nectar is so woven into the fabric of Ramadan that it makes 70% of its sales in the Holy Month (Janmohamed, 2016, p. 206), and popular food and beverage chains such as *PinkBerry* and *The Coffee Club*, have also capitalized on its popularity by creating *Vimto* frozen yogurt cups and milk cakes (Figure 6.7), which are specially for the Gulf market.

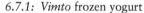

| 6.7.1: *Vimto* frozen yogurt | 6.7.2: *Vimto* milk cake |

Figure 6.7 The Reframing of British Soft Drink, *Vimto*, as a Ramadan Symbol

Photographs by the author

Here we can see Gulf nationals effectively reframing a product from the West to suit local customs and to symbolize Muslim identities, to the point where the origins are forgotten or irrelevant. However, as a side, notice that in both Vimto signs in Figure 6.7, English dominates, especially in Figure 6.7.2.

Imbalance of Old and New – Copying the West

While the blending of old and new was seen positively by some, others viewed such blending as unbalanced, with cultural aspects which accompany English dominating. Celebration of Western holidays, changes to ways of dressing, and choosing English movies/ TV/ music and greetings over Arabic ones were all discussed.

In the Emirati university student male focus group, it was not only the words of the participants but also the clothes they were wearing which significantly reflected cultural change regarding ways of dressing. Focus group members were happy to change traditional ways of dressing due to increased comfort and feeling more attractive in Western clothing. A sample of the discussion related to this can be seen in Example 6.29.

Example 6.29

RESEARCHER: Do you think that (English being used as a lingua franca between the UAE's multicultural population) has an effect on Emirati culture? For example, ways of dressing.
MALIK: Maybe, dressing. Here's an example (points to group Hamdan and Mansoor in T-shirts and jeans) (laughter).
TRANSLATOR: A perfect example
RESEARCHER: Yes. That's true.
ABDUL: I only wear this (kandoura) in uni.
TRANSLATOR: And you're not wearing anything on your head.

Another kandoura-clad focus group member, Omar, said he would not wear the kandoura outside university and another member, Mansoor (wearing a T-shirt and jeans), commented that Western clothing was 'a nice change' and he felt he looked more handsome. He stated that he only wore transitional clothes for religious holidays such as Eid. This reminds us of the third 'F' in Rubdy's (2016) theory of cultures being reduced to 'the four F's: *food, festivals, fashion* and *folklore*' (Rubdy, 2016) and celebrated superficially only on special occasions.

Some cultural changes brought about by 'copying the West' such as celebrations and music were said to be 'pushed on' to parents by the next generation who saw such events as normal, as voiced in Example 6.30. Some expatriates voiced similar views regarding the imbalance of 'old and new', seeing Western culture as the norm and local traditions as being 'superficially preserved' by the government in the form of museums, TV programs and events, rather than being core to Emiratis identities. It was felt this manufactured culture made Emiratis 'tourists in their own country' or 'culturally adrift', as voiced in Example 6.31.

Example 6.30

Even if you talk about occasions in the recent decades we don't have cakes, we didn't celebrate birthdays, or anniversary or Valentines. Nowadays our children push us to make a birthday for them or, because they see this one in the movies or in cartoons and most of their movies in English and they push their parents to celebrate their birthday.

(Anood, Emirati primary school teacher)

Example 6.31

They have a very strong social religious identity but to some extent they are as much tourists in their own culture as we are as it is being manufactured for them.

(Trevor, UK)

They always promote it (Emirati culture) don't they, you know the rich Emirati culture, but I'm not that convinced.

(Sebastian, UK)

Emirati cultural identity seems to be extraordinarily thin. They have very little connection to their past, beyond a few generic cultural symbols, Emiratis seems culturally adrift.

(Simon, USA)

6.4 A Conflict of Desires – Push and Pull

A final major theme in the data related to conflicts surrounding English. This often involved being pushed or pulled in different directions. Having to decide on the value of certain aspects of cultural identity individually is challenging, but it is equally challenging to receive mixed messages from society about the direction one should follow.

Mixed Messages

A 'conflict of desires' or feeling of being torn was described by both Emiratis and expatriates. Expatriate teachers commented that often mixed messages were given regarding how much cultural change was acceptable, leading to confusion and uncertainty about which path to take, as seen in Example 6.32.

Example 6.32

Cultural identity here is inextricably linked to religion, tribe and family, which are strong factors that are not changing so much. However, they are being pulled two ways now with the ever-increasing exposure to western ideals through media and the Internet.

(Lisa, New Zealand)

Identities are shifting and changing and moving and I think quite a few Emiratis probably do feel insecure because they think 'how can I be modern and progressive, educated and a high achiever, and keep my identity but at the same time embrace what is new and at the same time balance and juggle?' I think, particularly for girls (this is hard).

(Rachel, UK)

Expatriate teacher, Rachel (UK), went on to give further accounts of such challenges, when female students have dreams of a certain career, only to be told that working in a mixed environment is culturally inappropriate.

Linguistic and Cultural Conflicts in Families

A feeling of being pulled in different directions was discussed at length not only in relation to career goals but also in relation to home life, both in terms of language and culture. Emirati primary school teachers spoke of their school-age children using English so comfortably and naturally at home that certain family members were excluded from conversations. Descriptions of non-English-speaking older family members as 'mute' and 'isolated' indicated serious divisions caused by the dominance of English, as seen in Example 6.33.

Example 6.33

One day I was in the car with my husband and my kids. He is in KG2 (second year of Kindergarten), he talks with me in English and the father is like mute. He's not there, somebody is driving the car, it is not his father (laughs). And the conversation was there and we were talking and he asked his father 'isn't it like this?' and his father didn't answer, so I feel like yes, we are in the car but we are in danger, we are like isolated our father from dealing with us or joining us in our conversation about . . . so I taught the children the Arabic language at home and when my child starts to talk in English, I answer him in Arabic to ask his father to join us, you know, because it's scary because I need this relationship between us.

(Oshba, Emirati primary school teacher)

Example 6.33 indicates that English is causing relationships to be strained and damaged in families. Further personal accounts from Emirati university students described mothers and grandmothers needing to bring daughters or granddaughters on shopping trips and to hospital appointments due to not being able to get by without English as seen in Example 6.34.

Example 6.34

In malls, my mum can't speak English well so when she goes alone, she cannot deal with people in the shop so I have to go with her or my sister has to go with her to speak, to get the information that she wants.
(Sara, Emirati university student)

In Example 6.34, both Sara and her mother may experience a myriad of feelings. Sara on the one hand may feel 'proud to help' and on the other hand 'burdened or obligated'. Her mother may feel resentment, asking herself 'why can't I speak my own language in my own country?', as well as low self-worth and lack of independence and freedom (reliant on others).

Conflicting feelings also occurred when helping children with homework. Although Arabic is viewed as the 'home language' (as seen in Chapter 5 of this book), the homework from school often needs to be completed in English. Choosing English over Arabic when helping with homework caused tension and conflict in Emirati schoolteacher and mother, Lamya's household, as seen in Example 6.35.

Example 6.35

As an English teacher, I would be teaching my kids at home and my husband would come home and he would say everyone speaks English except him. I would be teaching them Math, English and Science and he will start to fight with us, you know, arguing. So, this is what I feel, to be honest. Because he's like, 'you have to teach them in Arabic' and I am like 'yes, but this is English. This is what our government asks in the schools. This is what they need'. This is the new generation.
(Lamya, Emirati primary school teacher)

Lamya's choice to use English with her children at home in order to help with homework may be seen by her husband as disloyal to their first language. Lamya feels she has little choice, however, as educational policies support English in education. Through homework, a language which may have stayed at school makes its way into the home. This leads Emiratis to separate Arabic from education, even in the home context, and by disengaging identities from home languages, the process of language loss is accelerated (Cummins, 1996). Further examples were given of younger family members being more comfortable using English than Arabic, or in some cases not being able to use Arabic. An illustration of this can be seen in Example 6.36.

Example 6.36

My brother he don't know how to write in Arabic, so he's lost that. (He's) seven. He just writes in English. But he speaks Arabic but he don't know how to write in Arabic. He don't know the letters. When my mother teaches him, she feels she will die. She wants to kill him.
(Nadia, Emirati university student)

Poor performance of young Emiratis in Arabic (and English – perhaps demonstrated by Nadia's frequent subject-verb-agreement errors in Example 6.36), is supported by results from the 'Progress in International Reading Literacy Study' (PIRLS) standardized test, which aims to measure students' ability to read and comprehend texts in their native language (Mullis et al., 2012), where Arabian Gulf students generally do not fare well. From the 51 countries which participated in the 2016 PIRLS, the Arabic-speaking Gulf nations scored notably lower than most other participating countries with the UAE ranking 43rd place, Bahrain 44th place, Qatar 45th, Oman 47th, and Kuwait 48th (Taha-Thomure, 2019, p. 4).

As well as low levels of ability, lack of interest in Arabic is also common in the region. Previous studies in the Gulf have presented accounts of youths' disinterest in Arabic, even at home. After multiple interviews with Emiratis as part of her research for a recent podcast on the status of Arabic in the UAE, Porzucki (2016) posed the question, 'is the new Emirati identity an English-speaking Arab?' One of many interviews with Emirati citizens was with a young woman named Dina who had attended an international school in the UAE. Dina explained that she grew up speaking English both at school and at home and therefore felt 'Arabic was not a priority'. She commented that when her parents tried to encourage her to speak Arabic it was similar to when other people's parents say, 'you should eat your vegetables'. She felt, 'great, but no thanks'. This demonstrates Findlow's (2006) fear of Arabic being relegated as 'non-useful' and Arabic culture being cast as 'other'.

In the present study, not only language rifts but cultural rifts in families were also commented on. Primary school teachers Rawda and Hessa's discussion in Example 6.37 demonstrates this.

Example 6.37

RESEARCHER: Do you think it (English) affects family life?

RAWDA: Yes, yes, yes, yes, yes. I'll give you an example. When I had my third baby recently, my son refused to go out with us. He says, 'I feel shy because we became a big family now' and he's in Year 3 only so, God almighty, he doesn't want me to come to the school with the baby.

HESSA: Did you tell him it's normal for Arab families?

RAWDA: Yes, I told him but you know. . .

HESSA: He's affected by. . .

RAWDA: He's affected by uh. . .

HESSA: His peers.

RESEARCHER: Umhum.

RAWDA: He says why do my friends all have small families? Why he's the awkward one?

In Example 6.37, Rawda talks of her son's embarrassment over the size of his family compared to his international classmates. Family size in the UAE is typically large, where having nine or ten siblings is the norm. The tension experienced between Rawda and her son in Example 6.37 reminds us of Mills' study (2004) where British-Pakistani mothers spoke of their children's embarrassment over them speaking Punjabi in the English-dominated setting of the UK, saying 'be quiet because everyone else is listening' (p. 178). Also, in Dovchin's (2019) study with Mongolian mothers living in Australia, feelings of shame over the first language were passed on to the children due to the Mongolian language being viewed as 'not necessary' and 'of no value' (p. 13). Accounts such as these, not only in the UAE context but in many other English-dominated areas, demonstrate a feeling of shame related to the L1 and local culture and a desire to change, which reminds us again of the final step in Oshba's stairs analogy (Figure 6.5).

To conclude, through analysis of data in this chapter, we can see that various layers of Emirati cultural identities are affected by English, both positively and negatively, leading to complex linguistic and cultural identities where 'wanted not welcome' or 'push-pull' relationships with English are often found. The findings revealed that new hybrid linguistic and cultural identities are emerging, although often not without challenges.

References

Ahmed, K. (2014). Language and identity in education. *The Fifth Annual Gulf Comparative Education Society Symposium Conference Proceedings: Locating the National in the international: Comparative Perspectives on Language, Identity, Policy, and Practice*, 104–111.

Canagarajah, S., & Dovchin, S. (2019). The everyday politics of translingualism as a resistant practice. *International Journal of Multilingualism*. https://doi.org/10.1080/14790718.2019.1575833.

Chianello, J. (1995). The Armani generation. *EYEtalian*, Winter, 14–17.

Clarke, M. (2006). Beyond antagonism? The Discursive construction of new teachers in the United Arab Emirates. *Teaching Education*, 17 (3), 225–237.

Crystal, D. (1997). Vanishing languages. *Civilization*, 40–45.

Cummins, J. (1996). *Negotiating Identities: Education for Empowerment in a Diverse Society*. Ontario, Canada: California Association for Bilingual Education.

Dovchin, S. (2019). Language crossing and linguistic racism: Mongolian immigrant women in Australia. *Journal of Multicultural Discourses*. https://doi.org/10.1080/17447143.2019.1566345.

Findlow, S. (2006). Higher education and linguistic dualism in the Arab Gulf. *British Journal of Sociology of Education*, 27 (1), 19–36.

Garcia, O. (2009). Education, multilingualism and translanguaging in the 21st century. In A. Mohanty, M. Panda, R. Phillipson, & T. Skutnabb-Kangas (Eds.), *Multilingual Education for Social Justice: Globalizing the Local* (pp. 140–158). New Delhi: Orient Blackswan.

Giampapa, F. (2004). The politics of identity, representation, and the discourses of self-identification: Negotiating the periphery and the centre. In A. Pavlenko, & A. Blackledge (Eds.), *Negotiation of Identities in Multilingual Contexts* (pp. 192–218). Clevedon: Multilingual Matters.

Hammine, M. (2019). Our way of multilingualism: Translanguaging to break a chain of colonialism. In C. Seals, & V. L. Olsen-Reeder (Eds.), *Embracing Multilingualism Across Educational Contexts*. Wellington, New Zealand: Victoria University Press.

Holliday, A. (2013). *Understanding Intercultural Communication: Negotiating a Grammar of Culture*. New York: Routledge.

Hopkyns, S. (2014). The effects of global English on culture and identity in the UAE: A double-edged sword. *Learning and Teaching in Higher Education: Gulf Perspectives*, 11 (2).

Janmohamed, S. (2016). *Generation M: Young Muslims Changing the World*. London: I. B. Tauris and Co. Ltd.

Jones, M. C., & Singh, I. (2005). *Exploring Language Change*. New York: Routledge.

Kramsch, C. (1993). *Context and Culture in Language Teaching*. Oxford: Oxford University Press.

Lawrence, M. (2015, July 9). What do Ramadan, Vimto, and 'Game of Thrones' have in common? *Al Arabiya*. Retrieved from: http://english.alarabiya.net/en/life-style/art-and-culture/2015/07/09/What-do-Ramadan-Vimto-and-Game-of-Thrones-have-in-common-.html.

Mathews, G. (2000). *Global Culture/Individual Identity: Searching for Home in the Cultural Supermarket*. London: Routledge.

Mills, J. (2004). Mothers and mother tongue: Perspectives on self-construction by mothers of Pakistani heritage. In A. Pavlenko, & A. Blackledge (Eds.), *Negotiation of Identities in Multilingual Contexts* (pp. 161–191). Clevedon: Multilingual Matters.

Modiano, M. (2001). Linguistic imperialism, cultural integrity, and ELT. *ELT Journal, 55* (4), 339–346.

Mullis, I. V. S, Martin, M. O., Foy, P., & Drucker, K. T. (2012). *PIRLS 2011 International Results in Reading*. Retrieved from: http://timssandpirls.bc.edu/pirls2011/international-results-pirls.html.

Orellana, M., Ek, L., & Hernandez, A. (1999). Bilingual education in an immigrant community: Proposition 227 in California. *International Journal of Bilingual Education and Bilingualism, 2* (2), 114–30.

Porzucki, N. (2016). *I'm Arab but I Don't Speak Arabic.* Retrieved from: www.pri.org/stories/2016-11-14/im-arab-i-dont-speak-arabic.

Romaine, S. (2008). Linguistic diversity, sustainability, and the future of the past. In K. A. King, N. Schilling, L. W. Fogle, J. J. Lou, & B. Souku (Eds.), *Sustaining Linguistic Diversity: Endangered and Minority Languages and Language Varieties* (pp. 7–21). Washington: Georgetown University Press.

Rubdy, R. (2016). *Cultural Globalization and Changing Perspectives on English as an International Language.* Paper presented at the Third International Conference on Language, Linguistics, Literature and Translation – Connecting the Dots in a Glocalized World, Sultan Qaboos University, Muscat, Oman.

Rubdy, R., & Alsagoff, L. (2014). The cultural dynamics of globalization: Problematizing hybridity. In R. Rubdy, & L. Alsagoff (Eds.), *The Global-Local Interface and Hybridity* (pp. 1–14). Bristol: Multilingual Matters.

Seymour, J. (2016). *Supporting Bi-Literacy Among Emiratis in Dubai's Private Schools: An Analysis of Current Arabic Language Policy.* Doctoral module assignment, University of Bath, UK. Retrieved from: https://bath.academia.edu/JoanneSeymour.

Taha-Thomure, H. (2019). Arabic Language education in the UAE: Choosing the right drivers. In K. Gallagher (Ed.), *Education in the UAE: Innovation and Transformation* (pp. 75–93). Singapore: Springer. doi:10.1007/978-978-981-13-7736-5_5.

Tomlinson, J. (1999). *Globalization and Culture.* Chicago: Chicago University Press.

Tse, L. (1998). Ethnic identity formation and its implications for heritage language development. In S. Krashen, L. Tse, & J. McQuillan (Eds.), *Heritage Language Development* (pp. 15–29). Culver City: Language Education Associates.

7 English Medium Instruction – Sociolinguistic Implications

'IELTS, I see it as a future killer' – marriage, jobs, university, travel all depend on it.

— Maha (26-year-old Emirati university administrative assistant, *pseudonym used)

In Emirati higher education, there is currently almost no choice but to study in the Medium of English (EMI), which is extreme in terms of language policies worldwide. In almost all English medium universities there are entrance exams, and usually this exam is the International English Language Testing System (IELTS). The opening quote in this chapter was said with a sigh of frustration by one of the Emirati administrative assistants in my department as she prepared for yet another try at gaining the IELTS band score necessary for acceptance onto her planned English medium Master's program. Equally, the Emirati university students and Emirati primary school teachers in the study depend on achieving a Band 5.5 and Band 6.5, respectively. The gatekeeper function and 'Wasta-like' status given to English (as tested through IELTS) and dire consequences of not achieving the required level affect not only Emiratis' academic careers and job choices but also their sense of self-worth and identity. As formal education occupies a large percentage of childrens', teenagers', and sometimes adults' lives and undoubtedly shapes minds, learning in the medium of English has multiple sociolinguistic implications. While EMI as a phenomenon has been on the rise globally, it has been identified as an under-researched area by the International Research Foundation (TIRF). This underlines the need for investigating the sociolinguistic implications of the phenomenon in various contexts. The chapter thus investigates key areas relating to EMI in the UAE such as perspectives on medium of instruction, teachers' linguistic backgrounds, and cultural content of courses. Answers to the questions 'Which medium? Which teachers? Which content?' are sought.

7.1 English Medium Instruction, Arabic Medium Instruction, or a Choice?

When asked about preferred medium of instruction, Emirati university students' responses varied, with the most popular options being a choice between 'EMI and AMI' or 'just EMI'. 'Just AMI' was chosen by less than a quarter of the students (Figure 7.1).

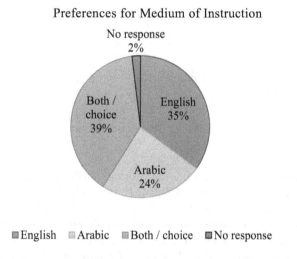

Preferences for Medium of Instruction

⬛English ⬛Arabic ⬛Both / choice ⬛No response

Figure 7.1 Emirati University Students' Medium of Instruction Preferences

The expatriate teachers were also asked to share their perspectives on medium of instruction in UAE higher education. Just over half of the expatriate university teachers (55%) felt that students should be given a choice to study through Arabic or English (a dual stream approach), or both mediums should be used. The expatriate teachers mainly commented on the benefits of EMI (55%), with some pointing out negative aspects (37.5%), and 20% taking a philosophical attitude to the phenomenon, stating they had no control over it or no strong feelings about it. The Emirati primary school teachers were not asked directly to comment on preferences for medium of instruction in higher education as they were only temporarily studying at the university. As primary school teachers, they were asked to comment on EMI in schools, however.

Both EMI and AMI Preference: 'A Balance is Good'

As seen in Figure 7.1, having both English and Arabic as a medium of instruction was the preference of most Emirati university students. Here the importance of both languages was recognized. Some stated a preference for the use of EMI for all subjects except Arabic and Islamic studies, which is the current practice. This supports findings in Chapter 5 where English is associated with education and Arabic with religion. Shamma's comment in Example 7.1 demonstrates such a division. Other participants protested the current 'choiceless choice' (Troudi & Jendli, 2011, p. 41) of EMI in Emirati higher education. As Troudi and Jendli (2011) point out, 'being a speaker of Arabic, an Emirati has no choice but to study his/her chosen university subjects in English. This is now a taken-for-granted reality and an uncontested practice in many Arab countries' (p. 41). In Example 7.1, Amina argues the injustice of this, stating that Emiratis should have the right to learn in both English and Arabic.

Example 7.1

Mix. For example, Arabic and Islamic in Arabic and others in English.
(Shamma, Emirati university student)

Both, because it's our rights.
(Amina, Emirati university student)

*Pseudonyms used for all participant names

Both Emiratis and expatriates stressed the need for choice and balance in relation to medium of instruction. Words such as 'balance', 'equal', 'choose', and 'choice' were frequently used, as seen in Example 7.2.

Example 7.2

A balance is good. If they have a balance it would be good.
(Alya, Emirati university student)

We should let students choose if they want to study major in Arabic or English.
(Sultan, Emirati university student)

I think it would be good if English was equal to Arabic.
(Nejood, Emirati university student)

A choice is always better. Choice.
(Graeme, UK)

I'd support a dual stream approach so some students could do their degrees in Arabic.
(Thomas, UK/Canada)

It was voiced that rather than being given a choice to study in English, it had been imposed on them and feelings of obligation and resulting resentment were present, as seen in Example 7.3.

Example 7.3

I feel that if the English language was not imposed on us in education and other things, I think it would be better.

(Layla, Emirati university student)

I don't like it because it is imposed on us.

(Alia, Emirati university student)

I am here because I am obliged, I don't have any the choice, nobody asked me whether you want to come here or not, you know. I'm happy to be here to study and develop my language but I have to choose.

(Khadija, Emirati primary school teacher)

An overall preference for choice regarding medium of instruction was also found in previous studies such as O'Neill's study (2014) where the majority of Emirati university students stated a preference for studying in English and Arabic equally (377 respondents, or 60.22%) 'over any other option' (p. 11). A move towards bilingualism in higher education was also found to be desirable in Belhiah and Elhami's study (2015, p. 17), in which 62% of the university students stated a preference for English and Arabic instruction.

EMI Preference: 'English is More Demanded'

A testament to the power of English in the UAE is that the second most popular preference for medium of instruction was learning solely in English (EMI). Despite the strong personal accounts relating to the fear of society losing the Arabic language (as seen in Chapter 6 of this book), on an individual level, the benefits of EMI seemed to overshadow such concerns. The primary reason for choosing EMI was its power in terms of accessing the job market and communicating in international business settings, as shown in Example 7.4. The necessity of English was described by many expatriate teachers as a 'necessary evil' and there being 'little alternative' due to its role as the world's lingua academia. Others, selfishly, felt it provided jobs for 'native-speaker' teachers, and it was 'too late' to turn back (Example 7.5).

Added to the power, prestige, and usefulness of English, further factors such as negative AMI learning experiences and the fact they had become accustomed to learning in English added to this preference.

Example 7.4

English, it's more demanded.
(Muna, Emirati university student)

You'll have a job. If you are in a meeting in a job I don't think any-one will talk Arabic, there's Egyptian, there's Indian, there's Emirati, there's Germany, they will not talk Indian, Arabic, they will talk all English.
(Sara, Emirati university student)

Most of the companies, ninety percent of the companies, they need English.
(Fahad, Emirati university student)

Example 7.5

English is the language of professional publications, textbooks, work environments, etc. If Emiratis want to be a part of this 'world', they, like every other country these days, require English as a tool.
(Alice, USA)

There's little alternative. Arabic medium education cannot offer any-thing like a comparable body of literature and is not suited to a num-ber of disciplines like Business. The nature of private institutes in the Gulf, whereby English is the medium of communication even among Arabic speakers, also means education has to be in English.
(Alexander, UK)

In this sense, EMI represents a 'chicken and egg' situation. The global status of English encourages more EMI to be used, resulting in greater comfort and confidence using English, which may lead some to prefer EMI over using local languages as the medium of instruction. Coleman (2006, p. 4) names this process, 'the Microsoft effect: once a medium obtains a dominant market share, it becomes less and less practical to opt for another medium, and the dominance is thus enhanced'. Simi-larly, Beacco and Byram (2003, p. 52) refer to this as 'a self-reinforcing upward spiral' operating in favour of English in education. Such a phe-nomenon is reflected in Example 7.6.

Example 7.6

English. It's much easier. I got used to it since high school. Everything was in English except Arabic and Islamic studies.

(Taif, Emirati university student)

English, because it is easier. At the same time, English is developing/ evolving/ progressing.

(Hamad, Emirati university student)

Hamad's comment in Example 7.6 reflects common language ideologies voiced by Emirati participants in Chapter 5 of this book where English is seen as part of the future, whereas Arabic is less flexible and associated with the past. With reference to the Microsoft effect of English (it has become the norm, so therefore the preference), Rahma speaks of her little brother's international school where English is the only way he can communicate with classmates and teachers (Example 7.7). In this sense, he has become used to using English and given the choice would probably rather 'carry on as normal' (in English).

Example 7.7

I go to their class, maybe five or six Emirati kids and all from the other countries. That's why they will talk Arabic with whom? Like even the teacher is English.

(Rahma, Emirati university student)

Preferences for EMI also related to associated teaching styles and nationality of teachers. Foreign teachers using English were desired due to their more innovative teaching style, as voiced in Example 7.8.

Example 7.8

In English, of course, because it helps me get educated and more thoughts and ideas.

(Maitha, Emirati university student)

The English way for the major. I think it's better than the Arabic because boring style for the study. The English has some fun and be better thinking.

(Masood, Emirati university student)

AMI Preference: 'Some Talented Mathematicians may be Poor Linguists'

Although only 38% of the Emirati undergraduate participants stated they would prefer to study in the medium of Arabic (Figure 7.1), reasons given for this choice were potent. These reasons included greater understanding, increased confidence and comfort, and the ability to be more creative in one's first language, as voiced in Example 7.9.

Example 7.9

I will be a creator and not afraid of things like grammar and vocabulary.
(Nouf, Emirati university student)

When you study your major in your own language, you will innovate more.
(Faiza, Emirati university student)

It makes us more comfortable.
(Yaseem, Emirati university student).

The expatriate teachers also pointed out that the extra cognitive load placed on students when studying through EMI was an 'unnecessary burden' (Example 7.10), especially considering the wide linguistic gap between English and Arabic. The fact that English uses an entirely different script and does not possess full one-to-one symbol-sound correspondence (Baker, 2017, p. 294) makes it 'phonologically opaque' (Cook & Bassetti, 2005, p. 7) and particularly difficult for Arabic learners. This, according to Baker (2017), together with other linguistically distant features, 'poses an additional load in an already challenging linguistic context . . . and may limit bi-literacy success' (p. 294).

Example 7.10

The impact (of EMI) is huge as creativity and research is very challenging in a foreign language.
(Youseff, Tunisia)

It has unnecessarily burdened students with years of extra study, and they end up being less literate in English and Arabic as a result.
(Abdulla, Canada)

Expatriate university teachers further questioned the logic and fairness of EMI as a gatekeeper to academic success, stating that it often caused 'untold suffering' in the form of a host of hurdles and obstacles placed in students' way. Expatriate teachers commented that not all students are natural language learners, and English should not be a barrier to success for those who struggle with the language, as seen in Example 7.11.

Example 7.11

(EMI is) unnecessary and possibly imperialistic. It causes the students untold suffering.

(Wendy, USA)

Some talented mathematicians may be poor linguists.

(Grace, UK)

English acts as a gatekeeper to students who may be bright, but not good language learners. Ideally, there would be other options for these kinds of students.

(Bella, UK)

Many of the students would probably be more successful if they were able to study their courses in Arabic, as this would allow them to focus on new content and ideas without the burden of having to operate beyond their level of linguistic ability.

(Janet, UK)

I heard them, especially boys, complaining so many times about the necessity of being good at English in order to do well in schools. English has put off so many of my Emirati students from pursuing their studies.

(Youseff, Tunisia)

EMI: Too Much, Too Early

The Emirati primary school teachers voiced concerns over the young age (four or five years old) at which EMI begins in the UAE, saying it is 'too much, too soon' causing students to become confused and for their first language to suffer, as seen in Example 7.12.

Others pointed out introducing EMI for all core subjects from the beginning of schooling was a policy which jarred with successful and established bilingual education models elsewhere, such as in Finland and Canada. As Lin and Man (2009) point out, the New School Model (NSM), as described in Chapter 2 of this book, is quite different from the prototypal models such as the Canadian school immersion model, where

---

Example 7.12

They started teaching (in English) from the KG and they still don't know their language, so when they introduce them to teach them English and Arabic in the one time, writing and reading in one time, that affects them in a bad way. Now in our schools, I taught Grade 5, I find that students, my students, wrote English from right side to left side and wrote Arabic from left side. That makes things confused and make the words like a reflection. When you write a word and put it in the mirror, you see the word in the mirror.

(Salwa, Emirati primary school teacher)

---

bilingual education is an elective choice made by middle-class parents. It is also unlike the selective approach in Hong Kong where only the academically skilled are selected according to examination results for bilingual education (Lin & Man, 2009). In contrast, all families whose children attend Abu Dhabi state schools do not have the choice of partial immersion (Baker, 2017, p. 291). As well as lack of choice, the UAE's approach is also more extreme regarding the age at which EMI is introduced. Malaysia's EMI policy (Swee Heng & Tan, 2006) and Brunei's (Lin & Man, 2009) also teach the 'hard or core subjects' of English, Mathematics, and Science in English but starting later in elementary school. In these countries too, English teachers are most often bilingual. However, in the UAE, the English-speaking teachers, unless newly qualified Emiratis, are usually not speakers of Arabic. Further challenges arise for Emirati families who are not always proficient in English as they struggle to support their children in the medium of English at home (Blaik Hourani et al., 2012), which was evident in the personal accounts of family rifts shared in the study, as seen in Chapter 6 of this book.

7.2 Importance of Teachers' Linguistic Backgrounds

The phenomenon of EMI is not only about the language of instruction. It also relates to the teachers who are hired to teach both content and language through the medium of English. Issues such as 'native-speakerism' (Holliday, 2006) as well as 'monolingual/bilingual teaching' become central to explore in EMI contexts, in terms of pedagogical and sociolinguistic implications.

The Emirati cohort were asked if they had preferences regarding the nationality of their English teachers. In the questionnaire, many different nationalities were provided as choices and participants were asked to tick as many boxes as they wished. The choices included English 'native-speaker' nationalities, their own nationality, other Arabic-speaking nationalities, and other European and Asian nations. There was also a space to include further desired nationalities (Table 7.1).

Table 7.1 Emirati Preferences for the Nationality of English Teachers

Nationality of English Teacher	Emirati University Students (%)	Emirati Primary School Teachers (%)	All Emirati Participants (%)
USA	78	42	74
UK	74	50	71
Canada	62	58	62
Australia	40	25	38
UAE	38	33	37.5
Germany	24	0	21
China	4	0	4
India	2	0	2
Egypt	2	0	2

Other Answers: Emirati university students – Russia, South Africa, anywhere, Africa (6%), Emirati primary school teachers – in general any person who has English as a second language (8%)

As can be seen in Table 7.1, there was a strong preference for English 'native-speaker' teachers especially from Britain, Australia, and North America (BANA). The fifth most popular choice was Emirati teachers. German teachers came next with India, China, and Egypt being relatively unpopular choices. The focus group sessions allowed both Emiratis and expatriates to reflect on the importance of EMI teachers' nationalities and linguistic backgrounds.

The Native-Speaker Fallacy in Full Swing: 'For Me Only UK or USA'

Shaped by the dominant ideology of monolingualism (Kinginger, 2004, p. 222) and the globally-entrenched 'native speaker (NS) fallacy' (Phillipson, 1992), which results in the belief that monolingual NSs intrinsically make the best language teachers, the findings showed an overwhelming preference for native-speaker (NS) teachers from Britain, Australia, and North America (BANA) (Table 7.1). In the focus groups, many made quite definite statements such as 'For me only UK or USA' (Fahad, Emirati university student). When probed for reasons, Emiratis voiced preferences for 'exonormative models' (models from outside) as opposed to 'endonormative' (models from within) (D'Angelo, 2014, p. 222) due to the perception that BANA teachers speak 'good, exact and right' English and that 'original English' is the best model, as seen in Example 7.13.

The belief that real or legitimate English is British or American standardized English, and that the most appropriate teacher is a 'native speaker' of English, privileges Western culture and can be described as 'white-dominant epistemological racism' where Eurocentric and US-centric beliefs are observed (Kubota, 2019). Expatriate teachers, from mainly BANA countries, were aware of their privilege in the eyes of the students. They commented on the respect students had for 'NS' knowledge of the language and desirable accents.

Example 7.13

Most of foreign people in our school now are from Canada and Britain. They are the most perfect English teacher because they talk the original language.

(Salwa, Emirati primary school teacher)

It should be original English.

(Reem, Emirati university student)

Especially British. I love to learn British accent.

(Alyazia, Emirati university student)

Some also commented on cultural aspects of their nationalities being appealing to students (Example 7.14).

Example 7.14

As a native speaker, I have the advantage of being/appearing an expert.

(Russell, Australia)

I think it has been an advantage. Emirati students seem to respect and listen and want to learn from American or Western English-speaking teachers in general.

(Henry, USA)

Advantage as a representative culture for English-speakers and therefore with some 'authority' when it comes to language teaching.

(Mary, Australia)

Students respect my knowledge of grammar and pronunciation.

(Grace, UK)

I think it has been an advantage in terms of how we are perceived by Emirati students. It is the one field in which they feel Emiratization would not work! They want to have native English teachers teaching them, and many young Emiratis students have often mentioned the value of acquiring a British/ USA etc. like accent.

(Carl, UK)

I think Emiratis, especially boys, like American things, cars, movies, food – many travel there – advantage!

(Jim, USA)

Not only were 'native-speaker' (NS) teachers placed on a pedestal but also 'non-native-speaker' (NNS) teachers were often ridiculed. It was voiced that NNS teachers, especially from India, Egypt, and China, were undesirable due to their accents and that having an Arabic-speaking teacher would tempt them to use Arabic more than English and as a result they would not be challenged enough (Example 7.15).

Example 7.15

Teachers from Africa or India, they have the language better than us but not like the original so the students will learn better from the British and Canadian.

(Shaikha, Emirati university student)

If they are from Chinese, they eat some letters.

(Najood, Emirati university student)

Some Egyptian guys say instead of 'the', 'ze'. So, when it is in your mind it's all 'ze' not 'the'.

(Abdul, Emirati university student)

If she is Arabic maybe sometimes she will talk Arabic with us and we will talk also Arabic, you know. And we should speak English. No Arabic.

(Reem, Emirati university student)

Expatriate teacher Joe's (Canada) experience in Example 7.16 supports the findings from the Emirati focus groups, where often non-native-speaker accents are mocked openly, in sharp contrast to the desirable British and North American accents.

Example 7.16

There was this video my students loved to show me of an Egyptian teaching English and they thought it was hilarious and they were making fun of the Egyptian English accent and I think it was supposed to be in Saudi, it was a cartoon and they thought it was absolutely hilarious. Teacher, teacher look and basically the gag was how these Egyptian English teachers are terrible because they have this particular accent and students thought it was funny. So, there is a perception among students that the accent matters.

(Joe, Canada)

Although a minority of expatriate teachers felt Emirati students attached 'more importance to a teacher's personality, enthusiasm and a positive learning environment' (Alina, UK), a majority reflected on witnessing the 'native speaker fallacy' where native speakers are automatically seen as better language teachers due to country of origin alone. In Example 7.17, the difficulty of combating the NS fallacy is commented on as well as negative images of Arab teaching styles confounding a preference for BANA teachers.

Example 7.17

If they have choices (NS vs NNS teachers), they will choose those (NS teachers) because it's in their heads.

(Sebastian, UK)

There is an association of Emirati teachers having a stick in their hands and you know, their understanding of Emirati teachers is different.

(Yonka, Turkey)

The expatriate teachers also commented on a larger-scale form of favouritism for BANA teachers with regard to hiring practices. Trevor (UK) went so far as to say being a native-speaker teacher was not just an advantage in the region, it was 'a prerequisite'. Joe (Canada) stated that although the merits of bilingual language teachers are well known amongst educators, 'institutionally at a macro level there is still a preference for Western'.

A further form of favouritism observed by the expatriate teachers related to race. As there is also a connection made between English and 'whiteness' (Copland et al., 2016, p. 9; Javier, 2016, p. 233), non-white teachers, regardless of first language, are often discriminated against. As Holliday and Aboshihia (2009, p. 669) point out, 'a growing number of teachers and researchers claim that there is a hidden racism within TESOL professionalism which is directed at so-called non-native-speaker teachers'. This does not apply to the same extent with European NNS teachers who often get NS jobs due to 'looking the part' (Holliday, 2008, p. 122). Although race was not mentioned as a factor when it came to preferences for English teacher nationality amongst the Emirati cohort, the fact that there was a far stronger preference for teachers from Germany than other NNS countries such as India, Egypt, and China, indicated perhaps an association made between 'whiteness' and English. Without probing further, however, one cannot be sure this was the case. From the perspective of the expatriate English teachers, however, English tended to be strongly connected to a certain 'image' which included being Caucasian. Teachers commented on past experiences of the racialization of English, as seen in Example 7.18.

Example 7.18

There was a Nigerian lady who trained on the CELTA at the British Council when she was with us and then when she started teaching, the students were up in arms, because A) she's black and B) she's not British, her accent is not British. Or not American or whatever.

(Tabitha, UK)

In Korea, they would complain, you know there were a lot of complaints if you weren't from the United States, Australia or the UK and you didn't look the part.

(Anna, USA)

In other global contexts such as Japan, similar incidents of racial discrimination have been found. For example, native English-speaking American teachers of Japanese descent working in Japan have experienced marginalization and discrimination (Kubota & Fujimoto, 2013), and according to an experimental study investigating Japanese university students' preferences for English teachers, the white race was significantly favoured (Rivers & Ross, 2013).

The Benefits of Teachers and Students Sharing Language and Culture

Although from Table 7.1 and Examples 7.13–7.18 it appears that the native-speaker fallacy is thriving in the UAE, in the Emirati primary school teacher focus groups, future goals seem to be focused on moving away the hiring of BANA teachers and towards the hiring of bilingual Emirati English teachers. The Emirati primary school teachers had high expectations for the next generation of Emirati teachers. It was hoped that future Emirati teachers would have excellent English, presumably due to the NSM running its course, thus being able to replace expatriate native-speaker English teachers (Example 7.19).

Example 7.19

I think also our generation depends on the new generation. The new generation is fluent talking in English and excellent and everything, and academic words they have it already. I think most of Emiratis, the new generation, their goals or objectives are more than bachelors. It's in Masters also and PhD at the moment, so I think they have a confidence to teach English in the future more than us as we are not established in a new technology and new media so they contact easily in English. The accent, they have everything that qualifies them to teach English in the future.

(Lubna, Emirati primary school teacher)

It was also felt that Emirati teachers would be desirable due to greater cultural understanding and their ability to act as role models (Example 7.20) for the students. It was voiced that by having Emirati teachers, 'we can save our culture' (Anood), 'she's attractive for the students' (Lubna), and 'it's not only a person or a device or the medium to talk in English it's a whole person itself so I prefer to be totally Emirati'(Khadija).

Example 7.20

I have an Emirati English teacher in my friend's school, all of the teachers are from foreign countries. Just one Emirati, she's teaching maths, English and science. She's a role model for Emirati teachers, teaching English and teaching math and science also. For example, when the visitors come to the school, the principal is American, she takes the visitors to this class because it's a model class. It's showing the school as a model school. When you saw other classes it's just foreign people teaching English.

(Lubna, Emirati primary school teacher)

Expatriate university English teacher participants also commented on the benefits of students and teachers sharing a language and culture. For example, with reference to his own language-learning experience, Sebastian (UK) stated a preference for being taught by a bilingual teacher who spoke his own language as well as the target language (Example 7.21).

Example 7.21

I loved French at school and I remember it really annoyed me when we had to go, when we had a teacher who only spoke in French, we had an actual, a proper French teacher. Before we always had an English guy and he taught and spoke French and I really enjoyed it. I was good at it as well and as soon as it went to that I just felt some frustration and a bit of resentment and that was it for me. Then my French just kind of, that was it. I remember thinking to myself, I actually loved it when I felt like I could communicate quickly with my teacher and he could help me.

(Sebastian, UK)

Cultural and linguistic barriers were also recognized by the expatriate teachers as being a salient negative aspect of teaching in the UAE. As Syed (2003, p. 339) states, 'Linguistic and cultural distance between learners and teachers is a serious factor in the Gulf EFL classroom'. Not speaking Arabic disadvantaged the expatriate teachers in many ways, as seen in Example 7.22.

Example 7.22

This (being a non-Arabic speaker) limits my ability to explain things at times.

(Russell, Australia)

Not knowing much Arabic makes me a bit less effective when teaching to a class who all share the same L1.

(Joanna, USA)

Feelings of 'us and them' and 'insider/outsider' dichotomies as well as being treated as 'just the hired help' were expressed (Example 7.23). Such feelings are perhaps amplified due to social stratification reversing traditional teacher-student power dynamics in the Emirates. Expatriate teachers are usually on temporary contracts (usually three or four years) and these contracts rather than being 'employment contracts' are essentially 'life contracts' as almost everything related to living is included in the package from housing, health insurance, children's school fees, annual travel expenses to the home country, and many other benefits. As an expatriate teacher colleague of mine casually commented, 'when you live in the Emirates, your job is your life'. This makes expatriate teachers fearful of cultural misdemeanours and the prospect of being deported as a result. The temporary nature of expatriate work can also lead students to view their expatriate teachers as 'hired help' rather than respected professors. Expatriate teachers in Hudson's study (2019, p. 255) reported that rather than being respected on the grounds of authority, skills, and knowledge, they felt 'disposable' as if they were 'second-class citizens', 'paid employees', and 'glorified housemaids' whose survival as a teacher depended on lax attendance monitoring and gaining high student evaluations. In this sense, while Emiratis are very much supported and secure in their country, their teachers are in a far less 'powerful' position. This phenomenon is commonly referred to as wearing 'golden handcuffs' as teachers' lack of power in the classroom is challenging but at the same time walking away is difficult for financial and lifestyle reasons. Such power relations between Emirati students and expatriate teachers can accentuate the 'us-them' dynamic, as voiced in Example 7.23.

Example 7.23

(I feel) disadvantaged as a non-Arabic 'outsider' who is less accepted, doesn't belong and hasn't a real stake in this country: just the 'hired help'.

(Mary, Australia)

> *I often feel there is a 'him and us' feeling in the class, a wall between the students and me. I think a native Arabic speaker, preferably Emirati, would be able to get closer to the students than I can.*
>
> (Vincent, UK)

> *Sometimes a distinct disadvantage. Not knowing their culture means I have made plenty of gaffes, and assumed things that might be true in my culture that are not actually true here.*
>
> (Lisa, New Zealand)

> *I think being a native-speaker of Arabic can help teach certain things better. I think a language teacher MUST be bilingual.*
>
> (Yousef, Tunisia)

Martin (2003) had a similar feeling to the teachers in Example 7.23 when teaching in UAE higher education. She states, 'Accustomed to being spoon-fed, students often treated teachers as paid servants' (p. 52). This could partly be attributed to social stratification and a 'servant culture' in the UAE. It also could be associated with students' perceptions of their expatriate teachers as lacking investment in Emirati education due to cultural and linguistic divisions.

A further factor which affects the 'us and them' feeling mentioned by many participants is the rentier nature of the Gulf States (Minnis, 2006) which serves to 'distort the relationship between educational achievement and financial reward' (Calafato & Tang, 2019, p. 137). Especially amongst male Emiratis, living in a patriarchal, rentier society that expects males to financially provide for their families (Abdullah & Ridge, 2011), academic success tends to be undervalued as it is often not as easy or as useful as *Wasta* for securing financial success (Alsheikh & Elhoweri, 2011; Jones, 2011). Such an attitude undermines the value of the mainly expatriate teaching force, in general.

Despite the cultural and bilingual advantages Emirati English teachers may have, teaching as a profession thus far has not been a popular local choice, partly due to its lack of prestige and comparatively low salaries, as explained in Chapter 3 of this book. To attract more Emiratis to the profession, with the aim of replacing foreign teachers, local newspaper *the Gulf News* (24 June 2012) recently announced that there would be a salary increase for government teachers 'in recognition of the critical role played by teachers in a nation's development' (Baker, 2017, p. 291). Whether this will be enough of an incentive remains to be seen.

7.3 Which English?

A further factor influencing EMI university education in the Gulf is the cultural content of courses, which has both pedagogical and sociological implications in terms of learning and belonging. After having discussed views on English teacher nationality, both Emirati and expatriate cohorts were asked to comment on preferences concerning the cultural content of English lessons. When asked if English was connected to Western culture, 97% of the expatriate university teachers agreed and many felt they, as teachers, represented the broader values of Western culture such as freedom, democracy, equality, and tolerance (Example 7.24). Others felt due to being global citizens, having mixed backgrounds, or having lived abroad for a long period, they were able to teach neutrally. Example 7.24 shows comments from the expatriate teachers on how English and Western culture are connected.

Example 7.24

I think the two (English and Western culture) are inseparable, especially with the rise of the internet, and the fact that so much information is presented in English, and student interest in Western culture.

(Alan, UK)

A lot. From Chaucer to Fast & Furious 7.

(Scott, UK)

Since English originated within a Western cultural setting, I think they are very connected. British colonialism and American superpower status did the rest.

(Heidi, Belgium /Australia)

Very much, despite it being used all over the world and being at least a secondary official language in parts of Asia and Africa, etc. It carries with it the baggage of colonialism and imperialism.

(Bella, USA)

During the focus group discussions, the Emirati primary school teachers felt very much that teachers carried cultures which influenced learners, going so far as to say, 'this teacher *is* a culture' (Khadija). It was felt that it was not only direct instruction that teachers gave but also other factors such as way of dressing which influenced learners. Diallo (2014, p. 3) agrees with this view, when stating:

The imported Western-trained language teachers in the UAE, like any other teachers elsewhere, are far from 'neutral'. They are highly positioned even before they enter local classrooms, given that they embody Western Judeo-Christian epistemologies, liberal views and secular traditions.

In other global contexts, English is also associated with Western culture. For example, in Selvi's (2019, p. 150) survey with teacher educators in Turkey and Northern Cyprus, two out of every three participants associated English with inner-circle countries and the cultures of inner-circle countries.

Perhaps to be expected from Emirati participants who generally favoured NS English teachers, there was a great interest in learning about Western culture as part of an English course with 75% of primary school teachers and 68% of university students wanting this (Figure 7.2).

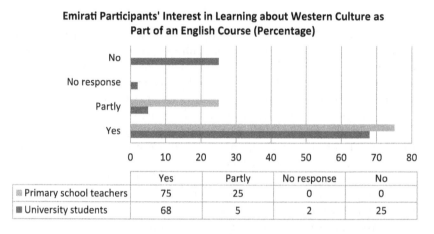

Emirati Participants' Interest in Learning about Western Culture as Part of an English Course (Percentage)

	Yes	Partly	No response	No
Primary school teachers	75	25	0	0
University students	68	5	2	25

Figure 7.2 Emirati Interest in Learning About Western Culture as Part of an English Course

'Putting a Frame' on Western Culture

The main reason given for interest in 'Western culture' as part of an English course was wanting to know how to deal with Westerners in order to interpret actions or 'put a frame on their culture'. Many gave general reasons such as a desire to learn as much as possible about a variety of topics, rather than specifically wanting to know about Western culture as indicated by responses such as 'why not?' (Example 7.25).

Example 7.25

It will help me to interpret their action, life style and it will help me to put a frame for their culture.

(Naeema, Emirati student)

When you know their culture, you know how to deal with them.

(Shamma, Emirati student)

> *Why not? It's interesting! Because I want to know more about how they think.*
>
> (Hafsa, Emirati university student)
>
> *Our Prophet Muhammad is pushing us to learn the other languages because it is easier to communicate. You can't live isolated in this world.*
>
> (Oshba, Emirati primary school teacher)

In Example 7.25, we see that religion was also given as a reason for wanting to know more about Western culture. For example, Oshba refers to Prophet Muhammad's wish for Muslims to learn new languages. Scholars have recognized the effect of religious *hadiths* (words of Islamic Prophet Muhammad) on attitudes towards language learning and gaining of knowledge. For example, Morrow and Castleton (2011, p. 329) point out, the Prophet taught Muslims to 'seek knowledge from the cradle to the grave' and Karmani (2005, p. 739) points out the importance of the *hadith* 'learn the language of your rivals (or others)'. In fact, Mahboob and Elyas (2014, p. 133) state that the similar *hadith*, 'he whoever learns other people's language will be secured from their cunning' is used as a motto by many English language centres in the neighbouring Kingdom of Saudi Arabia (KSA) to promote the study of English.

Intercultural Pragmatics

Others felt it was primarily important to show an interest in Western culture or the culture of their teacher to be respectful and make their teacher feel happy. Some were keen to point out that they were open to learning about Western culture if this were a choice, but not by force, and comments were made regarding cultural respect not being one-sided but rather reciprocal, as voiced in Example 7.26.

Example 7.26

> *It's okay for me but I prefer to make choice so if I want to learn about British or American culture, better give students choice. If we like we will learn, if not, so we have a choice.*
>
> (Sultan, Emirati university student)
>
> *It's better if they (expatriate teachers) also learn the Arabic language.*
>
> (Masood, Emirati university student)

The Emirati primary school teachers discussed the importance of inter-cultural pragmatics when learning a language, which refers to the way language is used in social encounters between people with different first languages who communicate in a common language, and usually represent different cultures (Kecskes, 2014, p. 15). It was deemed important by group members to understand English 'native-speaker' culture to show respect and understanding of cultural differences (Example 7.27).

Example 7.27

Respect, for example. How they show respect, for example. What specific phrases to use. For example, if I have to write a formal letter, for example apologize, we have to know what words they use. Maybe if I translate it from my own language word by word, it will be incorrect but if I know what they say and what's the proper way of saying or apologizing or saying thank you for example, that would help me.

(Lamya, Emirati primary school teacher)

Like we cannot travel without a male, like a father or a brother or a husband. If you are a Western woman, she can go anywhere by herself. They are more open than us. They can sit with a big group of males but in our culture we cannot. . . . In her culture that's fine but in my country it's not appropriate so my way of seeing her will not be negative, I will respect what she is doing and know that in her society that's fine, so it will be fine.

(Rawda, Emirati primary school teacher)

In contrast to Figure 7.2, where we see most Emiratis expressing an interest in learning about Western culture as part of an English course, the expatriate teachers perceived a general lack of interest, feeling that any interest was a 'nicety' rather than genuine (Example 7.28), which perhaps, consciously or unconsciously, deepened feelings of 'us and them' in the view of the teachers.

Example 7.28

I think some of the nice students I have might say, 'have a nice Christmas' as they are going out of the room but it's not like they are saying 'oooo what are you going to do', it's like they want to say it, they want you to have a nice time. It's not like they want to know exactly what I'm doing because I'll say to them, 'Eid Mubarak' and stuff like that. So maybe, you know it's an extension.

(Sebastian, UK)

Rather than showing curiosity about holidays, expatriate university teacher focus group members shared personal accounts of students showing curiosity about the negative and controversial cultural topics, or 'the decadence' (James, Australia) of Western culture, such as alcohol, drugs, and dating before marriage. We can see in Example 7.29, Joe recounting Emirati high school students he taught previously asking about drug addiction.

Example 7.29

It's the negatives of Western culture which they were curious about. They asked about drug use which they'd seen in movies in the West and I don't know, they don't understand the difference between socio-economic classes and all that kind of stuff.

(Joe, Canada)

Sebastian (UK) pointed out that although students may appear disinterested in Western culture, in general, if the topic has to do with the teacher's specific experience, interest is higher. He gave a personal account of such an instance in Example 7.30.

Example 7.30

Suicide came up once and there's a place where I'm from in East-bourne where basically, Beachy Head, a lot of people jump off. And the word just happened to come up and I said well this is where I'm from and they were really interested in it and I don't know, it wasn't so much that it was England, I think it was the concept at the time and because it relates to me as well.

(Sebastian, UK)

Looking to Asia

Rather than being interested in Western culture, which some found hard to distinguish from global culture, many Emirati university students stated a preference for learning about culture associated with Asian countries such as Korea, Japan, or China. Both Emiratis and expatriates commented on this, as seen in Example 7.31.

Figure 7.3 shows one of many 'Asian festivals' at the university in which the study takes place, which is what Rachel (UK) refers to in Example 7.31.

Example 7.31

I don't have interest in American or British culture, and I don't think there's an American/British culture that people will get interested about but I will love to learn Chinese or Korean culture.

(Hind, Emirati university student)

It's interesting because some other cultures are promoted in the university. I mean there's been a big focus on Korea. There've been various exhibitions downstairs and you know and language classes offered for free and come and learn about Korean culture, and I think that's kind of interesting.

(Rachel, UK)

Figure 7.3 Asian Culture Day at the University

Photograph by the author

There was a feeling amongst expatriate teachers that perhaps Asian cultures were viewed as less threatening, as accessing them was optional rather than obligatory in the case of English. Western culture associated with English could also be seen as anti-Islamic due to the complex history between the USA and Muslim countries, especially with Trump in power at the time of the study (Example 7.32).

> ### Example 7.32
>
> *Probably subliminally that message has been passed through through-*
> *out their childhood that it's very important to keep their culture*
> *distinct and separate and not to be influenced by cultures which are*
> *non-Islamic.*
>
> (Rachel, UK)
>
> *The West and how it is seen here is very different from, and I mean*
> *Korea might be more Catholic than the pope, some Koreans, but still,*
> *they don't get that, they think the values and morals in Korea are*
> *similar to their values if that makes sense.*
>
> (Yonka, Turkey)

Finally, a minority of Emirati undergraduate students who were not interested in learning about Western culture as part of an English course felt they knew about Western culture through movies and media, and they only wanted English for a future job. Expatriate English university teachers could also understand this view, stating that there were more important aspects of English courses, such as skills development, especially in an academic setting.

Think Globally, Teach Locally

After discussing interest in Western culture as part of an English course, participants were asked to comment on course content with regard to local vs. global topics. The majority (60%) of expatriate university English teachers felt English should be taught through a mixture of local and global topics. This desire to include the local and the global as part of course content is supported by Mahboob and Elyas (2014, p. 134) who recommend teachers 'think globally and teach locally'. Here English can be used functionally and pragmatically to think globally, but used, by choice, to live or teach locally, thus establishing a pragmatic link between the two identities (Narasimhaiah, 1991).

Local Topics: Connecting Information With Real Life

Previous studies support the notion that English can effectively be taught through local topics which tend to increase interest, engagement, and ownership (Gobert, 2014, p. 101). Many expatriate teachers stated that it was better to start with local topics and expand to global topics as students' level of English improved, as voiced in Example 7.33.

Example 7.33

Local topics provide a global springboard to go from familiar (local) to unfamiliar (global). It may lower cognitive load enabling them to focus on their language.

(Grace, UK)

Reducing the cognitive load, increasing the relevance and interest level, and avoiding many global topics which are 'taboo' in the Gulf context were further reasons given for emphasis on local topics (Example 7.34).

Example 7.34

I think that we are restricted greatly in terms of the topics that can be taught by external factors. Therefore, I think it makes more sense to teach English based on local topics.

(Carl, UK)

With reference to Carl's comment in Example 7.34, certain topics such as 'pets' (especially dogs as pets) and 'music' are considered 'haram' (religiously prohibited) in the Arabian Gulf. As teachers in the Gulf receive relatively little sociocultural training, they may be unaware of such taboos, and only learn which topics to avoid through trial and error. Freimuth (2014, p. 189) gives an example of when a number of students in her UAE university class refused to read a passage on people's love of dogs. Anecdotally, the topic of women doing cardiovascular or endurance sports tends to be disapproved of due to being considered unladylike, which I learned the hard way when sharing pictures of my first half marathon with groups of female classes. Similarly, teachers who choose to use songs as a teaching tool may receive complaints or have students walk out of the room and teachers doing practice IELTS exams may have students refusing to discuss the topic of music, which often occurs in Part 1 of the test. However, as Hudson (2019) points out, far from being a 'monolithic block', topics which offend some are embraced with curiosity by others.

Besides using local topics as a way of avoiding culturally taboo content, from the Emirati primary school teachers' point of view, local topics are helpful in the English classroom due to their relevance to real life as seen in Example 7.35.

Example 7.35

I think instead of having birthdays if we have, for example, about National Day and what do we wear and what's the traditional customs, in English, the kids will learn as well as it can be. . . . They are already learning the word, for example, dress and if it connected with our local dress and the shape of it or. . . . Connecting the information with the real life, this is very helpful. It will be very helpful for the students.

(Lamya, Emirati primary school teacher)

As seen in the opening quote in the chapter, the IELTS test is often unpopular with Emiratis who may encounter a double challenge in mastering not only the English language but also unfamiliar Western-biased content. According to Freimuth's (2016b) study, 65% of locations mentioned in the IELTS tests are situated in the English-speaking West. In addition to this, Western cultural objects and political/historical settings are predominant including Western idioms and cultural references such as *Holy Grail, Agatha Christie, igloos, canary in a mine,* and *gone off the boil.* Freimuth (2016a, p. 165) argues that the lens that frames IELTS is essentially Western, in that the designers of the exam and the test-writers originate from the West who employ their own Western-dominated perception of literacy to create the exam resulting in a 'one size fits all' mentality. The Emirati primary school teachers, who were on a sabbatical to take an intensive IELTS course at the university at the time of the study, expressed wishes that the high-stakes English tests be more locally relevant and indicated if this were the case, they would perhaps perform better and feel more comfortable. Canadian teacher, Abdulla, also comments on the extra challenge presented when students are faced with unfamiliar topics (Example 7.36).

Example 7.36

If it (data in IELTS test) is about our country it will be familiar for us so we can write about it. But another data maybe we don't have ideas about it. It will help us write.

(Seeta, Emirati primary school teacher)

If we talk about Task One (IELTS), if it was a process about something related to our culture like making yogurt, for example, most of us will know the process. We know the equipment, what it is called. It's related and interesting.

(Bashayer, Emirati primary school teacher)

> *Many texts rely heavily on culturally-specific knowledge. For example, I remember one IELTS-type listening text on the topic of Venice sinking. If you've never been to Venice, it would be very difficult to understand, and not just because of the language.*
>
> (Abdulla, Canada)

Such unfamiliar culturally-inappropriate content in the IELTS test has led many to push for an alternative more locally appropriate English test or to question the UAE's country-wide EMI policy in higher education, where so much rests on English proficiency and achieving a certain IELTS score.

Global Topics: 'You Don't Want to Feel Stupid When You Go Outside'

The main reasons for including global topics in English courses included the need to use English as a global language, to succeed in international exams such as IELTS, and not to heavily rely on Arabic words as tends to be the case when discussing local topics, due to no direct English translation. It was also commented on that local topics had been 'done to death' or 'over-emphasized' at school. University English courses should progress to global topics, it was felt by some (Example 7.37).

Example 7.37

> *Students don't want to learn about kanduras and abayas and local food because they've done that to death in high school.*
>
> (Joe, Canada)

> *It is necessary to use non-local topics with our students because of IELTS and because we want them to be globally aware.*
>
> (Rebecca, USA)

Despite comments made earlier about the Western-centric and challenging content of international English tests, some Emirati participants were resigned to the fact that global topics were likely to continue to dominate international tests and many desired world knowledge and ideas to become globally aware and succeed in international settings, as voiced in Example 7.38.

Example 7.38

You don't want to feel stupid when you go outside
(Nejood, Emirati university student)

If you ask about the issues, like vandalism, something that is new to our culture, I never mind to have some idea about this thing. So, when I travel, I have background about their culture. But about occasions, I don't think because we have occasions from our culture.
(Anood, Emirati university student)

Moving Forward

We can see from the data in this chapter that English Medium Instruction as it currently exists is not meeting the needs and wishes of many stakeholders. We see again the notion of 'wanted not welcome', which is present in relation to English in general society, also being applicable to English Medium Instruction in higher education. While EMI is wanted for the opportunities it presents, it is not entirely welcome due to its enforced nature and its gatekeeper status. Although Emiratis mainly want native-speaker teachers from BANA countries thus indicating monolingual and 'native-speakerism' ideologies, these teachers are not fully welcome due to cultural and linguistic divisions. Finally, the findings in this chapter suggest a preference for including both local and global topics in English courses rather than the current situation where Western-biased course content and assessments dominate.

References

Abdulla, F., & Ridge, N. (2011). *Where are all the Men? Gender, Participation and Higher Education in the United Arab Emirates.* Dubai: Dubai School of Government.

Al-Sheikh, N. O., & Elhoweris, H. M. (2011). United Arab Emirates (UAE) high school students' motivation to read in English as a foreign language. *International Journal of Language Studies, 5* (4), 53–68.

Baker, F. (2017). National pride and the New School Model: English language education in Abu Dhabi, UAE. In R. Kirkpatrick (Ed.), *English Language Educational Policy in the Middle East and North Africa* (pp. 279–300). Cham, Switzerland: Springer International Publishing.

Beacco, J., & Byram, M. (2003). *Guide for the Development of Language Education Policies in Europe: From Linguistic Diversity to Plurilingual Education.* Retrieved from: www.coe.int/t/dg4/linguistic/Source/FullGuide_EN.pdf.

Belhiah, H., & Elhami, M. (2015). English as a medium of instruction in the Gulf: When students and teachers speak. *Language Policy, 14,* 2–23.

Blaik Hourani, R., Stringer, P., & Baker, F. (2012). Constraints and subsequent limitations to parental involvement. *School Community Journal, 22* (2), 131–160.

Calafato, R., & Tang, F. (2019). Multilingualism and gender in the UAE: A look at the motivational selves of Emirati teenagers. *System*, 84, 133–144.

Coleman, J. A. (2006). English-medium teaching in European higher education. *Language Teaching*, 39, 1–14.

Cook, V., & Bassetti, B. (2005). An introduction to researching second language writing systems. In V. Cook, & B. Bassetti (Eds.), *Second Language Writing Systems* (pp. 1–67). Clevedon: Multilingual Matters.

Copland, F., Davis, M., Garton, S., & Mann, S. (2016). *Investigating NEST Schemes Around the World: Supporting NEST/LET Collaboration Practices.* London: British Council.

D'Angelo, J. (2014). The West/East paradigm and Japan's NS propensity: Going beyond the 'friendly face' of West-based TESOL. In R. Marlina, & R. A. Giri (Eds.), *The Pedagogy of English as an International Language: Perspectives from Scholars, Teachers, and Students* (pp. 221–237). Switzerland: Springer International Publishing.

Diallo, I. (2014). Emirati students encounter Western teachers: Tensions and identity resistance. *Learning and Teaching in Higher Education: Gulf Perspectives*, 11 (2).

Freimuth, H. (2014). *Cultural Bias on the IELTS Examination: A Critical Realist Investigation.* Unpublished Doctoral dissertation, Rhodes University, Grahamstown, South Africa.

Freimuth, H. (2016a). Revisiting the sustainability of the IELTS examination as a gatekeeper for university entrance in the UAE. In L. Buckingham (Ed.), *Language, Identity and Education on the Arabian Peninsula* (pp. 161–175). Bristol: Multilingual Matters.

Freimuth, H. (2016b). An examination of cultural bias in IELTS Task 1 non-process writing prompts: A UAE perspective. *Learning and Teaching in Higher Education: Gulf Perspectives*, 13 (1), 1–16.

Gobert, M. (2014). *Language Learner Literature and Identity.* The fifth Annual Gulf Comparative Education Society Symposium Conference Proceedings: Locating the National in the International: Comparative Perspectives on Language, Identity, Policy, and Practice, 95–103.

Holliday, A. (2006). Native-speakerism. *ELT Journal*, 60, 385–387.

Holliday, A. (2008). Standards of English and politics of inclusion. *Language Teaching Journal*, 41 (1), 119–130.

Holliday, A., & Aboshiha, P. (2009). The denial of ideology in perceptions of 'nonnative speaker' teachers. *TESOL Quarterly*, 43 (4), 669–689.

Hudson, P. (2019). A gin and tonic and a window seat: Critical pedagogy in Arabia. In M. E. Lopez-Gopar (Ed.), *International Perspectives on Critical Pedagogies in ELT* (pp. 241–263). New York: Palgrave Macmillan. http://doi.org/10.1007/978-3-319-95621-3_12.

Javier, E. (2016). 'Almost' native speakers: The experiences of visible ethnic-minority native English-speaking teachers. In F. Coupland, S. Garton, & S. Mann (Eds.), *LETS and NESTS: Voices, Views and Vignettes* (pp. 233–245). London: British Council.

Jones, C. W. (2011). *Economic, Social, and Political Attitudes in the UAE: A Comparison of Emirati and Non-Emirati Youth in Ras Al Khaimah.* Ras Al Khaimah: Sheikh Saud bin Saqr al Qasimi Foundation for Policy Research.

Karmani, S. (2005). TESOL in a time of terror: Toward an Islamic perspective on Applied Linguistics. *TESOL Quarterly*, 39 (4), 738–744.

Kecskes, I. (2014). *Intercultural Pragmatics*. New York: Oxford University Press.

Kinginger, C. (2004). Alice doesn't live here anymore: Foreign language learning and identity reconstruction. In A. Pavlenko, & A. Blackledge (Eds.), *Negotiation of Identities in Multilingual Contexts* (pp. 219–242). Clevedon: Multilingual Matters.

Kubota, R. (2019). A critical examination of common beliefs about language teaching: From research insights to professional engagement. In F. Fang, & H. P. Widodo (Eds.), *Critical Perspectives on Global Englishes in Asia* (pp. 10–26). Bristol: Multilingual Matters.

Kubota, R., & Fujimoto, D. (2013). Racialized native-speakers: Voices of Japanese American English language professionals. In S. A. Houghton, & D. J. Rivers (Eds.), *Native-Speakerism in Japan: Intergroup Dynamics in Foreign Language Education* (pp. 196–206). Bristol: Multilingual Matters.

Lin, A., & Man, E. (2009). *Bilingual Education: Southeast Asian Perspectives*. Hong Kong: Hong Kong University Press.

Mahboob, A., & Elyas, T. (2014). English in the Kingdom of Saudi Arabia. *World Englishes*, 33 (1), 128–142.

Martin, A. (2003). An experience of teaching in the United Arab Emirates. *English Today*, 19 (2), 49–54.

Minnis, J. R. (2006). First Nations education and rentier economics: Parallels with the Gulf States. *Canadian Journal of Education*, 29 (4), 975–997. http://doi.org/10.2307/20054207.

Morrow, J. A., & Castleton, B. (2011). The impact of global English on the Arabic language: The loss of the Allah lexicon. In A. Al-Issa, & L. S. Dahan (Eds.), *Global English and Arabic* (pp. 307–334). Bern, Switzerland: Peter Lang.

Narasimhaiah, C. D. (1991). *N for Nobody: Autobiography of an English Teacher*. New Delhi: B. R. Publishing Corporation.

O'Neill, G. T. (2014). Just a natural move towards English': Gulf youth attitudes towards Arabic and English literacy. *Gulf Perspectives*, 11 (1), 1–21.

Phillipson, R. (1992). *Linguistic Imperialism*. Oxford: Oxford University Press.

Rivers, D. J., & Ross, A. S. (2013). Idealized English teachers: The implicit influence of race in Japan. *Journal of Language, Identity, & Education*, 12, 321–339.

Selvi, A. F. (2019). Walking the talk but not walking the walk? Preparing teachers for global Englishes pedagogy. In F. Fang, & H. P. Widodo (Eds.), *Critical Perspectives on Global Englishes in Asia* (pp. 10–26). Bristol: Multilingual Matters.

Swee Heng, C., & Tan, H. (2006). English for mathematics and science: Current Malaysian language-in-education policies and practices. *Language and Education: An International Journal*, 20, 306–321.

Syed, Z. (2003). The sociocultural context of English language teaching in the Gulf. *TESOL Quarterly*, 37 (2), 337–341.

Troudi, S., & Jendli, A. (2011). Emirati students' experiences of English as a medium of instruction. In A. Al-Issa, & L. S. Dahan (Eds.), *Global English and Arabic* (pp. 23–48). Bern, Switzerland: Peter Lang.

8   New, Not Less – Embracing Complexities, Multiplicities, and Hybridity

It is normally supposed that something always gets lost in translation;
I cling, obstinately, to the notion that something can also be gained,

– Rushdie (1991)

Far from English being viewed as entirely negative, as the headlines at the start of this book would have the reader believe, local cultural identities are affected by English and accompanying culture on many levels and in multiple ways. It is clear from the findings that Emirati cultural identities are indeed multifaceted, socially-constructed, fluid, dynamic, and drenched with complexity. How Emiratis position themselves and are positioned by others are continually being molded and remolded according to different contexts and interaction. Depending on the context and interaction, certain aspects of identity receive greater levels of acceptance and value. For example, English-speaking aspects of identity are highly valued at university for access to future jobs and in many public domains. Positioning oneself as a confident English-speaker in such contexts leads to personal pride and acceptance from certain others such as teachers. In this sense, English is very much 'wanted'. Similarly, positioning oneself as an Arabic-speaker (Emirati dialect) in other contexts such as the home or with Emirati family and friends leads to greater levels of inclusion and acceptance. Here we see interculturality 'as doing' helps us to understand the complexities within cultural identities as we see how different aspects of identities are more salient according to the context, domain, or interaction patterns, thus emphasizing the plurality and fluidity within identity construction.

From the findings, we see that tensions arise mainly when reflective positioning (how one sees one's self) is at odds with interactive positioning (how one is seen by others). For example, young Emiratis may feel confident in speaking English and perhaps dressing in Western clothes at home as well as public places, but they may be positioned negatively by those seeing this behaviour as a betrayal of what it traditionally means to be Emirati. This was a scenario which often arose in the data.

The findings also revealed the dynamic nature of bicultural and bilingual identities. Tensions between self-chosen identities and interactive positioning were shown to lead to a lack of acceptance in both traditionally Arabic-only contexts (e.g., home) and English-only contexts (e.g., university). What has arisen from such tensions is hybridity where there is a need to create something new that is theirs alone. This can take the form of linguistic hybridity such as code-switching, translanguaging, and Arabizi, or cultural hybridity, where a new twist is added to a tradition (e.g., using social media to show henna designs), as mentioned by multiple participants. How such hybridity is viewed, however, varies according to individuals. In the case of the Emirati participants in this study, such linguistic hybridity was mainly seen to be negative, thus reflecting dominant 'double monolingual ideologies' in the region. Cultural hybridity was accepted or celebrated by some but opposed by others. In the concluding chapter of this book, three main suggestions are put forward in order to address key issues arising from the study:

1. Placing emphasis on a discourse of balance and inclusion
2. Greater acceptance of hybridity over purity
3. Changing the nature of English Medium Instruction as it currently exists

8.1 Discourse of Balance and Inclusion

Since the formation of the nation in 1971, striking a balance between maintaining traditions and embracing change has been an ongoing challenge for the UAE. Experiencing 'acute self-consciousness' (Findlow, 2005, p. 287) in its early years and being torn between looking inward 'in contemplation of the term "indigenous"' (Findlow, 2005, p. 287) and outward in terms of dramatic expansion with foreign influence, it is easy to see how mixed feelings over the pace of development and amount of English persist. Kazim (2000, p. 434) names three types of discourses in the present-day UAE: conservative, progressive, and moderate. The first aims to preserve past patterns, the second to embrace globalization, and the third to strike a balance between the first two. The results from the study reflect these discourses with an overall dominance for the third discourse involving a balance. The study also showed that this balance, especially in terms of Arabic and English, is not currently being addressed.

In order for Arabic to stay important, valued, and dynamic in the future, it is important to challenge the contrasting ways English and Arabic are currently viewed. It is clear that English is not, and cannot be, 'just a language' due to its overwhelming presence in multiple spheres of the Emirati participants' lives. English and its accompanying 'cultural tsunami', as Hatherley-Greene (2014, p. 2) powerfully describes it, dominate multiple domains. As explained in Chapter 2, sipping a coffee in a

Café Nero or *Costa Coffee* in one of Abu Dhabi's many shopping malls, positioned with a view of the shops, the vast majority of the words one sees are in English. The same can be said when sitting in one of Abu Dhabi or Dubai's many hospital waiting rooms. It is not Arabic, but English, that is heard in conversations between doctors, nurses, patients, and receptionists. This is not only an observation of the author who could perhaps be said to have 'a special eye or ear' for her own native language, English. Emirati participants commented on the dominance of English in public places throughout the study, which became especially noticeable when travelling to other countries where this was not the case, such as China. This sends out a strong message that Arabic is not important or necessary in public places, as was commented on by multiple participants in the study.

With regard to the image of Arabic and English, it is important for Arabic to be spoken, out of choice and with pride, by role models in the region. As Said (2011) comments with regard to the situation currently:

> Role models give the overall impression, even if unintentional, that Arabic is not important and neither is learning it. The people feel that using English presents them as sophisticated individuals and that Arabic has a place only in religion and religious discourse and not in everyday 'worldly' life.
>
> (p. 203)

This was commented on at length by Emirati participants, especially during the male university student focus group. Having clear role models such as leaders and actors using a high standard of Arabic and choosing to do so over using English would be an effective way to encourage another view of Arabic amongst the next generation. In the world of literature and research, the same applies. For example, Emirati sci-fi novelist Noura Al Noman sums up the difficulty Arabic writers face by stating, 'Too many young adults are abandoning Arabic literature and exclusively reading English; my six kids and I are a case in point'. When asked whether her latest book would be available in English, she honestly responded, 'If an English version is published I suspect no one will bother to read the Arabic' (Holland, 2014). Making Arabic the official language in 2008 has had little effect if everywhere one goes in the UAE speaking English is necessary to survive. In response to this, Said (2011, p. 205) suggests that Arabic needs to be the public language just as English is in multicultural Britain and America. This would certainly pave the way for the desired balance to be achieved. However, this should happen in a way that does not promote negative attitudes towards English or frame English as an enemy. Rather than sharp divisions such as 'only Arabic/ no English allowed' discourses or 'culture wars' (Kachru, 2017) that tend to emerge from current Arabic language initiatives (see Chapter 3), recognition and acceptance of linguistic multiplicity and cultural complexity would be a more effective way to prevent Arabic attrition and cultural fragility. Allowing both languages to be strong and complementary should be the focus.

Hand in hand with strengthening Arabic amongst Emiratis comes the need for the promotion of Arabic amongst the UAE's expatriate majority population. This would further serve to combat feelings of linguistic and cultural fragility. As Al-Issa and Dahan (2011, p. 18) explain, at present:

> The many foreigners, who come to the UAE to work, do so based on the knowledge that when they work here the language they will use will be English. Very few, if any, take the time to learn the language of the country: Arabic.

This includes the all too often main caregivers of Emirati children, nannies. Although often Arabic classes are provided free of charge to expatriate workers and parents (see Chapter 3), such classes tend to be short and infrequent. It is easy for expatriates to find more important priorities in their busy working weeks when knowledge of the language is not currently needed to live a full life in the UAE. Providing such classes, while a step in the right direction, may be too little, too late as once settled in the UAE, it is quickly apparent that attendance of such classes relies on interest rather than necessity. Making knowledge of Arabic a basic requirement before arrival would be more effective. This could be achieved by making an elementary-level Arabic language certificate a stipulation in employment contacts. Learning Arabic would also benefit expatriates in terms of building a deeper connection with the country. At present, the expression 'expat bubble' is commonplace in the UAE and relatable for most foreign residents. As Coleman (2006) suggests, without knowing and using the language of the country one is inhabiting, one spends this time 'as tourists, skimming the surface of their host country, without deeper involvement' (p. 9). In the field of education, Burkett (2016, p. 10) suggests simple 'classroom Arabic' training for expatriate teachers which would expose teachers to the language they might hear in the classroom. This would also act as 'a gateway into further study of Arabic' (Burkett, 2016, p. 10). Emirati participants in the study at various points stressed they would very much welcome their expatriate English teachers taking a step such as this.

Not only the majority expatriate population but also Emiratis themselves need to intensify efforts to strengthen the Arabic language in the form of concrete action rather than merely 'policy talk' (Aydarova, 2012, p. 285). In Mouhanna's UAE-based study (2016) investigating perspectives of university content teachers on EMI, particularly Arabic-speaking teachers commented on the need 'to apply real and practical measures, beyond lip service, to the preservation of Arabic in the academic sphere in the UAE' (p. 204). As seen from the findings of the study, there appears to be a mismatch between ideals and reality. The need to strengthen the Arabic language was frequently mentioned throughout the study, especially for the next generation. Yet when asked about which language they would prefer as the medium of Emirati tertiary education, Arabic was the least popular choice after 'both English and Arabic' and 'only English' and when asked about the importance of English the response was unanimously affirmative.

A further example of a discrepancy between words and actions relates to clothing choices. Many participants saw Western clothes as a negative effect of English or Western culture and indicated it was a cause for concern, yet in the male university student focus group, participants openly discussed their personal preferences for Western clothing while wearing T-shirts adorned with English slogans. Relating to Arabic loss, Said (2011) stresses the need for actions to match words or sentiments, when stating:

> The Gulf Arabs themselves must believe that Arabic as a language is their language and instead of expressing dissatisfaction that they are losing the language, they should make efforts at both individual and group levels to promote the use of Arabic.
>
> (p. 204)

To change attitudes towards Arabic and for it also to be connected with education and the wider world, greater effort needs to be channelled into including local culture in education and teaching Arabic well. Ahmed (2011) suggests:

> When all that is around one is seemingly foreign, as is increasingly the case in the UAE and many of the Gulf countries, any mention of one's own culture, no matter how simple, may help to maintain it. Issues such as student vulnerability, personal worth, and alienation need to be examined.
>
> (p. 131)

Currently, there appears to be a disconnect between goals and reality in this area too as often local themes are minimally or superficially present in the curriculum structures. Rather than using excessive censorship to remove Western cultural content which Hudson (2012) warns can result in 'dull, anodyne lessons that are demotivating for both teachers and students' (p. 16), adding local cultural content would be preferable. Scotland (2014, p. 36) argues that, 'English language teaching pedagogy needs to be decentered; it needs to adopt a local approach'. In this sense, English needs to be modified and used on local learners' own terms and needs. This could be achieved through the use of regionally themed textbooks, which are becoming increasingly popular, and by using local newspapers in lessons, and centring projects around relevant and culturally accessible topics. Steps in this direction are already happening. In 2016, the Abu Dhabi Education Council (ADEC) spearheaded the 'Haweyati Program' (My Identity Program) which covers topics such as culture, society, values, Arabic, citizenship, and history. It was successfully piloted in 50 private schools in Abu Dhabi and has now been introduced in all schools (Zaman, 2017).

Steps also need to be taken to counter the current gatekeeper status of the IELTS exam, which, as discussed in Chapter 7, is viewed by many as culturally inappropriate, cripplingly powerful in Emirati society, or even 'a future killer'. This is especially true for the vast majority of Emirati female university students who will not have the opportunity to study abroad where IELTS is a necessary qualification, due to cultural constraints. Freimuth (2016, p. 172) suggests, 'A better-more local-solution needs to be found to address this dilemma of assessment'. This could involve, commissioning IELTS to 'create a localized version of their exam where test-writers collaborate with local education experts to inform them of the topics and skills needed to operate in an academic English-medium learning environment in the UAE' (Freimuth, 2016, p. 172). Since the completion of the study, the Ministry of Education has created the Emirates Standardized Test (EmSAT) as a measure of students' English proficiency. However, IELTS continues to run alongside this exam and in fact the university in which the study takes place has expanded its involvement with IELTS to the point where it has become an official testing centre for both students and members of the public.

The study revealed many negative learning experiences connected with the way Arabic is taught in schools. Addressing this would boost interest in Arabic as a language of education. Badry (2011) comments on the current discrepancy between the quality of English and Arabic teaching by stating:

> For Arabic to remain part of the identity of young and future generations in the UAE (and elsewhere in the Arab world), the same efforts exerted in teaching English must be brought to bear in improving the teaching of Arabic.
>
> (p. 112)

Often demotivating authoritative and rule-based ways of teaching are found in many Arabic language classrooms (Taha-Thomure, 2008, p. 191). These experiences result in negative stereotypes of Emirati teachers, or Arabic teachers in general, with 'a stick in hand' as stated by expatriate university teacher, Yonka (see Chapter 7). To tackle such negative stereotypes, Taha-Thomure (2019) has identified seven very worthwhile ways in which the teaching of Arabic could be strengthened. Firstly,

Taha-Thomure (2019) suggests increasing the time allocated to Arabic, especially in private schools where Arabic is treated as a 'special subject' rather than a medium of instruction, and where lessons do not exceed 45 minutes. Secondly, increasing the rigour is needed as many parents of non-native learners say their children study Arabic for years without being able to fluently speak, read, or comprehend. Thirdly, leadership practices need to be addressed as in most private schools, the leadership teams are non-Arabic speaking Westerners who are unable to direct the learning of the language in a meaningful way. Fourthly, currently in private schools, Arabic is not integrated into other areas of school life such as music, newsletters, artwork, etc. Changing this dynamic would alter the perception that Arabic is just a subject. Fifthly, improving the quality of Arabic teachers is held necessary. Currently, there is a large divide between highly-qualified English teachers often recruited at international job fairs, and under-qualified Arabic teachers who are hired locally after an Arabic language test and a short interview. The sixth change needed according to Taha-Thomure (2019) is an improvement to the quality of Arab language curricula. Most curricula available in schools are textbook based without innovative digital resources. Finally, more professional development needs to be provided for Arabic-language teachers in the region. Taha (2017) explains that most of the training takes place in English, or not at all. Following these steps with regard to the teaching of Arabic in schools would, Taha-Thomure (2019) argues, 'propel forward a field that has been stagnant for decades' (p. 7).

In addition to improvements to the quality of Arabic teaching in schools, Seymour (2016) argues that the home environment is also key to fostering strong Arabic language skills through 'Family Language Planning' (p. 9). As stated by multiple Emirati participants, this is often a struggle, especially for the younger generation who often prefer to use English over Arabic, even at home. Starting early and at home is even more essential given that the main concern shown in the study was not Arabic loss amongst the Emirati participants (aged between 18 and 58) so much as Arabic loss amongst the younger generations. To address this concern in a practical and concrete way involves parents, teachers, and society as a whole investing in Arabic as a language of the future. However, this should not be in the form of 'Arabic only' house rules which leave children feeling obliged or under pressure to use the language in the same way children feel they must eat their vegetables. Such 'all or nothing' methods tend to be counterproductive. Rather, a flexible attitude towards bilingualism is required as elaborated on in the following section.

8.2 Hybridity Over Purity

It is important to challenge the perception by some, as seen in the study, that English is subtractive. As English shows no sign of retreating in the

Gulf countries due to its gatekeeper status, Belhiah and Elhami (2015, p. 21) stress the importance of Emiratis seeing it as 'an ally to Arabic' rather than a competitor. Instead of viewing English as an aggressor, as was seen in the many newspaper headlines at the start of this chapter, scholars such as Pennycook (2010) and Canagarajah (1999) see English as 'too complicated to be considered benign or evil' (Block, 2004, p. 76). In this sense, English is viewed as a 'Hydra-like language' having many heads, representing diverse cultures and linguistic identities (Kachru, 2006, p. 446). To utilize this characteristic of English, Holliday (2014, p. 1) suggests students use their existing cultural experience to 'stamp their identities on English' rather than carrying the 'common anxiety that English represents a culture which is incompatible with their own'.

There are, indeed, authentic and visible signs of this happening in the region, despite the binary positions of English and Arabic promoted by local journalists. Hybridized forms of English and Arabic are being used inside and outside the classroom. For example, it is common to hear 'Allah Lexicon' (Morrow & Castleton, 2011, p. 307) punctuating conversations in English. Arabic words such as *Yani* (I mean), *Insh'Allah* (God willing), and *Wallah* (I promise) are very much a feature of local English conversations as well as more substantial code-switching or translanguaging. Indeed, numerous examples were given of such hybridity by participants in the study (Chapter 6) as well as examples of translanguaging and *Arabizi* (use of English letters and numbers to represent Arabic sounds) being used in popular culture (such as T-shirt designs as seen in Chapter 3). Here, we see the lines between the languages blurring. Distinct linguistic identities are starting to form where linguistic repertoires rather than individual languages are used. As Kramsch (2018) states, 'There is no doubt that translingual practices are as genuine, authentic, and natural as the monolingual practices of the now outdated monolingual native speaker' (p. 26).

The 'ordinariness' of linguistic hybridity in multilingual contexts has been recognized by many scholars (Blommaert, 2015; Canagarajah, 2013; Dovchin, 2017; Dovchin & Lee, 2019; Kramsch, 2018). As Dovchin and Lee (2019, p. 2) state, 'there is nothing exotic, odd, or perhaps even "exciting" about linguistic creativity'. However, despite the commonplace nature of translingual practice, Emirati participants in the study mainly expressed negative attitudes towards such practice, especially in the case of the Emirati primary school teachers. For example, the use of *Arabizi* was viewed as a form of English pollutant to the Arabic language, and many expressed wishes for the languages to be used in isolation, such as Arabic at home, and English at the university. Such viewpoints reflect dominant monolingual ideologies in the region. Findings from other studies in the UAE echo such attitudes. For example, in Palfreyman and Al-Bataineh's (2018) study Emirati university participants used the words 'wrong', 'inarticulate', and 'disaster' to describe mixing languages, thus seeing translanguaging as a bilingual deficit. Translanguaging was seen to violate linguistic integrity and was even called an 'Arab-franko language' (Palfreyman & Al-Bataineh, 2018). Similarly, in Al-Bataineh and Gallagher's study (2018) with Emirati undergraduates majoring in Education, a strong objection was expressed to the use of translanguaging in storybooks for young learners, where Emirati undergraduates 'were ambivalent if not downright hostile' (p. 12) towards its use for ideological, linguistic, and pedagogical reasons. Although, in today's age there is prestige attached to being multilingual due to the recognized cognitive benefits that can accrue as well as multilingual practices 'having become the hallmark of people living in a network society' (Kramsch, 2018, p. 25), such prestige does not appear to extend to linguistic hybridity. As the mixing of languages in multiple ways is seen as above all else 'creative', Gramling (2019) points out that the question 'is creativity viable?' runs through the minds of many. In this sense, linguistic hybridity may be viewed as experimental or exciting in informal social settings but due to institutionalized monolingualism (as discussed in Chapter 3) it remains taboo or unfeasible in more formal contexts such as university classrooms.

To combat such beliefs, many scholars (Buckingham, 2015; Davies, 2006; O'Neill, 2016; van den Hoven & Carroll, 2016) argue that embracing hybridity and diversity over two 'pure' and separate languages should be encouraged in multiple settings. Van den Hoven and Carroll (2016, p. 54) suggest promoting Arabic languages with a focus on linguistic complexities that exist in the UAE, arguing that although Emirati Arabic is spoken by a minority of the population in the UAE, it is less likely to be threatened by English if it is celebrated and allowed to adapt and change. O'Neill (2016) proclaims that rather than translingual practice such as *Arabizi* being a threat to Emirati Arabic, it 'may be key to its survival' (p. 36). Indeed, the primary aim should be to 'encourage avenues of belonging which are not exclusionary or segregated, and the promotion of identity which values hybridity, not purity' (Davies, 2006, p. 1037).

Such inclusive ideologies, where linguistic hybridity is embraced, can be incorporated into classrooms to benefit students both pedagogically and sociologically. Embracing linguistic hybridity in classrooms 'makes links for the classroom participants between the social, cultural, community, and linguistic domains of their lives' (Creese & Blackledge, 2010, p. 112) and allows teachers to see the world through youths' eyes and create alternative learning opportunities (Dovchin, 2018). By embracing linguistic hybridity, language varieties that learners already have are validated as part of their cultural identities (Kramsch, 2018, p. 27) which is ultimately more 'democratic' (Norton, 2000). In this sense, by using their multilingual resources, learners can 'tap into what they already know about a language to take up, refashion, and personalize their new language' (Schulze et al., 2019, p. 39). Here, affirming learners' full linguistic repertoires serves to provide an empowering education. Further benefits of embracing linguistic hybridity include encouraging reflexivity and appreciation of the nuances of meaning between linguistic systems (Kramsch, 2018). For example, some concepts are not easily translatable and the use of the original word is more precise or culturally appropriate. For instance, the Arabic concept of *Wasta* (a form of social capital or favouritism) is not easily translated into English, nor is the German concept of *Bildung* (educational self-development rather than training). As Heidt (2015, p. 3) explains, *Bildung* (from the German verb 'bilden', to build) is a notion which is unparalleled in other nations and thus has no direct translation into English.

However, supporting the use of translingual practices in the classroom can be challenging for teachers in the face of official or de facto 'English-only' policies, as well as the immeasurable and unknown nature of combining languages in formal teaching and learning. Convincing students who hold entrenched monolingual ideologies to embrace the practice of translanguaging in educational settings can also be a challenge. To combat de facto 'English only' policies, teachers can create a space for translanguaging by becoming bottom-up policymakers in their own classrooms. This can be achieved by recognizing the benefits of translingual practice, and 'purposefully designing and implementing opportunities for using the languages of choice' (Wei, 2017). Hornberger (2005) talks of 'opening and filling up ideological and implementational spaces' where teachers and community members make space for and choose to implement multilingual educational practices and more favourable ideological spaces in the face of restrictive policies. In this sense, classroom instruction can 'affirm students' identities and challenge patterns of power relations in the broader society' (Cummins, 2014, p. 5). If teachers embrace such practice, students' attitudes towards translingual practice in formal settings may follow suit. By taking the initiative of endorsing translingual practice, teachers are effectively 'prestige planning' (Carroll, 2017, p. 178) as they are actively working to change deficit ideologies surrounding the mixing of languages in EMI classrooms. Prestige planning is especially important in post-colonial contexts where such ideologies may be particularly ingrained (Baldauf, 2004; Zhao & Liu, 2010).

In addition to teachers acting as policymakers, research which places a priority on translanguaging through classroom-based investigations should be encouraged as this would give stakeholders insights into how such pedagogies can be implemented in the future (Conteh, 2018, p. 446). Carroll (2017) predicts that the current 'explosion of research' on the benefits of tranlanguaging may have the potential to disrupt monolingual ideologies. An example of an action research project on translingual pedagogy in the UAE can be seen through Steinhagen and Aljanadbah's (2019) study, in which their Emirati university students were given the choice of using Arabic or English for reading academic papers, discussions, and writing. They found the students responded positively to the inclusion of both languages in classroom materials as well as the provision of structured translanguaging spaces. Similarly, in the context of the Dominican Republic, Schulze (2016) found that by incorporating his Spanish-speaking students' love of reggaeton music, they were able to draw on topics and language which were familiar to them with positive learning outcomes. In the context of Puerto Rico, Mazak et al. (2017) successfully used translanguaging to counter hegemonic tendencies of English in higher education, as did Daryai-Hansen et al. (2017) in the context of Denmark.

Schulze et al. (2019) suggest a range of ways translanguaging spaces can be provided in classrooms for the four skills of reading, writing, listening, and speaking. For example, having students read an article in their first language, and then discussing it in the target language or having more proficient English-speakers use their first language to translate words or concepts for peers empowers students to use their linguistic skill sets. For brainstorming ideas and taking notes, using full linguistic repertoires rather than only the target language allows for unhampered creativity. Promoting translanguaging through speaking activities also prevents breakdowns in communication and reduces levels of frustration (Schulze et al., 2019). Using bilingual or translingual texts would also act as a powerful counter-discourse to 'English only' policies. Finally, for linguistic hybridity to be embraced, it needs to be recognized as a 'social fact' (Blommaert, 2019) rather than as taboo. As Makalela (2019) states, simultaneous use of more than one language is normal and should be normalized. Indeed, in the age of superdiversity, monolingualism is the anomaly, rather than multilingualism or translingual practice (Gramling, 2016).

8.3 Rethinking English Medium Instruction as it Currently Exists

Currently, the 'choiceless choice' (Troudi & Jendli, 2011, p. 41) surrounding English as a medium of instruction in Emirati higher education is problematic. EMI as a 'one size fits all' educational policy clearly does not suit all learners' needs, abilities, and wishes. It is suggested here that rethinking EMI as it currently exists is necessary. This involves something larger than changing policies, but rather the underlying ideologies of monolingualism, native-speakerism, and neoliberalism also need to be challenged, as well as placing an emphasis on choice and agency regarding medium of instruction.

Challenging Monolingual Ideologies and Native-Speakerism

The Emirati cohort's general preference for 'native-speaker' teachers and 'native-speaker' models is not unique to the area. This phenomenon, known as the 'native speaker fallacy' (Phillipson, 1992b) or 'native speakerism' (Holliday, 2006), as discussed in Chapter 7, can be seen in many areas of the world. As Sung (2015, p. 43) points out, even in Hong Kong, which is known as 'Asia's World City', native-speaker norms are still entrenched in its ELT practices. In Hong Kong's case this is 'largely owing to its colonial history' (Sung, 2015, 43), but in general, preferences for native-speaker teachers may be related to 'deep-seated stereotypes of non-native varieties of English', as Lippi-Green (2012) theorizes. The perception of 'native speaker' (NS) and 'non-native speaker' (NNS) teachers as different species or that 'native speakers are from Venus (and) non-native speakers are from Mars'(Selvi, 2016, p. 57) is further exacerbated by the labels 'NS' and 'NNS' themselves which, despite much criticism, continue to be the most commonly used terms in the field. These divisive terms clearly disempower NNSs by emphasizing what they lack by the use of the prefix 'non' in the title. Furthermore, as Kubota (2019, p. 14) argues, NNSs are often perceived as a homogeneous group, rather than appreciating that they come from diverse backgrounds with regard to gender, age, nationality, and sexual identity, all of which may impact teaching experiences. Such misconceptions and prejudices overshadow the many advantages bilingual or multilingual language teachers possess.

Phillipson (1992a) points out the irrelevance of the native-speaker ideal in today's era of globalization and superdiversity. Firstly, the NS fallacy dates back from 'a time when language teaching was indistinguishable from culture teaching' (Phillipson, 1992a, p. 13). The primary reason for learning English was assumed to be familiarizing oneself with the culture that English originated from, being able to read its literature, and preparing for contact of some kind with that culture. However, learning another culture is no longer the prime reason for learning English in today's world. As Bailey (2006) points out, in today's world, English is most often used 'to communicate with other non-native speakers rather than with native speakers' (p. 296). This is certainly the case in the UAE. It therefore makes sense to say that adhering to NS norms is 'no longer valid in light of the current demographics of the world's English-using population' (Lowenburg, 2000, p. 67). In fact, in the age of superdiversity, Jenkins (2016, p. 4) states 'Native speakers are at a disadvantage when in a lingua franca situation' due to being less adaptive to different forms of English and using culture-specific idiomatic and 'flowery' language.

Such truths are very much recognized in the world of TESOL as was demonstrated by Silvana Richardson's plenary talk on the NS fallacy at the 50th anniversary IATEFL conference in Birmingham (April 2016), as well as in Garton et al.'s (2016) edited volume which presents a collection of current perspectives on native-speakerism in the final chapter (pp. 247–266) from scholars such as Kirkpatrick, Phillipson, Kramsch, Jenkins, Llurda, Mahboob, and Pennycook, who each discuss the importance of discrediting the automatic view of the 'ideal NS teacher'. However, despite such awareness amongst scholars and researchers, as well as recently-established advocacy groups for NNS teacher rights, universities in the Gulf and worldwide still seem to see NS teachers as a 'better business draw' (Medgyes, 1994, p. 72). This unjust reality was commented on at various points by the expatriate university English teachers in the study.

Rather than placing value on, often non-Arabic-speaking, NS teachers, the strengths of bilingual teachers should be given greater recognition. As indicated previously, rather than speaking one's mother tongue in the English language classroom being viewed as 'interference', multilingualism and translingual practice should be viewed as creative and enabling (Rubdy, 2016). This was emphasized in Deena Boraie's (2015) plenary speech at the *21st TESOL Arabia Conference*, entitled *Shifting Sands of Teaching and Learning English* when she stressed the need to move away from the traditional 'English only: Arabic forbidden' classroom policy and towards one of choice. This clearly points towards the importance of valuing different languages as a rich resource to be drawn upon in the classroom rather than something to be discouraged. This can be achieved by looking beyond Western education models where a 'monolingual lens has been the norm' (Carroll, 2017) and by EMI universities actively hiring teachers who share similar language backgrounds to their students. Carroll (2017) suggests that during the interview phase of the hiring process, linguistic practices be a major consideration.

Providing Choice and Agency Around Medium of Instruction

Continuing with the importance of 'choice', allowing university students to decide whether they complete their degree in English or Arabic would further enhance feelings of ownership. This element of choice, described by university student Amina as 'our right' (Chapter 7), was clearly desired by the majority of participants in the study and is supported by findings from previous research in the region (Belhiah & Elhami, 2015; O'Neill, 2014).

As Findlow (2006, p. 21) states, it is not 'acceptable to force students to study in a foreign language when so much is at stake competitively'. Although, this does not reflect the sentiments of all Emiratis, a choice regarding medium of instruction would overall be welcomed. Numerous alternative suggestions to the current situation were advocated by participants. These were often inspired by looking at other countries' educational policies and included suggestions of a dual stream approach where students could choose either English or Arabic tracks, English electives running parallel to degree courses in Arabic, and certain degrees being taught in particular mediums. Currently, Troudi and Jendli (2011, p. 41) stress the need for EMI to engage in self-criticism, stating:

Without theorization and without awareness of mother tongue and bilingual education, EMI will continue to alienate the very participants it claims to serve and empower in the first place. These are the students who have no right to choose the language of their instruction. Instead of an over-reliance on received knowledge about the status of English and fashionable trends in international education, educationalists in contexts such as the UAE need to consider the quality of the learning experience of the students.

The study's findings certainly support the need for such self-criticism throughout EMI education in the UAE, and particularly in higher education, where little choice exists.

8.4 Conclusion – the Big Picture

This book contributes to a growing body of research on English as a global language and its sociolinguistic implications. While much research exists on multilingualism and translingual practice in superdiverse European migration hubs and Spanish-English educational contexts in the USA, comparatively little research exists on global south or periphery contexts such as the United Arab Emirates. This book has aimed to help fill such a gap by sharing the perspectives of Emirati university students, Emirati primary school teachers, and expatriate university English teachers' on the impact of global English on layers of cultural identity in the UAE. By examining pertinent related topics, the book also provides an extensive account of attitudes towards global English and EMI, as well as how the languages English and Arabic are symbolized.

The main beneficial outcomes of this study have arisen from the varied perspectives presented from three distinct participant groups, which is a feature previous researchers in the region have called for (Solloway, 2016; Mouhanna, 2016). A further strength of the study is the depth of qualitative data obtained and me of detailed personal accounts candidly shared, allowing me to delve deeper into issues previously explored on a more general or surface level. A final strength of the study was the pilot study which greatly helped shape the main study in terms of the design of the data collection tools and recognizing the need for bilingual support.

It is also important to be aware of any inherent limitations. This study was limited by its context-bound nature and its imbalanced number of males and females. Firstly, the current study was conducted only at one state university in Abu Dhabi. The university students were also educated in state schools rather than private schools. Findings from this study should therefore not be interpreted as representative of all Emirati university students, all Emirati primary school teachers, and all expatriate university English teachers in the UAE. Secondly, the Emirati participants were mainly female reflecting the male/female balance at the university, meaning male views were under-represented. This was difficult to avoid due to low numbers of male students enrolled in the foundation program at the time of the study. Based on the study's limitations, several suggestions for further research can be made. Firstly, in order to gain a full picture of the phenomenon of English in the Emirates, it would be beneficial to conduct research country-wide. Furthermore, it would be fascinating to gain the perspectives of an even wider sector of Emirati society. This would involve gaining the views of university students (even number of males and females), university students' parents and grandparents, students and faculty at private universities, and also management. Due to the complexity of the topic under investigation there is a sense that there is still more to explore.

The suggestions made in this concluding chapter are not limited to the UAE context, of course, as the discussion of the effects of English on cultural and linguistic identities in this chapter are relevant to multiple contexts around the world where English plays a major role in society and/or in education. Throughout this book, parallels have been drawn between the context of the UAE and similar scenarios found in other global settings ranging from neighbouring oil-rich Gulf nations, to the Far Eastern metropoles of Singapore and Hong Kong, to Western migration hubs such as the UK, USA, Canada, and Australia. Shared contextual factors between Emiratis' language use in the UAE and those living in diasporic communities were also highlighted in terms of public/private divisions. Furthermore, as has been discussed at various points in the book, the growing phenomenon of EMI globally makes many of this chapter's suggestions highly applicable and relevant to a wide variety of contexts. Although physical distance many separate nations and indeed every context has its own sociolinguist reality, major themes in this book such as the notion of English being 'wanted not welcome', push-pull relationships with English, cultural implications of English, and issues of choice and agency surrounding cultural and linguistic identities are global rather than national issues. It is hoped that the perspectives voiced in this book will be heard not only by fellow scholars but also by educational policy-makers and language-planners. As Ahmed (2014, p. 107) points out, it is often the case that various

> fears and anxieties may continue to be addressed in conferences and research panels and symposia, (but) if they are not acknowledged and addressed on the political levels and implemented in curricula, they may result in only heightening awareness of such issues and not much else.

Here the message is a call for action rather than merely academic discussions of such issues.

As alluded to in the opening quote in Chapter 3, English like water is difficult to direct, control, or resist; rather, as a global language it naturally merges and mixes with other languages and cultures. To embrace and take advantage of such inherent fluidity, both linguistically and culturally, effectively 'flips the script' (Schulze et al., 2019, p. 39) or changes the power dynamic between the global and local. Here we see that 'owning' cultural and linguistic identities which are hybrid, multifaceted, and complex involves moving away from tradition language use and ideologies. Such new and modern cultural and linguistic identities in the UAE may be different from how they once were in pre-oil days, however difference or newness does not make such identities any less Emirati or any less valid. As Dr. Temple Grandin (2012) famously points out with reference to inclusion, 'different is not less'. In this sense, cultural and linguistic hybridity and inclusive language policies, especially in education, should be embraced and distanced from the deficit positions they currently hold. This is very much the message of this concluding chapter's opening quote, where an emphasis is placed on what can be gained rather than what is lost. It is clear from the findings of the study that just as water continues to flow, language, especially in the UAE's particularly fast-paced and superdiverse environment, never stops moving. It is therefore important to regularly revisit the topics investigated in this book.

References

Ahmed, K. (2011). Casting Arabic culture as the 'other': Cultural issues in the English curriculum. In C. Gitsaki (Ed.), *Teaching and Learning in the Arab World* (pp. 119–137). Bern: Peter Lang.

Ahmed, K. (2014). Language and Identity in Education. *The Fifth Annual Gulf Comparative Education Society Symposium Conference Proceedings: Locating the National in the international: Comparative Perspectives on Language, Identity, Policy, and Practice*, 104–111.

Al-Bataineh, A., & Gallagher, K. (2018). Attitudes towards translanguaging: How future teachers perceive the meshing of Arabic and English in children's story books. *International Journal of Bilingual Education and Bilingualism*. https://doi.org.10.1080/13670050.2018.1471039.

Al-Issa, A., & Dahan, L. S. (2011). Global English and endangered Arabic in the United Arab Emirates. In A. Al-Issa, & Dahan, L. S. (Eds.), *Global English and Arabic* (pp. 1–22). Bern, Switzerland: Peter Lang.

Aydarova, O. (2012). If lot "the lest of the West," Then "look East": Imported teacher education curricula in the Arabian Gulf. *Journal of Studies in International Education*, 17 (3), 284–302.

Badry, F. (2011). Appropriating English: Language in identity construction in the United Arab Emirates. In A. Al-Issa, & L. S. Dahan (Eds.), *Global English and Arabic* (pp. 81–122). Bern, Switzerland: Peter Lang.

Bailey, K. (2006). *Language Teacher Supervision*. Cambridge: Cambridge University Press.

Baldauf, R. B. (2004). Issues of prestige and image in language-in-education planning in Australia. *Current Issues in Language Planning, 5* (4), 376–389.

Belhiah, H., & Elhami, M. (2015). English as a medium of instruction in the Gulf: When students and teachers speak. *Language Policy,* 14, 2–23.

Block, D. (2004). Globalization and language teaching. *ELT Journal, 58* (1), 75–77.

Blommaert, J. (2015). *Ethnography, Superdiversity and Linguistic Landscapes: Chronicles of Complexity.* Bristol, UK: Multilingual Matters.

Blommaert, J. (2019). Formatting online actions: # justsaying on Twitter. *International Journal of Multilingualism,* 16, 112–126.

Boraie, D. (2015, March). *The Shifting Sands of Teaching/Leaning English. 21st TESOL Arabia Conference 2015.* Paper presented at TESOL Arabia 2015, Dubai, United Arab Emirates.

Buckingham, L. (2015). Commercial signage and the linguistic landscape of Oman. *World Englishes, 34* (3), 411–435.

Burkett, T. (2016). Emirati students' cultural norms and university teachers' awareness: A socio-cultural gap? *Perspectives, 24* (1), 5–11.

Canagarajah, A. S. (1999). Interrogating the 'native speaker fallacy': Non-linguistic roots, non-pedagogical results. In G. Braine (Ed.), *Non-Native Educators in English Language Teaching* (pp. 77–92). London: Lawrence Erlbaum Associates.

Canagarajah, A. S. (2013). *Translingual Practice: Global Englishes and Cosmopolitan Relations.* New York: Routledge.

Carroll, K. S. (2017). Concluding remarks: Prestige planning and translanguaging in higher education. In C. M. Mazak, & K. S. Carroll (Eds.), *Translanguaging in Higher Education: Beyond Monolingual Ideologies* (pp. 177–185). Bristol: Multilingual Matters.

Coleman, J. A. (2006). English-medium teaching in European higher education. *Language Teaching,* 39, 1–14.

Conteh, J. (2018). Key concepts in ELT: Translanguaging. *ELT Journal,* 72, 445–447.

Creese, A., & Blackledge, A. (2010). Translanguaging in the bilingual classroom: A pedagogy for learning and teaching? *The Modern Language Journal,* 94, 103–115.

Cummins, J. (2014). Language and identity in multilingual schools: Constructing evidence-based instruction policies. In D. Little, C. Lieung, & P. V. Avermeat (Eds.), *Managing Diversity in Education: Languages, Policies, Pedagogies* (pp. 3–23). Bristol: Multilingual Matters.

Daryai-Hansen, P., Barford, S., & Schwarz, L. (2017). A call for (trans)languaging: The language profiles at Roskilde University. In C. M. Mazak, & K. S. Carroll (Eds.), *Translanguaging in Higher Education: Beyond Monolingual Ideologies* (pp. 29–49). Bristol: Multilingual Matters.

Davies, L. (2006). Education for positive conflict and interruptive democracy. In H. Lauder, P. Brown, L. Dillabough, & A. H. Halsey (Eds.), *Education, Globalization and Social Change* (pp. 1029–1037). Oxford: Oxford University Press.

Dovchin, S. (2017). The ordinariness of youth linguascapes in Mongolia. *International Journal of Multilingualism,* 14, 144–159.

Dovchin, S. (2018). *Language, Media and Globalization in the Periphery: The Linguascapes of Popular Music in Mongolia.* New York: Routledge.

Dovchin, S., & Lee, J. W. (2019). Introduction to special issue: 'The ordinariness of translinguistics'. *International Journal of Multilingualism.* doi:10.1080/149 0718.2019.1575831.

Findlow, S. (2005). International networking in the United Arab Emirates higher education: Global-local tension. *Compare,* 35 (3), 285–302.

Findlow, S. (2006). Higher education and linguistic dualism in the Arab Gulf. *British Journal of Sociology of Education,* 27 (1), 19–36.

Freimuth, H. (2016). Revisiting the sustainability of the IELTS examination as a gatekeeper for university entrance in the UAE. In L. Buckingham (Ed.), *Language, Identity and Education on the Arabian Peninsula* (pp. 161–175). Bristol: Multilingual Matters.

Garton, S., Copland, F., & Mann, S. (2016). Opinions and positions on native-speakerism. In F. Coupland, S. Garton, & S. Mann (Eds.), *LETS and NESTS: Voices, Views and Vignettes* (pp. 247–263). London: British Council.

Gramling, D. (2016). *The Invention of Monolingualism.* New York: Bloomsbury.

Gramling, D. (2019). On reelecting monolingualism: Fortification, fragility, and stamina. *Applied Linguistics Review,* 1–18. https://doi.org/10.1515/applirev-2019-0039.

Grandin, T. (2012). *Different, Not Less.* Arlington: Future Horizons.

Hatherley-Greene, P. (2014). The cultural border crossing index: Implications for higher education teachers in the UAE. *Learning and Teaching in Higher Education: Gulf Perspectives,* 11 (2).

Heidt, I. (2015). Exploring the historical dimensions of *Bildung* and its metamorphasis in the context of globalization. *L2 Journal,* 7 (4), 2–16.

Holland, J. (2014, February 5). The Emirati sci-fi novelist Noura Al Noman on Arabic versus English. *The National.* Retrieved from: www.thenational.ae/arts-culture/books/the-emirati-sci-fi-novelist-noura-al-noman-on-arabic-versus-english-1.314138?videoId=5740140880001.

Holliday, A. (2006). Native-speakerism. *ELT Journal,* 60, 385–387.

Holliday, A. (2014). *Using Existing Cultural Experience to Stamp Identity on English.* Retrieved from: http://adrianholliday.com/articles.

Hornberger, N. H. (2005). Opening and filling up implementational and ideological spaces in heritage language education. *Modern Language Journal,* 89 (4), 605–609.

Hudson, P. (2012). 'Shabbery' and 'banattitude': Western ELT professionals' perceptions of the role of gender in English-medium higher educations in the Gulf. *Learning and Teaching in Higher Education: Gulf Perspectives,* 9 (2).

Jenkins, J. (2016). Interview in Morrison, L. (2016). *Native Speakers Are the World's Worst Communicators.* Retrieved from: http://www.bbc.com/capital/story/20161028-native-english-speakers-are-the-worlds-worst-communicators.

Kachru, B. B. (2006). World Englishes and culture wars. In B. B. Kachru, Y. Kachru, & C. L. Nelson (Eds.), *The Handbook to World Englishes* (pp. 446–471). Hoboken, NJ: Wiley Blackwell.

Kachru, B. B. (2017). *World Englishes and Culture Wars.* Cambridge: Cambridge University Press.

Kazim, A. (2000). The United Arab Emirates A.D. 600 to the Present: A Socio-discursive Transformation in the Arabian Gulf. Dubai: Gulf Book Center.

Kramsch, C. (2018). Is there still a place for culture in a multilingual FL education? *Language Education and Multilingualism,* 1, 16–33.

Kubota, R. (2019). A critical examination of common beliefs about language teaching: From research insights to professional engagement. In F. Fang, & H. P. Widodo (Eds.), *Critical Perspectives on Global Englishes in Asia* (pp. 10–26). Bristol: Multilingual Matters.

Lippi-Green, R. (2012). *English with an Accent: Language, Ideology and Discrimination in the United States*. New York: Routledge.

Lowenburg, P. H. (2000). Non-native varieties and the sociopolitics of English proficiency assessment. In S. Hall, J. Kelly, & W. G. Eggington (Eds.), *The Sociopolitics of English Language Teaching*. Clevedon, Buffalo, Toronto, Sydney: Multilingual Matters Ltd.

Makalela, L. (2019). *Ubuntu Translanguaging: Making Sense of Simultaneous Disruption and Stability in 21st Century Multilingual Encounters*. Plenary talk at Languaging in Times of Change Conference, University of Stirling, Scotland, September 26–27.

Mazak, C. M., Mendoza, F., & Mangonez, L. P. (2017). Professors translanguaging in practice: Three cases from a bilingual university. In C. M. Mazak, & K. S. Carroll (Eds.), *Translanguaging in Higher Education: Beyond Monolingual Ideologies* (pp. 70–90). Bristol: Multilingual Matters.

Medgyes, P. (1994). *The Non-Native Teacher*. London: Macmillan Publishers.

Morrow, J. A., & Castleton, B. (2011). The impact of global English on the Arabic language: The loss of the Allah lexicon. In A. Al-Issa, & L. S. Dahan (Eds.), *Global English and Arabic* (pp. 307–334). Bern, Switzerland: Peter Lang.

Mouhanna, M. (2016). *English as a Medium of Instruction in the Tertiary Education Setting of the UAE: The Perspectives of Content Teachers*. Doctoral thesis, University of Exeter, UK. Retrieved from: https://ore.exeter.ac.uk/repository/handle/10871/23758.

Norton, B. (2000). *Identity and Language Learning*. Harlow, England: Longman.

O'Neill, G. T. (2014). Just a natural move towards English': Gulf youth attitudes towards Arabic and English literacy. *Gulf Perspectives*, 11 (1), 1–21.

O'Neill, G. T. (2016). Heritage, heteroglossia and home: Multilingualism in Emirati families. In L. Buckingham (Ed.), *Language, Identity and Education on the Arabian Peninsula* (pp. 13–38). Bristol: Multilingual Matters.

Palfreyman, D., & Al-Bataineh, A. (2018). 'This is my lifestyle, Arabic and English': Students' attitudes to (trans)languaging in a bilingual university context. *Language Awareness*, 27, 79–95.

Pennycook, A. (2010). The future of Englishes: One, many or more. In A. Kirkpatrick (Ed.), *The Routledge Handbook of World Englishes* (pp. 673–687). London: Routledge.

Phillipson, R. (1992a). ELT: The native speaker's burden? *ELT Journal*, 46 (1), 12–18.

Phillipson, R. (1992b). *Linguistic Imperialism*. Oxford: Oxford University Press.

Richardson, S. (2016). *The 'Native Factor', the Haves and the Have Nots*. Plenary session at IATEFL Conference (April 14), Birmingham, UK.

Rubdy, R. (2016). *Cultural Globalization and Changing Perspectives on English as an International Language*. Paper presented at the Third International Conference on Language, Linguistics, Literature and Translation – Connecting the dots in a glocalized world, Sultan Qaboos University, Muscat, Oman.

Rushdie, S. (1991). *Imaginary Homelands: Essays and Criticism 1981–1991*. London: Granta.

Said, F. F. S. (2011). Ahyaan I text in English 'ashaan it's ashal': Language in crisis or linguistic development? The case of how Gulf Arabs perceive the future of their language, culture and identity. In A. Al-Issa, & L. S. Dahan (Eds.), *Global English and Arabic* (pp. 179–212). Bern, Switzerland: Peter Lang.

Schulze, J. (2016). Understanding the persuasive writing practices of an adolescent emergent bilingual through systematic functional linguistics: A case study. *International Journal of Learning, Teaching, and Research*, 15 (10), 163–179.

Schulze, J., Ittner, A., & Marquez, E. (2019). Translanguaging in the multilingual classroom: From theory to practice. *WAESOL Educator*, Summer, 38–40.

Scotland, J. (2014). Operating in global educational contact zones: How pedagogical adaptation to local contexts may result in the renegotiation of the professional identities of English language teachers. *Teaching and Teacher Education*, 37, 33–43.

Selvi, A. F. (2016). Native or non-native English-speaking professionals in ELT: 'That is the question!' or 'is that the question?' In F. Coupland, S. Garton, & S. Mann (Eds.), *LETS and NESTS: Voices, Views and Vignettes* (pp. 53–69). London: British Council.

Seymour, J. (2016). *Supporting Bi-literacy Among Emiratis in Dubai's Private Schools: An Analysis of Current Arabic Language Policy*. Doctoral module assignment, University of Bath, UK. Retrieved from: https://bath.academia.edu/JoanneSeymour.

Solloway, A. (2016). *English-medium Instruction in Higher Education in the United Arab Emirates: The Perspective of Students*. Doctoral thesis, University of Exeter, UK. Retrieved from: https://ore.exeter.ac.uk/repository/handle/10871/26316.

Steinhagen, T., & Aljanadbah, A. (2019). *A Dalton Plan Classroom for Translanguaging in Higher Education in the UAE*. Presentation at the 2nd Applied Linguistics and Language Teaching Conference, Dubai, March 7–9.

Sung, C. C. M. (2015). Implementing a Global Englishes component in a university English course in Hong Kong. *English Today*, 31 (4), 42–49.

Taha-Thomure, H. (2008). The status of Arabic language teaching today. *Education, Business and Society: Contemporary Middle Eastern Issues*, 1 (3), 186–192.

Taha-Thomure, H. (2017). Arabic language teacher education. In A. Gebril (Ed.), *Applied Linguistics in the Middle East and North Africa* (pp. 267–287). Amsterdam: John Benjamins. doi:10.1075/aals.15.12tah.

Taha-Thomure, H. (2019). Arabic language education in the UAE: Choosing the right drivers. In K. Gallagher (Ed.), *Education in the UAE: Innovation and Transformation* (pp. 75–93). Singapore: Springer. doi:10.1007/978-978-981-13-7736-5_5.

Troudi, S., & Jendli, A. (2011). Emirati students' experiences of English as a medium of instruction. In A. Al-Issa, & L. S. Dahan (Eds.), *Global English and Arabic* (pp. 23–48). Bern, Switzerland: Peter Lang.

Van den Hoven, M., & Carroll, K. S. (2016). Emirati pre-Service teachers' perspectives of Abu Dhabi's rich linguistic context. In L. Buckingham (Ed.), *Language, Identity and Education on the Arabian Peninsula* (pp. 39–58). Bristol: Multilingual Matters.

Wei, L. (2017). Translanguaging as a practical theory of language. *Applied Linguistics*, 39, 9–30.

Zaman, S. (2-017, May 16). Haweyati programme will teach Emirati culture and heritage across all schools. *The Gulf News*. Retrieved from: https://gulfnews.com/uae/education/schools-in-abu-dhabi-to-focus-on-national-identity-1.2028232.

Zhao, S., & Liu, Y. (2010). Chinese education in Singapore: Constraints of bilingual policy from the perspectives of status and prestige planning. *Language Problems and Language Planning*, 34 (3), 236–258.

Index

Page numbers in *italic* indicate a figure and page numbers in **bold** indicate a table on the corresponding page.

214   *Index*